THE MAKING OF LONDON

THE MAKING
OF LONDON

THE PEOPLE AND EVENTS THAT MADE IT FAMOUS

ALAN BROOKE
AND
DAVID BRANDON

PEN & SWORD
HISTORY

AN IMPRINT OF PEN & SWORD BOOKS LTD.
YORKSHIRE - PHILADELPHIA

First published in Great Britain in 2023 by
PEN AND SWORD HISTORY
An imprint of
Pen & Sword Books Ltd
Yorkshire – Philadelphia

ISBN 978 1 39908 467 3

Typeset in Times New Roman 11/13.5 by
SJmagic DESIGN SERVICES, India.
Printed and bound in the UK by CPI Group (UK) Ltd.

Pen & Sword Books Limited incorporates the imprints of Atlas, Archaeology,
Aviation, Discovery, Family History, Fiction, History, Maritime, Military, Military
Classics, Politics, Select, Transport, True Crime, Air World, Frontline Publishing,
Leo Cooper, Remember When, Seaforth Publishing, The Praetorian Press,
Wharncliffe Local History, Wharncliffe Transport, Wharncliffe True Crime and
White Owl.

For a complete list of Pen & Sword titles please contact
PEN & SWORD BOOKS LIMITED
47 Church Street, Barnsley, South Yorkshire, S70 2AS, England
E-mail: enquiries@pen-and-sword.co.uk
Website: www.pen-and-sword.co.uk

Or
PEN AND SWORD BOOKS
1950 Lawrence Rd, Havertown, PA 19083, USA
E-mail: Uspen-and-sword@casematepublishers.com
Website: www.penandswordbooks.com

Contents

Timeline   vi

Map of Central London   x

Introduction   xi

Chapter 1   The Shaping of a City: From Roman to
             Norman Conquest   1

Chapter 2   Medieval London: From Norman to Tudor Conquest   10

Chapter 3   Trading and Commercial London   28

Chapter 4   London 1500–1700: Medieval City to
             Modern Metropolis   45

Chapter 5   Eighteenth-century London: 'Full of Wonders and
             Wickedness'   68

Chapter 6   Unruly London: 'If you do not want to live among
             wicked people, do not live in London'   90

Chapter 7   Victorian London: 'The dust and din and
             steam of town'   105

Chapter 8   London 1914–2000: A Tumultuous Century   143

Chapter 9   Twenty-first-century London: From Promises
             to Pandemic   173

Sources   186

Acknowledgements   188

Index   189

Timeline

Romans to Normans

AD 43	Romans settle and build Londinium.
AD 61	Queen Boudicca of the Iceni tribe attacks and burns London.
c. 180	Roman Wall built around the city.
410	Romans withdraw from London.
490	Saxons occupy London.
604	First St Paul's Cathedral built at Ludgate.
c. 750	Monastery of St Peter is founded, later to become Westminster Abbey.
842	London raided by Vikings.
886	English rule restored – Danes ousted by Alfred the Great.
1066	January, Harold crowned king, beginning the coronation of sovereigns in Westminster Abbey.

Medieval London

1066	December, William I, Duke of Normandy crowned King of England.
1078	Tower of London's White Tower built.
1123	St Bartholomew's Hospital and Smithfield market established.
1133	First annual Bartholomew Fair at Smithfield.
1176	Construction of first stone-built London Bridge begins (completed 1209).
1189	City's first mayor elected.
1240	First parliament in Westminster.
1265	Covent Garden market established.
1290	Jews expelled from the City – a ban not lifted until 1657.
1348	Black Death reaches London by autumn.
1381	Peasants' Revolt, led by Wat Tyler – many buildings destroyed.
1476	William Caxton sets up first printing press in England at Westminster.

Reformation to Restoration

1532	Palace of Whitehall built, the largest in Europe.
1536	Anne Boleyn executed at the Tower of London.
1537	Dissolution of Monasteries: Charterhouse dissolved.
1540	Thomas Cromwell executed on Tower Hill.
1559	Elizabeth I crowned at Westminster Abbey.
1571	Royal Exchange opened.
1598	John Stow's classic *A Survey of London* published.
1600	Population of London around 200,000.
1605	Guy Fawkes attempts to blow up Parliament.
1621	First Hackney coach recorded.
1642	Outbreak of Civil War.
1649	Charles I executed at Banqueting House, Whitehall.
1652	First coffee house opens in London at Cornhill.
1660	Monarchy under Charles II restored.
1663	Theatre Royal, Drury Lane opened.
1665	First recorded death from Great Plague in London.
1666	September, Great Fire of London starts in the City.
1684	Downing Street built in Westminster.
1688	December, 'Glorious Revolution' – William of Orange enters London.
1694	Bank of England founded.

Eighteenth-century London

1703	Buckingham House (Palace) built (Royal residency in 1762).
1711	The present St Paul's Cathedral officially completed.
1736	Gin Act passed in an attempt to stop the 'Gin Craze'.
1739	Building of Westminster Bridge begins (completed 1750).
1752	Mansion House, residence of the Lord Mayor of London, completed.
1759	British Museum in Bloomsbury opened.
1760s	Large part of the City Wall and the ancient gates of the City removed.
1780	Gordon Riots destroy many buildings in London.
1783	Last public execution held at Tyburn.
1798	Marine Police Force is founded on River Thames: the first organized police force in Britain.

Nineteenth-century London

1801	First census records London's population at just over one million.
1807	Gas first used to light Pall Mall.
1816	First Vauxhall bridge opened, first iron bridge over the Thames.
1820	Cato Street (Marylebone) Conspiracy to murder cabinet exposed.
1826	University of London established.
1829	Metropolitan Police begin operations.
1832	Cholera epidemic spreads in London.
1836	London–Greenwich, first public passenger railway service in London.
1837	Euston Station, London's first mainline railway terminus opened.
1838	National Gallery in Trafalgar Square opened.
1851	Great Exhibition opens at The Crystal Palace in Hyde Park.
1863	World's first underground railway opened between Paddington and Farringdon.
1868	Last public execution in England takes place at Newgate.
1875	Completion of thirty-year construction of London's sewer system.
1880	Royal Albert Dock opened.
1888	The 'Jack the Ripper' murders in Whitechapel.
1894	Tower Bridge completed.

Twentieth-century London

1901	Population of Greater London 6.5 million
1906	The Ritz in Piccadilly opened.
1907	The Central Criminal Court (Old Bailey) opened.
1909	Selfridges opened.
1915	German Zeppelins bomb London.
1919	The Cenotaph, Whitehall, unveiled as temporary memorial.
1922	British Broadcasting Company transmits programmes from Strand.
1923	First Football Association cup final held at Wembley Stadium.
1933	London Underground diagram designed by Harry Beck.
1940–5	Bombs dropped on London kill nearly 30,000 people.
1951	Festival of Britain on South Bank near Waterloo.
1952	'Great Smog' causes disruption and kills thousands of people.
1968	Anti-Vietnam demonstrations in Grosvenor Square.

1970s	Series of IRA bombings in London.
1986	Greater London Council (GLC) abolished.
1999	Official opening of the Millennium Dome.

Twenty-first-century London

2000	Tate Modern opened on Bankside. Ken Livingstone becomes first directly elected Mayor of London.
2003	Congestion charge introduced.
2005	July, fifty-six people killed in four suicide bombings on London Transport.
2007	New Wembley Stadium opened. Eurostar terminal opened at St Pancras.
2012	Shard building completed. London Olympics held in Stratford.
2016	First Muslim, Sadiq Khan, elected Mayor of London.
2020	February, first COVID-19 case in London. COVID-19 pandemic in London. April, NHS Nightingale Hospital opened in ExCel Centre.
2021	COVID-19 restrictions lifted.

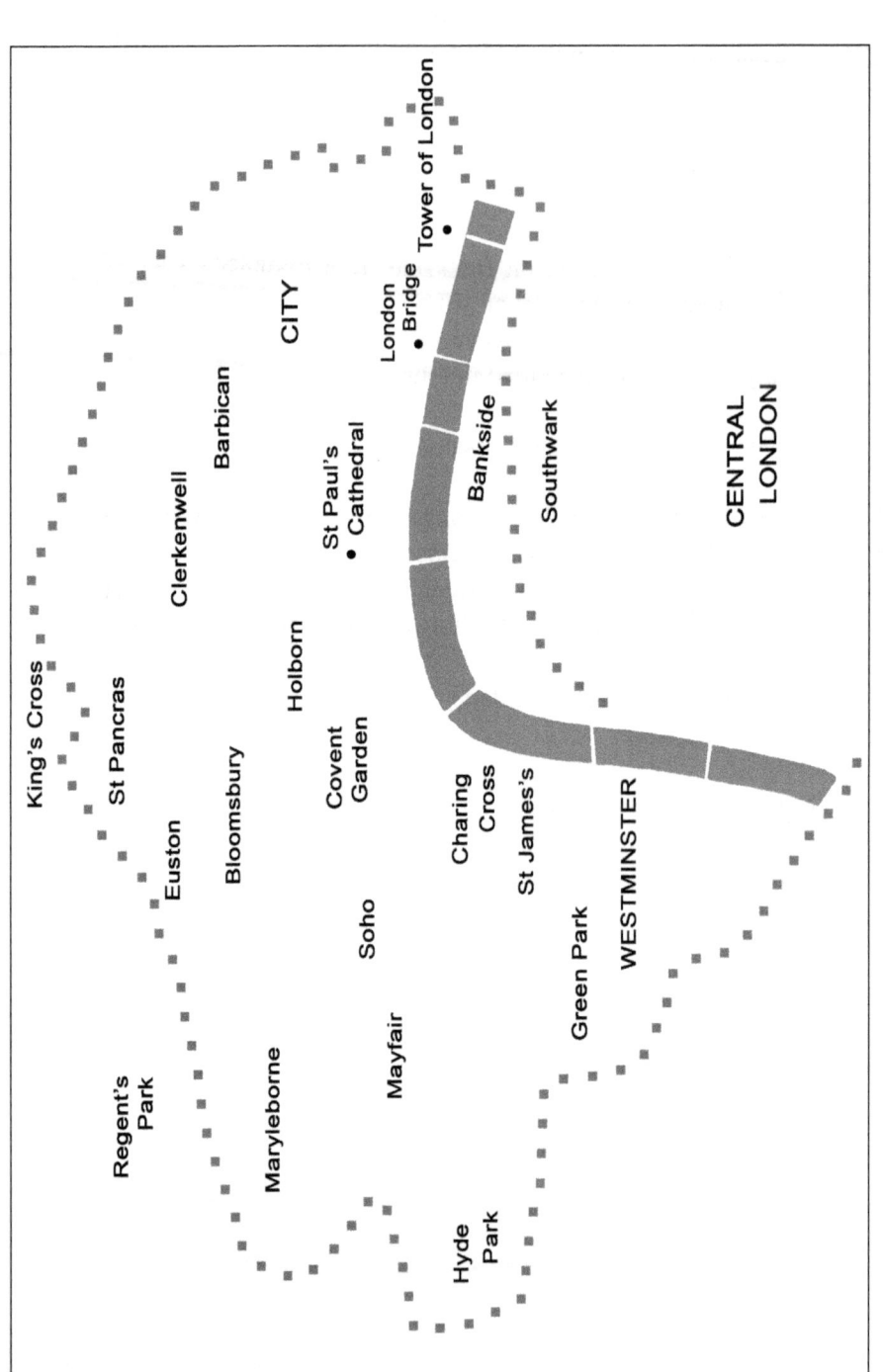

Central London

Introduction

London is the capital of the United Kingdom and far away its largest city. It is also unquestionably a world city. However, reaching an exact definition of London is not easy. That entity which currently is officially termed 'Greater London' consists of twelve inner and twenty outer boroughs. The district historically known as the 'City of London' has jealously guarded its right to remain different and largely independent. It is not one of the thirty-two boroughs. When 'The City' is mentioned in the news, for example, it is this ancient core of the capital, the famous 'Square Mile' now largely given over to the world of banking and finance, rather than the much larger spatially but more amorphous 'Greater London', which is being referred to. When the authors mention 'The City' it is always in this historical sense. Greater London covers an area of just over 600 square miles with a population of around nine million. As a more-or-less continuously built-up area, it has absorbed parts of Hertfordshire, Essex, Buckinghamshire, Surrey and Kent and continues its outward and seemingly inexorable physical growth. The thrall of London, of course, extends much further and a case could be made for its influence across the British Isles never having been greater and more pervasive than it is now in the twenty-first century.

For the purpose of this book the authors focus on what may loosely be called 'central London'. We take this to be bounded in the east by the area around the Tower of London, Hyde Park to the west, Regent's Park to the north and parts of Southwark across the Thames, to the south. This is suitable for our purposes. Inevitably other districts will appear in the narrative where events involve an interaction between them and central London.

The main purpose of this book is to offer a short introductory narrative history of London from Roman times to the present. Inevitably with such a vast topic we need to be selective in our coverage and the approach reflects the authors' particular spheres of interest as historians. There is a massive existing literature devoted to London's fascinating history. In recent years gifted authors such as Roy Porter, Peter Ackroyd and Jerry White have given us wonderfully informed, rich and readable general histories of the capital. We cannot hope to emulate the breadth of content these authors have been able to include in their works. Instead, we submit what we hope is an accessible history that may stimulate the reader new to the subject sufficiently to go on to find out more elsewhere.

The approach is largely chronological and concentrates less on individual so-called 'great figures' of history but more on the lives of ordinary Londoners and on how they lived and what they saw and sensed. Samuel Johnson, the famous diarist and devoted Londoner, wrote, 'It is not in the showy evolutions of buildings but in the multiplicity of human habitations which are crowded together, that the wonderful immensity of London exists.' For us, this remains a valid observation. We do not, therefore, attempt to survey the complex development of London's built environment.

This has been done many times and is extremely interesting but perhaps more relevant to students of architecture or of what has become known as 'heritage'. The present authors prefer to emphasize the human element in the study of the past. We hope that readers enjoy what follows as much as we enjoyed writing the book.

Chapter 1

The Shaping of a City

From Roman to Norman Conquest

The history of London effectively started with the Roman invasion of AD 43. For the following 400 years London, or Londinium as the Romans named it, was on the periphery of the Roman Empire and was the largest city in Britannia. Sea transport linked it to Europe and a network of roads connected it to many of the major towns of Britain. In the thousand years from the Roman occupation, London was a settlement founded by the Romans then occupied by the Saxons, conquered by the Danes, and ruled by the Normans.

The area that was occupied and fortified by the Romans, and later became known as the City, is located on the northern bank of the River Thames and was mostly, but not wholly, within the ancient defensive Roman Wall. Today, the boundaries of the City are marked with cast-iron dragons that stretch north from Temple and the Tower of London on the River Thames to Chancery Lane in the west and Liverpool Street in the east. It covers an area of 1.12 square miles and is known as the 'Square Mile'. Like all great cities London grew and spilled beyond the city walls and eventually into the large areas of countryside around it.

This chapter will focus on London between the Roman occupation in the first century AD to the arrival of the Normans in the eleventh century. However, some brief but important pre-Roman points of information need to be made. Towns and cities are shaped by their physical landscape and the geological features of London have provided it with many advantages. Above the various strata of geological time lies 650 feet of chalk and on top of the chalk lies the London clay, which in turn is topped by gravel and brick-earth. Although it is one of the most shrinkable of soil types, it does have important benefits. One is that these types of clay soils are easy to tunnel, hence it was a bonus in the building of the underground rail system, started in the nineteenth century, as well the labyrinthine subterranean network that runs under the capital. However, there is less clay on the south of the Thames, which accounts for fewer Underground lines. Another benefit is that the clay provides the good bricks that are evident in so many of London's buildings. The clay also bears witness to the skeletons and fossils of creatures that once inhabited this terrain – sharks, rhinoceros, giant deer, wolves and crocodiles.

Another significant feature in the shaping of London's history is the River Thames. When the Romans arrived, they would have seen a much wider and shallower river as well as a landscape similar to the marshy flats around the coast of East Anglia. The Thames was approximately five times wider at high tide compared to now and being tidal made it easily accessible for ships. It was inevitable that the Romans would soon construct a bridge across the Thames, which they did in the second century AD. The location of the Thames estuary gave access to continental Europe and was a vital factor in the centuries of trade that followed, notably with many of the richest cities in the Low Countries – Antwerp, Brussels and Ghent. In addition, the development of the Roman city, Londinium, was closely associated with the significance of its riverside as a port.

From prehistoric times the Thames ran through a broad valley, fed by streams including those from Hampstead and Highgate. There was an abundance of islands in the Thames now commemorated in names like Battersea and Bermondsey (*ea* or *ey* denoting Anglo-Saxon for island). The Thames, and its tributaries, linked up with many waterways. These waterways proved beneficial to trade, as did the development of a network of highways. From the south-east, Watling Street (modern Edgware Road) continued north to St Albans, Chester and the north-west, whilst Ermine Street linked London with Lincoln and York.

Long before the Romans, evidence of earlier human activity has been found at Brentford, Hampstead and Putney and of Bronze Age bridges and Iron Age forts near the River Thames. However, there is little evidence of earlier settlements at what was to become Londinium. In the first century BC Julius Caesar described the area around London as consisting of tribal civilizations, largely populated and studded with homesteads.

Whilst Rome was built on seven hills, Londinium could only boast two small hump-back hills, today called Cornhill and Ludgate Hill. Between them ran the Walbrook, one of the many 'lost' rivers or streams of London. Although neither hill is very high, the land was at least well drained. Centuries later, on the western side, the first St Paul's Cathedral was built at Ludgate and to the east the church of St Peter upon Cornhill stands. It is believed that the church of St Peter stood on the remains of an earlier Roman temple dedicated to the goddess Diana.

A century after Julius Caesar's short-lived incursion into Britain, the Romans returned and began their occupation under Emperor Claudius in AD 43. Within four years the Roman army soon gained control of much of the south-east of Britain and Londinium was established. The origins of the name, Londinium, are uncertain and much speculation has been offered varying from mythical to Celtic origins. Whilst Rome's mythical foundation is based on the wolf children, Romulus and Remus, London does have its own legends, albeit probably less well known. A discredited myth stems from Geoffrey of Monmouth's *History of the Kings of Britain* written in 1136. Monmouth suggested that London was named after Lud, a king of Britain in pre-Roman times who was reputedly buried at Ludgate. A statue of Lud and his sons can be seen in the porch of St Dunstan-in-the-West church on Fleet Street.

London's own legendary twins are Gog and Magog, originally known as Gogmagog and Corienus who became the guardians of the city. According to the myth they represented warriors in an assumed war, which resulted in the founding of the city, New Troy. Their statues have stood for many centuries within the Guildhall with the current pair carved by David Evans in 1953. Other statues of the twins have been used in pageants from the fifteenth century such as the Lord Mayor's show. The two figures that strike the hours on the famous clock of St Dunstan church in Fleet Street are assumed to be Gog and Magog.

Romans

Within a decade of their occupation the Roman settlement was, according to the Roman historian Tacitus, 'filled with traders and [was] a celebrated centre of commerce'. The city started as it meant to continue. However, in violent and uncertain times Londinium found itself under attack. In AD 60/1 a group of East Anglian tribes including the Iceni under the command of their queen, Boudicca (whose statue can be seen on Westminster Bridge, near the Houses of Parliament) headed south destroying Colchester then descended on London and sacked the town, reputedly killing many people. Most of what we know about Roman London is based on archaeological evidence and such evidence has found few human remains in relation to this attack, suggesting that the population may have had plenty of warning to escape the invasion. Nonetheless, Londinium was destroyed and burned to the ground, which is evident in the bright red oxidized iron in the burnt clay and the layers of charred debris stretching to the opposite side of the river. Here houses, granaries and workshops flanked the road leading to the crossing.

The Romans were quick to seek revenge, eventually crushing the revolt before starting to rebuild Londinium on a much grander scale. It seemed that the attack had kick-started a golden age. From the beginning of the second century Londinium could boast a temple, an amphitheatre, a large basilica (public building) where Leadenhall now stands, a large fort in the north-west (Cripplegate was the northern entrance), public baths, shops, sewers, timber-framed buildings built in the formal piazza patterns and timber quays which were constructed along the Thames.

Crossing the Thames may have been possible by means of a ford when the tide was low but it was the Romans who built the first London Bridge in order to consolidate their conquest. We know little of the first bridge but it could have been a military pontoon or floating bridge or even a rope ferry connecting the two banks. There may have been a bridge elsewhere, possibly near Westminster, where the Thames was shallower and narrower.

The Thames between Southwark on the southern side and Londinium on the northern had the advantage of being tidal which allowed sailing vessels to access wharves on an incoming tide. On the Southwark side of the river workshops and bakeries started to emerge which prompted Tacitus to claim that the settlement was 'crowded with merchants and goods'. A bridge linking Southwark with the city was essential and evidence of a bridge made of timber piles and decking has been dated to between AD 80 and 90. This Roman bridge was located about sixty metres east of the current London Bridge.

Roman London was strategically important and needed to defend itself against all types of marauders. Given the threat of pirate and Barbarian attacks, Londinium's defences were made more secure by the construction of a wall built between AD 180–230. It was made of ragstone, a hard sedimentary rock extracted from Maidstone in Kent, and brought to London on the Thames by boat. The wall that encircled the Roman city stretched over two miles in length from Tower Hill in the east to Blackfriars in the west. It was one of the largest building projects undertaken in Roman Britain and its course remained relatively unchanged for some 1,500 years. Included in the wall was a complex of towers, defensive ditches and bastions as well as the city gates. The names of the old city gates (built and rebuilt over the centuries), Aldgate, Aldersgate, Bishopsgate, Cripplegate, Ludgate, Newgate and Moorgate (the latter was expanded from a postern or smaller gate in the early fifteenth century) are familiar to us as parts of the City of London that still bear their names. Like the wall that enclosed them, they provided continuity in the city's history from around AD 200 to the eighteenth century (although they were regularly repaired and rebuilt over the centuries). When the gates were finally dismantled and demolished, they were sold off and all we have now are plaques that bear testimony to their location. Remains of the Roman Wall can be seen at the Barbican and on Tower Hill.

Throughout their history the city gates played an important function in the control of trade, defence, regulating access, representing the prestige of the city and as a point for collecting taxes. In addition to the daily flow of traffic, there were processions, curfews and occasional rebellions. The gates also displayed public information including announcements, tax and toll schedules, legal texts as well as the gruesome body parts of recently executed felons, intended to serve as a warning to potential transgressors.

From the beginning, Londinium was an ethnically cosmopolitan town. Most of the population within the wall consisted of Roman immigrant citizens and their slaves (slavery was central to the Roman economic system). However, over time many of the native British adapted to the Roman lifestyle mostly speaking Latin patois by the second century. Information from graves suggests that the average height of Roman Londoners was 5 feet 6 inches (male) and 5 feet 2 inches (female). Further evidence from the Museum of London shows that skulls and facial bones were probably native Britons. Most of the citizens worked as labourers, craftsmen or shopkeepers. The amphitheatre (discovered in 1988 in the Guildhall Yard and can be visited) provided brutal entertainment including executions – an entertainment that was to continue as a popular public spectacle elsewhere in London down to the nineteenth century. We know from excavations that the Romans used the area beyond the wall as a cemetery down to the late fourth century, mainly east of what is now Finsbury Circus.

Londinium expanded by the end of the first century, replacing Colchester as the provincial Roman capital. The peak and golden age of the Roman city came during the second century AD with a population of around 50,000 – a figure that would not be achieved for many centuries. About AD 368 the name Londinium was changed to Augusta (Imperial – a common name among provincial capitals) and can be seen on coins during this period.

However, it was one of decline from thereon for the Roman city. Buildings fell into disrepair and with Rome under threat it could no longer defend its distant provinces and Britain was left to protect its own interests. In AD 410 troops were withdrawn, thus marking the end of Roman London. The deserted city soon fell into ruin and would experience occupations and raids from Saxons, and Vikings (a seafaring people primarily from Scandinavia – Denmark, Norway, Sweden).

As buildings became derelict, the population declined and trade routes dwindled. Such a loss of importance meant that Winchester eventually became more significant. Nonetheless, despite this decline no other town out of the hundreds in the Roman Empire has had a greater influence than London on human affairs. However, for the next few centuries, what remained of the city would reside in the territory of the Kingdom of the East Saxons – Essex.

Anglo-Saxons – Vikings – Normans

In the 200 years after the Romans left Londinium records tell us very little about the period. From the fifth to the eleventh century, we see a pattern emerging: one group of people arrive, establish a settlement, rename the place then leave or are driven out. Sometimes they defended themselves from an attacking party. Between 842 and 1016 the Vikings attacked London on at least twelve occasions. The earliest known raid came in 842 although it was not necessarily the first. New settlements established themselves outside the old Roman city. By 886 the *Anglo-Saxon Chronicle* stated that King Alfred (848–99, king of the West Saxons and later king of the Anglo-Saxons) founded Lundenburg. However, it is difficult to know how populated the city was during the Anglo-Saxon and Viking periods. In Cnut's time (1014–35) it was probably between 10,000 and 12,000.

The Angles and Saxons from northern Germany were among the first post-Roman arrivals to settle in eastern Britain with some establishing themselves on the banks of the Thames. Whilst these settlements were to the west of the Roman city, the Cathedral of St Paul's was built in 604 within the walls of Londinium by the East Saxons – probably the only change within the old city since the Romans. Meanwhile, the Saxon settlement of Lundenwic (*wic* meaning a port or a place of trade as in Aldwych – 'old wic') developed west of the Roman ruins in modern-day Covent Garden. Excavations in 1985 and 2005 uncovered an extensive Anglo-Saxon settlement dating back to the seventh century, which stretched along the northern side of the Strand to the present-day Trafalgar Square. Commenting on this expansion the historian Bede recorded in 730 that London was the 'metropolis of the East Saxons'.

Trade from the Thames and its access to the sea, as well as the roads leading from London, also benefitted the Anglo-Saxons. In 730, Bede described London as 'an emporium for many nations'. The street pattern of Roman London was overlaid by the Anglo-Saxons and has survived up to recent times. Hence, the Anglo-Saxon legacy to London, in this sense, is more direct than the Roman. This can be seen for example in the curves of Lombard Street and Fenchurch Street which were probably through routes between some of the Roman ruins. Sadly, the past few decades have seen large numbers of medieval streets disappear and replaced by dual carriageways which have destroyed many of the surrounding lanes and old alignments.

The *Anglo-Saxon Chronicle* records that London had been under Viking occupation in 871 but they left for Northumbria the following year. This allowed Alfred the Great, king of the Anglo- Saxons, to extend his power to London in the area of what is now the City and along Fleet Street as far as Aldwych. Despite a series of Viking raids in the mid-ninth century, English control of London changed in 886 when Alfred began an urban renewal by restoring the Roman city as a fortress, re-fortifying the walls, creating a new street plan east of St Paul's Cathedral, and making improvements to the quayside along what is now Queenhithe. The old Roman city became known as Lundenburh (*burh* denoting a fortified town) marking the beginning of the history of the City of London. Alfred's grandson, Athelstan (or Æthelstan) became, according to some historians, the first king of England from 927 to 939.

There are references to a bridge across the River Thames at the time of King Edgar (959–75), and also in relation to a series of Viking attacks. The most famous of these invasions, which is worthy of a Nordic saga, was in 1014 when the Saxon bridge was pulled down by the Norwegian prince Olaf, who was aiding King Aethelred (Ethelred the Unready), in regaining London from the Danes. Olaf Haraldsson, who became king of Norway in 1015, descended on London with ninety-four ships. Fitting his ships with a wicker roof, he rowed up to the bridge where, under a barrage of stones and arrows, the attackers, according to *St Olaf's Saga* (written around 1230) 'fastened cables around the piles which supported the bridge; then with all their ships rowed downstream with all their might'. The bridge collapsed, Aethelred attacked the fort and was eventually acknowledged as king. *St Olaf's Saga* is the earliest account of the bridge collapsing and is assumed to be the origin of the nursery rhyme 'London Bridge is Falling Down' although this has been disputed.

Aethelred died shortly after and it was left to Cnut, son of Sweyn Forkbeard, to finally gain control of London and all England in 1016. Two years later he gained accession to the Danish throne thus bringing England and Denmark together. Another legend from the twelfth century is that of Cnut trying to stop the tide, which, according to the story, he wasn't: he was showing that mortals could not perform such tasks, only God could.

Westminster

London not only expanded to the north of Cheapside but also further to the west. There had been an abbey at Westminster since the eighth century which became known as the 'west minster' to distinguish it from St Paul's Cathedral – the 'east minster'. In the decade after 1042 King Edward the Confessor (step-son of Cnut) began rebuilding the abbey to provide him with a royal burial church. It was finally consecrated in December 1065 although the king was too ill to attend and died a few days later. After his burial in the abbey his successor Harold was crowned there, thus beginning the coronation of every sovereign (Edward V and Edward VIII were not crowned) in Westminster Abbey. Since 1560 it has not been a cathedral, abbey or parish church. It is a 'Royal Peculiar' (the Collegiate Church of Saint Peter at Westminster) under the jurisdiction of a Dean and Chapter and subject only to the Sovereign and not to any archbishop or bishop.

When Edward the Confessor moved his seat of royal authority from the walled City to Westminster, it was an event of huge importance. It eventually established Westminster as the centre of government whilst the walled City became the centre of commerce and trade and gained a significant measure of civic authority.

After his victory at Hastings in 1066, William the Conqueror secured Kent and southern England. While eventually laying waste to most of the country, he 'came friendly' to London, recognizing the liberties of its citizens, pledging to defend their freedoms and fortified the City against barbarian attack. When William first arrived, he found the entrance to the City from the south heavily defended. With his troops he took a detour and eventually established himself at Westminster Palace. After a mixture of negotiations, promises and bribes, William won over prominent Londoners and nobles. The gate at Ludgate was opened and his troops finally entered the City. William was crowned king of England at Westminster Abbey on Christmas Day, 1066. Following the Norman invasion, the defence of the City was reinforced with the construction of Baynard's Castle, Montfichet's Tower on the western side and the Tower of London in the east, the latter of which was to become the most powerful fortress in Britain.

There was no fixed capital town in England and kings moved from place to place taking their court with them. Winchester was where the royal treasury and financial records were stored but this changed from around 1200 when these functions moved to Westminster and royal government became increasingly established and centered there. Most of London's population in Norman times was of Anglo-Saxon origin but within a few decades it was a cosmopolitan place where Danes, Germans, Norwegians, French and Normans mingled. The majority of Londoners lived in timber-framed houses roofed with thatch or sunken-floored huts, which made them vulnerable to regular outbreaks of fire. Streets were narrow and undrained with all manner of filth sloshing about. Life in the City continued more or less uninterrupted despite the conquest, except that plots of land were given over to Norman noblemen.

The Norman Conquest brought to an end almost 500 years of invasions and finally established the political unification of the nation as well as the possession of London.

Chapter 2

Medieval London

From Norman to Tudor Conquest

London enjoyed a far greater national importance in 1500 than it had had in 1100. Its population had grown considerably mainly because of inward migration in the area traditionally known as the City. London even then had the reputation of being cosmopolitan. Foreigners had settled in London in considerable numbers, many of them from France, Flanders and Italy. There was a sizeable Jewish quarter. Visitors from the provinces commented on the visible foreign and Jewish presence, not always favourably. This was the period during which London established its position as the nation's capital – the undisputed centre of England's political, legal, governmental, economic, commercial and cultural life.

London had the advantages of being the focus of roads, the lowest bridging point of the Thames and of proximity to the sea. This gave it easy access to many parts of Europe and it had developed into a thriving port. The Thames itself was navigable far upstream. London's commercial importance grew vigorously especially from the late fourteenth century. As a port it secured a major share of English seaborne trade as the London-dominated associations of wool exporters and cloth-merchants virtually monopolized the country's two main export products. Particularly strong trading links were established with the flourishing port of Antwerp. As waterborne traffic grew on the Thames, land was reclaimed on the north side of the river between the Tower and the outlet of the Fleet River. Excavations have shown the existence of many quays of stone or timber and a host of stairs and landing places which would have served the many ferries and commercial vessels which crowded the river at this point.

The shape of the continuously built-up area was still very much dictated by the Roman walls and the Saxon and early Norman street patterns. The City itself had become more densely populated within the constraints imposed by the walls although some extra-mural suburban development had taken place. Westminster was a distinct community with green fields between it and the City and was very different in character. It was dominated by the abbey and the royal palace and, lacking the constraints of walls, was far more spaciously laid out. It had an air of affluence, being a centre of what we would now call the service sector. The royal court and the district's governmental and administrative functions led to the growth of businesses catering for the well-to-do, especially in hospitality and luxury retailing. Southwark, the Borough and Bankside, across the Thames, were communities with a character of their own. They were also places of much disrepute.

Churches and public buildings were mostly built of stone which had to be brought in from some distance. Timber-framing and plaster infill constituted the structure of most buildings. By 1500 increasing amounts of brick construction were to be seen. Thatch was banned in the City from the fifteenth century as being a fire hazard although this did not stop fires being a common feature of London life.

The Church

The Church had a massive visual, spiritual and economic presence in the City of London. It possessed in St Paul's one of the greatest cathedrals of Christendom, the seat of the Bishop of London who, like most prelates of the time, combined great spiritual and temporal influence. Many abbots and bishops from the provinces had business that frequently brought them to London and several had town houses on a grand scale. The Cathedral was a magnificent building in the Norman style with a central tower topped by a tall spire, two small western towers, transepts and an ambulatory at the east end. It stood on one of the highest points in the City which made it a focal point in distant views. It was the scene of splendid religious and civic ceremonies at which the growing number of rich City bankers and merchants ostentatiously displayed their finery alongside their supposed piety. In Westminster, the Abbey, also a striking building, was already associated with ceremonies involving royalty.

The monastic orders had a strong presence by 1250. They often benefitted from the largesse of royalty or plutocrats hoping that financial contributions might guarantee their passage to Paradise. These orders returned something to society by providing accommodation for numbers of elderly and indigent people as well as offering some basic health care.

Distant views of the City showed a forest of spires and steeples. Its parish churches were further evidence of the place of religion in the life of the people. The number of parish churches in the City is estimated at 110 in 1300. Some had names that seem strange today such as All Hallows Staining, St Benet Fink, St Dionis Backchurch, St Margaret Moses, St Michael Paternoster Royal, St Nicholas in the Shambles and St Giles without Cripplegate. The existence of so many parish churches meant that the communities they served were small and closely knit and the influence of their incumbents often considerable. Many underwent frequent alterations or rebuilding in the latest fashionable styles and were paid for by bequests from parishioners terrified of death and hoping for God's recognition of their generosity.

The Church was not without its critics, however. Some challenged the value of its teaching and ethical practices and the worldly wealth accumulated by the institution itself and many of its senior figures. Others questioned its support of royalty and the aristocracy and the obedience it demanded from the people for kings and barons who were perceived as exploiting and living off the labours of the commonalty. Many of these critics were known as Lollards and were persecuted by the Church as heretics.

The Watermen of London's River

The Thames was London's main thoroughfare. This meant that the men who operated the traffic on this waterway were important members of the community. They had skills which were highly valued but also rights and privileges which they jealously guarded. The roadways of the City of London and those that connected it to outlying places were poorly maintained, sometimes impassable and frequently hazardous because of the depredations of footpads and other highway robbers. For royalty, grandees and their entourages the Thames provided the most practical way to move between Westminster, Whitehall, Bridewell, the Tower and Greenwich. It also provided the most efficient means for the carriage of goods through London and for those who, business or pleasure, needed to move from one part of London to another. Watermen therefore played a crucial role in facilitating the life of England's largest city. Vessels of all kinds were crammed on the Thames. A great deal of muscle power and skill was required to shift masses of people and huge quantities of merchandise and other necessities up and down and across the river. This gave the watermen considerable bargaining power, and they were not averse to making use of it.

From piers and river stairs, the cry of 'Oars!' was heard for centuries, keeping watermen and their wherries in constant demand. They were rough-and-ready men, highly skilled at their trade. They possessed their own slang, largely incomprehensible to outsiders and were always ready to engage in banter and raillery with their passengers and others on the river. When necessary, they were equally ready to use their fists. They were exclusive, keeping their numbers down to give themselves some rarity value and usually the job was handed down from father to son. As traffic on the river built up over this period, the watermen became notorious for charging what they thought a passenger was able to pay. Impoverished-looking fares might have a long wait if numbers of evidently affluent fares wanted to use the services of the watermen who happily gave them preference. In the sixteenth century, they had become so arrogant in their behaviour that it became necessarily to regulate their activities closely.

St Mary Overy Stairs (also spelt Overie, it means St Mary 'over the river' to which Southwark Cathedral owes its origins) on the Southwark side of the river not only serviced a cross-river ferry but was also a point of embarkation for those requiring journeys taking them under London Bridge. This could be extremely hazardous given the very strong currents generated where the river passed through the bridge's piers. It was not unlike shooting rapids and such a journey taxed the skills of the watermen to the utmost, casualties being high. Some young bloods and men-about-town hired small vessels to shoot the bridge in a show of bravado. It was foolhardy and many paid the price. Some watermen made a speciality of navigating the bridge. They were an elite, being known as 'bridge-shooters'. Few lasted long to enjoy the quietude of old age.

London Bridge

The bridge, like much of London at the time, was originally built of timber. Between 1077 and 1136 eight great fires swept through the City, doing some damage to the bridge. In 1091 London was hit by a ferocious storm which destroyed at least 600 homes. It was followed by a great surge like a tidal wave which coursed down the Thames bearing with it a mass of uprooted trees and other bulky debris which hit the bridge with such force that most of it collapsed. Two years later there was a great freeze. The river was totally frozen and horses and heavily laden wagons were able to cross, much to the chagrin of the watermen. When the thaw came the bridge was again largely destroyed as huge chunks of melting ice battered its piers.

In 1176, a construction began on stone bridge which was to serve as London's sole bridge for over six centuries. This bridge was thirty years in the building and over those years its wooden predecessor remained in use. The new bridge was the handiwork of Peter de Colechurch, a priest who clearly doubled as an accomplished civil engineer. He designed the bridge in such a way that it became less of an obstacle to debris floating down the river. Fortification was also built into the new bridge which had a drawbridge to allow shipping to pass. Over time houses, shops and places of worship were built on the bridge. By the standards of the time, the bridge was a prodigious feat of engineering and it aroused awe and admiration immediately, not only from the humble citizenry but also from artists which helps to explain why it has been portrayed so frequently during its chequered history. London Bridge remained the only road crossing of the Thames in London until the eighteenth century.

The existence of the bridge and the nature of its construction strongly influenced the location downstream of the complex system of riverside wharfs and warehouses that constituted the Pool of London. These were a crucial factor in London's commercial development and its prosperity until they were partially superseded by the opening in the nineteenth century of enclosed docks further down the river.

Trade and Business

The major exports of medieval England were raw wool and woollen cloth. It was on the fleece of the sheep that England and London's rise to economic eminence was based. Tax on exports of wool helped to pay for London Bridge. London had the lion's share of this export trade and much of it went to the clothmaking centres in the Low Countries and Italy. In turn merchants from those countries brought their considerable capital and financial skills to organizing this trade. Many of them settled permanently in London.

A mass of imported goods came into England including fine textiles, spices, furs, some manufactured products such as knives and armour, and food and copious quantities of wine from France. After the Hundred Years' War from the 1330s to the 1450s, English-manufactured woollen cloth became the preeminent export item and London enjoyed the premier position in this trade. The leading merchants created cartels which made life difficult for small competitors. Continuous growth in London's import and export business was by no means automatic and boom periods were interspersed with slumps, especially when there was disruption caused by war. Imports largely entered the City via Watergate, Queenhythe, Dowgate and Billingsgate, each associated with a particular trade. Much of the export business was handled by Billingsgate and Dowgate.

London was a major retail centre and Westcheap in the City, later called Cheapside, is recorded as having around 400 retail outlets in 1300. A great deal of industrial activity also went on in the City with particular trades clustered together. Butchers, for example, were dominant in Eastcheap and the Shambles, skinners around Candlewick Street and Walbrook and brewers and dyers in The Bailey. Street names often reflected the local trade. Examples were Cordwainer Street, Poultry, Milk Street and Garlickhythe.

By the sixteenth century outside the City wall at Bishopsgate there were over 300 inns and brothels along with bull and bear baiting rings, skittle and bowling alleys. William FitzStephen described Smithfield in 1174 as a 'celebrated rendezvous' where country traders came to sell cows, sheep, pigs and agricultural goods.

Plague and Pestilence

Whenever epidemic diseases occurred in London, they thrived in the unholy alliance of overcrowding, filthy sanitary conditions and inadequate and polluted water supplies. The Thames had traditionally provided most of London's water supply but by the thirteenth century there were conduits containing fresh water from springs and streams on the high ground to the north of London. Access to this relatively clean water was, however, mostly only available to the better-off. Many other conduits carrying water and the Thames itself were supplies that constituted a threat to health. While this was understood empirically, the existence of disease-bearing pathogens was of course unknown as were measures to ensure that water was safe to consume. In 1597 an old woman who looked after a conduit near St Paul's and one of her friends were placed in the pillory charged with having 'at night entered the conduit, washed themselves and evacuated their bowels therein'. This was clearly regarded as unacceptable behaviour even with scanty scientific knowledge of the time.

In the late thirteenth century official instructions were issued that the Walbrook, a small tributary of the Thames flowing through the City, should be 'made free from dung and other nuisances' but a century later it was reported to be blocked by 'filth and dung'. In 1290, the White Friars who had their base a hundred yards west of the Fleet complained that the stench from this turgid watercourse was stronger than the smell of the incense they burned and had caused the death of one of their brethren.

The state of the streets added to the array of disgusting odours that assailed the nostrils of Londoners. They did not like the stench but regarded it simply as something they had to put up with, as an inescapable part of London life, always at its worst when the weather was hot and dry. There was no attempt to maintain hygiene either by the authorities or by individuals. People simply threw all their household refuse including excrement out into the roadway where it mixed with other filth. When it rained, the streets turned into an evil-smelling muddy morass which could not be avoided by pedestrians. Included in the stench exuded by this foul concoction would be the waste from slaughter-houses, tanneries, breweries and the other industrial premises which were cheek by jowl in the City's densely packed streets. Rats found rich pickings in the streets and acted as vectors of various diseases.

From 1309 there had been official ordinances about the disposal of sewage and offal within the City but they were largely observed in the breach. For example, people continued to keep pigs, these being given to rooting about in the miry mess. The City's citizens carried on blocking gutters and conduits with semi-solid ordure, throwing dead or unwanted animals into the nearest watercourse or simply dumping all sorts of rubbish in the nearest convenient spot. There were several public latrines whose users could not afford to be unduly modest since they were mostly perched on stilts over the edge of the Thames or its tributaries. The Thames was considered as one of the filthiest rivers in Europe, being little more than a vast open sewer in which much of the decaying matter was washed downstream when the tide ebbed only to come back as the tide turned. It should be remembered that the Thames was considerably wider and shallower in those days and its flow markedly slower. Records show that many people drowned in the Thames, often falling in when it was dark. It would not have been a pleasant way to go.

All this shows why Londoners were so prone to epidemic and endemic diseases such as plague, cholera, typhus, smallpox and tuberculosis. Virulent and often fatal disease was accepted as part of London life. Disease was no respecter of social class with rich and poor living close together in the densely packed City. Those living in Westminster and its environs tended to be healthier because there was considerably more open space. Few Londoners lived to any great age.

Most dreaded of all was bubonic plague. Buboes or large swellings in the lymph nodes, appeared to be followed by high temperature, fever, intolerance of bright light, inflammation of the kidneys, vomiting, splitting headache, coma, internal bleeding and heart failure. Once the buboes had appeared, the victim was not long for this world, usually dying in the utmost distress after about five days A few lucky patients experienced burst buboes – and survived.

Plague is usually spread by rats and their associated fleas (*Xenopsylla cheopsis*). When the host rodent dies, the fleas go off in search of new food supplies and are equally at home sucking human blood and leaving a free deposit of the lethal bacterium *Yersenia pestis*. Two other forms of bubonic plague were known: pneumonic and septicaemic. The former is more infectious than bubonic plague. It attacks the lungs and can spread very rapidly through droplets expelled by the sufferer into the atmosphere by coughing and sneezing. The rarer septicaemic plague which, as its name suggests, involves blood-poisoning, and almost always involved death within twenty-four hours of contraction.

The major visible transmitter of plague was the black rat (*rattus rattus*) which likes to live near humans. All that was needed was the flea, infected rats, closeness to humans living in overcrowded pestilential conditions and, preferably, warm, humid summer weather. London provided all these and, additionally, houses built of wood, plaster and straw providing ideal living and breeding conditions for rats.

The worst outbreak of bubonic plague to affect England was that known as the 'Black Death' which raged in Europe from 1347 to 1351. It is thought to have arrived by ship at Melcombe Regis in Dorset and was then carried along the road by travellers, reaching London with steady but inexorable speed. It is estimated that between February and May 1349, about 50,000 Londoners died. This would have been as much as two-thirds of its population at that time.

The immediate reaction to the approach or arrival of the plague was understandable panic. In this and later visitations of the plague many of those who could afford to do so fled London in the frequently forlorn hope of eluding the terrifying scourge. Frequently they unknowingly already carried it with them.

Such was the lack of knowledge of disease-bearing pathogens that the scared and disorientated populace cast around desperately trying to find an explanation for these horrifying events. Many ascribed them to supernatural activity. They argued that it was a punishment from God for human sin. This easily morphed into a search for human scapegoats which included the parents of children born out of wedlock, people with what we now call behavioural problems and Jews. It was easy to whip up anti-Semitic sentiment. The Jews were, for example, accused of spreading plague by deliberately poisoning the wells. No one stopped to question the fact that they were likely to drink the same water supplies and were just as likely to contract plague as anyone else.

Well known as money-lenders in the medieval period a Jewish presence is remembered in place names such as Jewry Street in Aldgate and Old Jewry in the City, locations for the medieval Jewish community. In 1275 Edward I decreed that Jews could no longer loan money for a living. The Statute of the Jewry also required Jews to wear badges to identify themselves. Having run up large debts waging war abroad, Edward was under pressure to raise money. In order to persuade Parliament to raise taxes he offered to barter the remaining Jewish population. In the Edict of Expulsion of 1290, Parliament granted Edward a tax of £116,000. The expulsion was the culmination of over 200 years of increasing anti-Semitism in England. All Jews (around 3,000) in England were required to leave by November of that year and were not readmitted until the 1650s. Their financial role was taken over by Lombard bankers from Italy in Lombard Street and whose symbol was the three golden balls, the origin of the pawn shop.

London's population was traumatized by the plague and society's normal mores broke down under the strain. Sick people ran groaning or screaming around the streets, often suddenly dropping dead. Mobs broke into houses, ransacking and pillaging; defenceless females were raped and people openly copulated in the streets. The authorities were overwhelmed by the quantity of bodies requiring burial and many cadavers simply rotted in the gutters. Scavenging animals rooted among the corpses and scavenging humans went through their clothes to seize anything that might be of value. They often sealed their own deaths in doing so.

Crime

London, consisting of the City but also Westminster, Southwark and the suburbs, was a Mecca for the criminal classes. It offered unique opportunities for criminal activity. Its size was relevant. At the end of the fifteenth century its population can be estimated at 60,000. Norwich, then the second most populous settlement, had 12,000.

How London grew is reflected in the history of its crime. The resident population was not able to maintain let alone increase its numbers. Smallpox, typhoid and other endemic and epidemic diseases regularly carried away swathes of its inhabitants. The growth of its population was caused by large-scale immigration. People migrated to London from the provinces, in what was frequently the forlorn hope that by doing so, they would make their fortunes. Many came to London forced by desperation. They included dispossessed cottagers, jobless rural labourers, stigmatized unmarried mothers and many other victims of desperate circumstances. Generally, London's incomers were young, single, rootless and poor. Often failing to find legal employment, they had little to lose by joining the criminal underworld of the social and ethnic melting pot that was medieval London.

London and Westminster as England's commercial and administrative centres attracted a host of wealthy visitors as well as residents, many of whom made easy targets. There was a huge concentration of portable and easily stealable wealth. The absence of effective policing and the number of criminal jurisdictions (the City, Westminster and Middlesex), the sheer numbers and ever-changing nature of its populace and the opportunities London offered for relative anonymity, made it very difficult to prevent let alone detect criminal activity and bring its perpetrators to justice. Crime was etched into London's fabric.

Back in the twelfth century, an English monk had written:

> if you come to London pass through it quickly. Each race brings its own vices and its own customs to the city. No one lives in it without falling into some kind of crime. Every quarter of it abounds in grave obscenities. Whatever evil or malicious thing that can be found in any part of the world, you will find it in that one city. Actors, jesters, moors, magicians, smooth-skinned lads, flatterers, pretty boys, pederasts, beggars, quacks, belly-dancers, sorceresses, extortioners, night-wanderers, buffoons ... if you do not want to dwell with evildoers do not live in London.

Many of those arriving in London were totally destitute and had little option but to turn to begging and criminal activity. However, the punishment for vagrancy was crude and cruel. A vagrant on first conviction would be burned through the gristle of the right ear with a hot iron and then secured to the back of a cart and whipped through the streets. On a second conviction, the left ear would be burned and another humiliating whipping would be administered. On a third conviction, the vagrant would be hanged in public. The same punishments were administered on men and women displaying a touching regard for equal rights.

However, it was not equal rights when it came to punishment for poisoning. Women poisoners were burned, males boiled alive. A multiplicity of offences such as coin-clipping, rape, horse theft and theft of items valued at forty shillings or more carried a mandatory death sentence. These brutal punishments were intended as deterrents. In the absence of effective policing, few offenders were brought to justice and so it was thought necessary to make an example of those who were caught and convicted.

Public unrest involving riots was a feature of medieval London life. More than that, riots have continued to be a feature of the life of the capital.

In the City it was difficult to ignore the presence of the apprentices. They were often behind outbreaks of disorder. They were given to swaggering around the streets hurling abuse randomly but especially at those clearly belonging to ethnic minorities. They were not averse to taking on other bands of apprentices in free-for-alls which often led to broken heads and broken limbs.

Riots could occur almost spontaneously. It might only take a foreigner to catch the eye of an apprentice and the shout would go up of 'Prentices-Clubs! Prentices Clubs!' whereupon dozens of apprentices would emerge from nearby premises for an insult to one apprentice was seen as an insult to all. One example will suffice to show how quickly a serious incident could blow up. An apprentice was arrested after he had stabbed an Italian for a supposed insult. The cry went up and a horde of apprentices appeared and rescued him. The authorities brought up reinforcements. A crowd gathered, eager for action, supporting the apprentice because they saw nothing wrong in him attacking a foreigner. A general melee broke out and the crowd moved on to attack the homes of well-to-do Italians, looting them, beating up the occupants and then firing the houses. The Lord Mayor brought in more men and a running battle ensued in which many on both sides were killed. Several rioters were later hanged. Such was the social volatility of the streets of the City.

The part of London most notorious for criminal and licentious behaviour was on the southern side of the Thames in the Southwark and Bankside areas. The City fathers, building up their trade and commerce from the fourteenth century, required the semblance of social stability, even of respectability, to inspire confidence in their business enterprises. They cracked down on street crime and the more boisterous activities that took place in the streets and alleys. Life became increasingly difficult for the City's underworld and in dribs and drabs many of its criminal activists fled across the river to Southwark where the City authorities had no jurisdiction.

Southwark was a seething den of criminality and vice. Every form of sexual preference was catered for in the district's brothels or 'stews' as they were commonly known. Many of the female sex workers were known as 'Winchester Geese' because they operated in hovels profitably owned by the Bishopric of Winchester. It was ironic that other stews were owned by William Walworth, Lord Mayor of London, who had been very most active among the City's rich in attempting to get the most blatant vice transferred across the river and conveniently out of sight. Southwark was largely allowed just to get on with doing what it did best.

The brothels, inns of ill-repute, bear gardens and other sordid delights of the South Bank did a roaring trade and brought considerable profits for their owners. The brothels of Bankside increased from seven in 1381 to eighteen by 1506 but there were concerns about the serious spread of sexually transmitted diseases, not least syphilis. The relative immunities enjoyed by Southwark and Bankside came under scrutiny but although some were legally withdrawn, nobody, including Londoners of the fifteenth and sixteenth centuries, has ever found an effective way of eradicating demand for and the provision of the kind of services that were on offer.

The City gates often doubled as prisons as well as places of accommodation. At Ludgate the upper rooms were used as a City gaol from 1378 for freemen and women charged with minor offences. Newgate became inextricably linked with the notorious prison as the medieval gateway was used for housing some of the most violent criminals. Other buildings were added and the prison was extended and rebuilt many times. In the absence of a prison in the northern part of the City any of the gates could be utilized when necessary. In 1262 some men who had broken into the Jewish quarter of the City were subsequently imprisoned in Newgate and Cripplegate. In 1311 when the Pope decreed to disband the Order of the Knights Templar, many were rounded up and arrested with six Templars imprisoned in Cripplegate. In addition, the gates functioned to police entry into the City. The City authorities appointed sworn keepers to the City gates who were responsible for opening and closing them. At Cripplegate in 1375 Porters of the City Gates were warned that they would suffer the pain of the pillory should they allow a leper to be brought into the City. Aldgate was the easternmost gate into the City and one of the original Roman gates. Some gates had apartments such as Aldgate where Geoffrey Chaucer (c. 1340–1400) lived from 1374 to 1386 whilst he was a customs official.

In a sense crime is eternal. In the medieval period we can see a variety of crimes, the perpetration of which has only changed over time to reflect the evolution of technology. Confidence tricksters still thrive today, as do quacks, pickpockets, card-sharpers, racketeers and forgers

The Peasants' Revolt

The feudal society of medieval England was typified by the relationship between lords who owned the land and peasants who worked upon it. Serfs, or peasants, had little or no legal rights. During the fourteenth century there was a fall in economic growth, a decline in the population caused by the Black Death in 1348, severe legislation (the Statute of Labourers, 1351) which inflicted heavy penalties on those demanding higher wages and the imposition of a poll tax. All these factors created a growing unrest towards those in power, notably the Church and the governing classes. Parts of Kent and East Anglia were in open revolt and on 12 June 1381 an army of Kentish and Essex rebels was camped at Blackheath. The rebels pledged their loyalty to the 14-year-old King Richard II and emphasized that their grievances were aimed not at him but at his corrupt advisers. Led by Wat Tyler, the rebels drew up a list of demands which included the abolition of serfdom.

Next day the rebels advanced on London where they had the sympathy of the mass of the citizenry for the gates of the City were opened for them. Rebels streamed in from elsewhere to join them. The group around the King decided to make some concessions to appease the rebels and then, when the time was right, to seize and kill their leaders and suppress the uprising. The rebels withdrew to draw up additional demands and arranged another meeting for the evening of 15 June at Smithfield in the City. The King appealed to the huge crowd of peasants that they should trust him to deal with their grievances and return to their homes. Accounts of what happened next are confused and contradictory. Lord Mayor Walworth, a leader of the hardliners opposed to any concessions, struck down Wat Tyler. A large force of soldiers appeared and most of the peasants then dispersed, believing that the concessions had been granted. They were soon to be disabused as a wave of brutal repression was launched with known ringleaders slaughtered and many hundreds of others killed.

The hugely unpopular poll tax which had ignited the uprising was abolished but the days of feudalism were numbered as the country's economy began to evolve from a rural and agricultural model to one with a commercial, mercantile and increasingly urban base. In terms of the history of London, the Peasants' Revolt had horrified the authorities and produced a profound and continuing fear of mass action that could threaten order and property.

Street Life

The streets, alleys and yards of medieval London were alive with seething masses of humanity. Streets were a bedlam of noise and much business was done there; communal feats and carnivals were performed; hell-raisers swaggered along from one tavern to the next; all manner of games and sports were played; agitators made speeches and were roundly abused or cheered by the crowds; people under punishment were placed in the pillory, whipped at the cart's tail or hauled to a place of execution such as Tyburn. When victories were celebrated, oxen might be roasted in the streets, bonfires ignited and barrels of wine emptied into the conduits – free for any and everybody to sample – and they did. People fought, flirted and often fornicated in the streets. The homeless slept on the streets where criminals of all kinds conducted their nefarious activities. Livestock was driven through the streets, horses and mules were everywhere, all adding to the ordure. Semi-feral cats, dogs and pigs rooted contentedly in the mire and muck alongside scavenging birds such as storks and crows. Occasionally a horse or a bull would break free and run amok, causing chaos. Those in upstairs workshops and dwellings gaily threw unwanted matter out of their windows and into the street.

Despite the capricious climate, the stench and the noise, being out on the streets was often preferable to staying inside the dark and noisome hovels so many of them inhabited. Communal feasts, carnivals and celebrations were held on the streets. Drunkards and hellraisers caroused. Grown men as well as children played games in the street and exercised at sports. In the days before newspapers, news of invasions, battles, rebellion and treason, was cried through the streets.

At Shrovetide there was cock-fighting and football which often degenerated into a general scrimmage without rules. On many Sundays in spring, the young sons of nobles met the sons of more humble citizens in the fields just north of Cheapside where they engaged in mock battles which not infrequently turned into the real thing. In summertime there was improvised street tennis, cricket, archery, wrestling and javelin-throwing. In the winter there was bull-baiting and bear-baiting, battles of boars against hogs, and a variety of Christmas revels. On the frozen swamps of Moorfields young men engaged in ice sports such as skating, the skates being the shin bones of animals fixed under the boot. One game involved skating towards each other as fast as possible and, in passing, attempting to crack the opponent on the head with a sturdy staff made of wood. Less robust and lethal were miracle plays and other activities associated with faith.

The scene for much of the bull- and bear-baiting was Bankside, Southwark, on the southern side of the river. These 'entertainments' were immensely popular except of course for the poor animals. Bulls would be set upon by several dogs specially bred to clamp tenaciously on to their victims. In fact, the dogs were victims themselves because they were frequently gored by the bulls and, in the frenzied excitement, bitten and ripped by their canine fellows. Sadly, the enraged and bloodied bulls could give a good account of themselves but the 'fun' usually ended when they finally expired from pain and exhaustion along with some of the dogs. The 'sport' with the bears was, if anything, even more barbaric. They were chained loosely to a strong post after having been hooded and blinded whereupon several men would attack them with whips. With one swipe a bear could disembowel an attacker. Crowds would be wild with excitement as bets were laid on how many dogs the bull might manage to kill or how long it would take the men with whips to subdue the bear.

Almost as inexplicable, although less repulsive, was a contest in the fourteenth century between the Scottish Earl of Crawford and the English Lord Wells to decide who was tougher, the Scots or the English. The contest took place on London Bridge to the accompaniment of an excited crowd and a fanfare of trumpets. Mounted on horses the two men charged each other repeatedly. Crawford took so many blows and broke so many of his lances without being unseated that spectators were sure that he was fastened to his saddle. He obligingly dismounted briefly to prove them wrong, quickly remounted and charged Wells so forcefully that he unhorsed him and he fell to the ground unconscious. Crawford then dismounted once more, ran to his fallen rival, embraced him tenderly and visited him daily until he had recovered from his injuries. The outcome of the contest was not mentioned but we can surmise that it was an away victory for the Scotsman.

Food and Drink

Most Londoners often did not have the facilities to cook anything substantial and would send a joint of meat or their own prepared pies and puddings to a cookshop. There were many of these and they were equipped with large ovens. They also operated as 'takeaways'. They could offer a wide selection of their own pies, puddings, baked and roasted meat. A tariff from a cookshop of 1378 shows that 'best roast pig' could be had for 8d., three roast thrushes cost 2d. and ten eggs just a penny.

It is not surprising that recipe books of the time deal with how to make tainted meat edible. Washing in vinegar was one of the favourite methods. Herbs and spices helped to disguise the taste of rotten meat. Much use was made of salting which could greatly prolong the life of meat or fish but not provide any great treat for the taste buds. Many families even in the densely populated City owned at least one pig. These shared the home and were allowed to forage in the streets. Some became extremely corpulent but it did them little good because the practice was for them to be slaughtered in the autumn and then salted to provide a supply of meat through the winter months.

Fish was consumed on a considerable scale, both fresh and preserved. Much sea fishing was done in the Thames estuary and along the coasts of Kent and Essex for the London market. The tidal Thames where it flowed through London, despite being filthy, contained a wide variety of fresh and saltwater fish and there were Londoners who made their living catching fish in the Thames and then selling them around the streets. Among those commonly consumed were salmon, then very common even in the Thames, sprats and eels. It is interesting to note that, as early as the mid-sixteenth century, there were regulations about the size of the mesh in the nets being used. These had to be of a size that would allow small fish to escape and therefore conserve stocks. Oysters and mussels were plentiful and inexpensive. However, 'fish' for Londoners often meant herrings from the North Sea in almost inconceivable quantities and which were frequently consumed salted or pickled.

The Roman Catholic faith to which most people belonged decreed that fish was to be consumed on Fridays and on various other days of the year, particularly those associated with religious festivals. This obviously created a large-scale demand for fish which could not always be met from what we would think of as orthodox sources. There are records of the authorities condemning and destroying unfit fish and punishing those who tried to sell it. Londoners may have built up some degree of resistance to the effect of consuming tainted food. It was thought that even the smell of rotting fish was harmful and a cause of various ailments. It was permissible on designated days to eat certain other creatures which were classified as 'fish'. These included barnacle geese and puffins, for example, considered to be fish because they lived on or close to the sea. Perhaps more extraordinary, on the permitted list were beavers because their tales were thought of as fishlike.

Fresh milk, unless it could be obtained from sources very close to London, was little used because of its highly perishable nature. In the earlier part of the period milk came largely from sheep and goats but later cow's milk was more widely used because it was less hard work to milk one cow than, say, ten sheep. Much milk went into the production of cheese and there was a considerable trade especially in Cheshire cheese which came by sea via small coastal vessels. Milk was also used in the production of butter, large amounts of which were salted and could be kept throughout the winter. Milk was recognized for its nutritional value but experience taught that it was dangerous once it started to go off. For that reason, great store was set by mothers nursing their own children or, failing that, employing the services of a wet nurse if they could afford to do so. However, it was widely believed that the moral and physical character of the infant would be greatly influenced by the milk it imbibed at the breast. If the wet nurse was a drunkard, for example, or regarded as simple minded, then the infant would take on such characteristics. If there was a trace of blood in the milk when the baby suckled, it was believed that it would grow up to be a murderer.

Bread was baked in the home or in communal ovens and was a staple item of diet. Only the better-off could afford the best quality white bread made from wheat. The commonest bread was called maslin and was made from a mixture or wheat and rye flour. Off-white and brown breads were often used by the wealthy as trenchers or plates. By cutting large stale loaves into thick slices with a slight hollow in the middle, food was scooped onto these trenchers and then eaten.

Given the importance of staple items of diet, the authorities took measures to try to ensure quality and price control from at least the thirteenth century. The bakers of underweight loaves would be consigned to the pillory or might find themselves drawn around the streets on a mule-drawn hurdle with examples of the offending loaves hanging around their necks. The punishment was intended to be humiliating and the offenders would be assailed by verbal insults and a variety of missiles. This was not confined to bakers. In 1366 John Russell of Billingsgate was found guilty of trying to sell thirty-seven pigeons described as 'putrid, rotten, stinking and abominable'. He was placed in the pillory and the pigeons were burnt by his feet. There were sharp practices associated with the production of wine. Sometimes 'body' would be added to thin French wines by the addition of starch, gum or sugar. In 1350 John Penroe was found guilty of selling 'unsound' wine. His punishment was being forced to drink an excessive amount of his own substandard concoction, having the rest poured over his head and then being forbidden from trading as a vintner.

There were rules of etiquette at the dining table, at least for those with money. People sitting down to dine were abjured not to play with their hounds, not to scratch themselves on the head and especially not on what were coyly described as the 'privy parts'. On no account was the nose to be picked and it was the height of inappropriate behaviour to blow one's nose on the tablecloth. Belching seemed to be regarded as mildly rude but breaking wind was seen as exceptionally discourteous to fellow-guests and the hosts.

Etiquette entered into the carving of roast joints. Meat, poultry and game were never simply 'carved'. A joint was dismembered with different words applied to different animals. Deer for example were 'broken', swans were 'listed', chickens 'spoiled' and peacocks 'disfigured'. A young squire in his teens aspiring to gain the knightly skills would carve for the company and be expected to know correctly how to carve carcasses of such varying size and anatomical detail as an ox and a blackbird, even something as small as a finch.

There had been a long tradition of trade in spices and much use seems to have been made of pepper, ginger, mace and cloves. There were many culinary delights which have now fallen into disuse but they provided some very tasty items before the age of additives. These included a sauce composed of bread, vinegar, chopped sage, mint, garlic, thyme and parsley which was an excellent accompaniment for baked eggs or, mixed with grapes, served with roast pigeon. Verjuice was the general name for the juice extracted from sour fruits or vegetables among which were crab apples, rowan berries, gooseberries and sorrel. London was surrounded by countryside and even its poorest inhabitants could get out into the meadows, woods and hedges and glean a natural bounty of wholesome food items.

The wealthy would drink ale, cider, perry and metheglin which was a kind of mead, and wine. Although some wine was produced in southern England, by the fourteenth century there was a flourishing trade in wine imported from northern Europe, especially from France and the Rhineland. When malmsey, a sweet wine from Crete became popular in the fifteenth century, a considerable trade developed in this commodity. London's many drinking places varied from decrepit hovels to travellers' inns, which would also serve ale. In the less fashionable establishments, brewing was usually done on the premises by the woman of the house, who was known as a brewster. Much of this ale would have been of formidable strength. It was known as 'recreational' ale, drunk in order to cause intoxication but other ale would be much weaker and consumed by adults and children alike for thirst-quenching purposes –this beer being safer to drink than water. Ale was dark and unhopped and often flavoured with herbs.

Chapter 3

Trading and Commercial London

By 1500 London had come to dominate England and Wales. By the end of the seventeenth century, two-thirds of England's town dwellers lived in London. It grew not only rapidly but more or less continuously whereas most other European capitals had periods of stagnation or even decline. It was England's centre of government and administration, a leading international trading city and a major manufacturing base. Until 1801 population figures are estimates but they clearly indicate the process that was at work. The population doubled to 400,000 between 1600 and 1650, rose to 675,000 in 1750 and 900,000 in 1801, this being the date of the first official census.

London's population growth was phenomenal given its almost continuously high rate of mortality, especially in the early eighteenth century. As a seaport and focus of inward migration, infectious diseases were endemic in overcrowded conditions. People came from all parts of the British Isles but also from foreign countries, near and far. Immigration as an issue in London history is dealt with elsewhere but here it suffices to say that immigration made a major contribution to London's rise to the status of a world city. Countryfolk, especially from East Anglia, and Irish and Welsh people and to a lesser extent Scottish, arrived in the capital, many convinced that in London they would improve their economic circumstances. The majority managed to eke out a frugal, often semi-criminal existence in that huge human mass which constituted the London poor. Others, perhaps more unscrupulous, came and blended quickly into the criminal underworld. For migrants into London who had skills that were in demand, good remuneration was indeed available and they could enjoy a comfortable living. London has always housed a disproportionately large number of the extremely rich: acute extremes of wealth and poverty have always been, and remain a feature of life in the capital.

London's Jewish communities, consisted of Sephardic Jews from Spain and Portugal, many of whom pursued various business ventures with some becoming extremely rich. In the early eighteenth century, Ashkenazi Jews arrived from central Europe. Many arrived with only the clothes they stood up in and somehow survived in the semi-underworld of districts like

Whitechapel. In the late seventeenth century, French Huguenot refugees from religious persecution arrived, also in the East End, and set up in specialized occupations such as silk-weaving, watch-making and, with some success, in what would now be called 'financial services'. The Jewish and Huguenot communities, while maintaining a strong tradition and identity, contributed significantly to the economic prosperity of London. Large-scale inward migration from an increasingly wide variety of sources has had a seminal influence in giving London the character it has today.

Those who lived elsewhere, especially in the counties close to London, increasingly found, as it grew, that their lives were bound to the capital by the demand it created for what they produced, be it food, fuel or any of a massive range of artefacts. Activities such as dairying, market gardening, stock-rearing and fattening, sea-fishing and many others were aimed almost exclusively at the London market. Much of the coal mined in the north-east of England was destined for London and quarries such as those on the south coast at Portland prospered as grand buildings were erected in London to house government and important commercial businesses. These commodities arrived in London by road, river and later, canal. London's demand was enormous. It has been estimated that in the eighteenth century, its inhabitants consumed fourteen million mackerel annually!

The London rich created a demand for luxury goods. In 1765 Josiah Wedgwood, the Staffordshire potter, opened a showroom in Grosvenor Square which proved so successful that within a few years he moved twice to new premises, each larger and more opulent than its predecessor. He had the business acumen to understand that relatively small amounts of high-priced quality goods sold on the London market to the rich produced more profit than large quantities of lower-quality goods sold to poorer consumers in the Midlands. Not only did the rich of London provide a market for luxury goods but the presence of emporia in London full of *haute couture*, *objets d'art* and other goods considered desirable by the rich elite, attracted affluent visitors from the provinces and from abroad. Between them rich visitors and rich residents constituted a demand for a range of services such as clubs, theatres and libraries. To pander to the needs of London's rich came doctors, quacks and charlatans, architects, actors, artists, lawyers, bankers, moneylenders and financial advisors and many slippery confidence tricksters eager to part the rich from their money. As the functions of the royal court and of state administration expanded, politicians, bureaucrats and functionaries proliferated.

For all that London was evolving into the prototype of the modern world-city, the machinery to administer the growing metropolis lagged behind the ever more complex needs of its expanding and diverse population. By the eighteenth century the City guilds which had enjoyed such a potent economic influence were becoming obsolescent. They had exercised stringent control of such areas as apprenticeships in their trades and what would now be called the terms and conditions of their employment but the new economic activities that were developing around London away from the City had little time for what were increasingly seen as restrictive practices. Consequently, many of the livery companies were evolving into male socializing bodies enjoying a self-indulgence in outdated rituals with some charity fund-raising.

Local government in London was a pot mess. Creaking structures dating back to medieval times were proving increasingly inadequate for dealing with the breadth of issues, some old but intensifying and others novel, raised by the burgeoning of London's population. The City had long been ruled by its autocratic Corporation. It had historic responsibility for markets, the Port of London, the Thames both upstream and downstream from London, and the right to levy duties on the movement of coal for a distance of twelve miles from the City. Its writ did not, however, extend to long-established villages close by such as Hammersmith, Chelsea, Paddington, Marylebone and St Pancras let alone to other districts like Westminster which were experiencing growth and its attendant problems. Nor did the City seem to have any wish to extend its jurisdiction to adjacent newly developing areas. Parish vestries in these and other localities varied in the responsibilities and jurisdiction they carried.

The parish was long established as an organ of local government and had considerable jurisdiction and responsibility. Every middle-class householder was expected to take on parochial responsibilities such as attempting to maintain law and order or looking after the indigent poor. The role of the ecclesiastical bodies in caring for the ill, the aged and vulnerable was virtually extinct. The growing layer of people who were victims of economic change found themselves stigmatized for the 'crime' of being poor with no real support structure except the workhouses which parishes were allowed to run from 1722. The conditions were such in these establishments that only the most desperate threw themselves on their tender mercies of the poor law overseers.

The area loosely called London, with a population approaching one million in the late eighteenth century, was run by a hotchpotch of bodies which jealously guarded their often historically conditioned areas of jurisdiction. They wanted little to do with each other and were hostile to the idea that they should be rationalized and modernized. The infrastructure essential for supporting the population of a large city in an advanced country was yet to be established and when it did so, there was a large element of trial and error.

Communications by Road

The location of London made it into a natural hub of physical communication. Even in Roman times London and its bridge were the focus of roads to and from ports on the Kent coast, Colchester, York and Scotland, Chichester, Exeter, Bath, Gloucester, Wroxeter and Chester among other places of importance. These roads were initiated by the Romans primarily for military purposes. After the Roman occupation ended, these roads tended to deteriorate over time and did not necessarily serve the places which were becoming economically important.

Travel overland by wheeled vehicles remained difficult until scientific methods of road construction and maintenance began to develop from the eighteenth century. However, as economic activity grew, the demands of trade and commerce led to increasing amounts of vehicular traffic on the roads, much of it passing to and from London. By the mid-seventeenth century, wagons, often drawn by oxen, were running regular scheduled services from London to places such as York, Manchester and Exeter. They lumbered along at a pace we would now regard as funereal. The state of the roads, dustbowls in hot weather and muddy morasses when it was wet, retarded potential economic growth.

The dire state of the roads did not prevent the development of an increasingly complex network of passenger-carrying stagecoaches from the mid-seventeenth century. By 1705 London was linked to no fewer than 180 provincial towns. Travel by coach was slow by later standards, expensive and hazardous, not only because of the depredations of highwaymen but also on account of the foolhardy speed which was required in continuous attempts to reduce journey times. Thus, the journey between London and Manchester which had taken three days in 1750 had been reduced to a mere eighteen hours in 1836. The fastest and most expensive journeys were made in those coaches licensed to carry the Royal Mail. No further accelerations were possible until railways appeared on the scene. They slashed travel times, reduced fares and enhanced safety, resulting in the long-distance stagecoach system going into terminal decline, unable to compete with the iron horse.

Stagecoaches were seriously big business during their peak which lasted from around 1750 to the mid-1830s. London, as was only to be expected, was the hub of the stagecoach network. The owners of the coaches mostly operated out of what became specialist coaching inns located in the City although there were a handful in Southwark and Borough on the south side of the Thames. Three companies dominated London's coaching business. William Chaplin was based at the Swan with Two Necks, the White Horse, the Spread Eagle and the Cross Keys. By the 1830s Chaplin had 2,000 employees, sixty-eight coaches and 1,800 horses. His major rivals were Benjamin Worthy Horne based at the Golden Cross, George and Blue Boar, the Bull and the Old Bell, and Edward Sherman whose main centre of operations was the Bull and Mouth.

From London, Royal Mail and long-distance stagecoach services radiated like the spokes of a wheel. Particularly long routes served places as far away as Penzance, Pembroke, Holyhead, Carlisle, Glasgow and Thurso. This demanding marathon took about six days. Most provincial towns of any importance were on the long-distance network and it is easy to forget that there were a host of short-haul coaches joining various parts of the expanding metropolis and others serving places within a radius of, say, thirty miles from London. Since vast numbers of carriers' wagons, both long and short distance, also used the coaching inns for their business, these places could be the scene of frenzied activity.

Before the coming of the railways in the 1830s, primitive though roads and their associated services may seem by today's standards, they played a critical role in furthering the prosperity of London and enhancing its role as the country's capital. They were arteries for transporting the products and produce that London needed and in turn allowed London's own goods and services to be consumed in the provinces. At the expense of local centres, London was able to use the road system to extend the governmental influence of Westminster and its ideological and cultural domination. The unequivocal assertion of the authority of London was essential for the task of creating a unified nation-state and national market for the circulation of commodities. London became the focus of decision-making on matters of national importance and the overall wealth of its citizens was increased by the concentration in the capital of the bulk of the nation's movers and shakers.

The Thames – London's Super Highway

In the absence of an effective system of administering and maintaining the roads, wherever possible for the carriage of goods in bulk, water transport was a better option. The Thames provided an ideal link with the North

Sea and the English Channel with the added advantage that it penetrated deep into London's hinterland with tributaries that could be navigated by small vessels. London developed both as a seaport, an inland port and an entrepot. An almost continuous run of quays, wharves and warehouses lined the Thames where it passed through London. Most of them concentrated on handling specific types of merchandise or produce being imported or exported. At the same time, much transshipment took place on the Thames as cargoes were moved from river craft, mostly lighters, to larger ocean-going vessels. This was because there was frequently insufficient space at these wharves for the number of vessels that wanted to use them.

It was always commerce which provided the driving force of London's development into a world city. Britain became the trading nation par excellence and went on to control the largest empire ever seen. The hub of the wealth which made Britain temporarily the most powerful nation in the world was to be found in the City and in the port. Britain became an intensively industrialized economy exporting manufactured goods across the world but it was in London that the decisions were taken and the money raised and committed that made all this possible. For much of the period up to the mid-nineteenth century it was also the port handling the bulk of the county's imports and re-exports. In 1700 about 80 per cent of imports were handled in London and 69 per cent of exports. Imports through London quadrupled in both the seventeenth and eighteenth centuries. At the end of the eighteenth century the value of goods exported through London was more than that of all the other ports combined. In the nineteenth century ports on the west coast boomed because of the massive growth of trade with the Caribbean and the Americas but London still virtually monopolized trade with mainland Europe, India and the Far East. The Thames played a vital role in London's growth into a world city.

Coal had been shipped down the coast from north-east England to London at least as early as the thirteenth century. It was usually called seacoal. As London grew the demand for coal increased to the extent that the 200 colliers operating on the Thames around 1600 had become 1,200 by 1850. Coal was used for domestic purposes and by London's industries, many of which clustered along the banks of the Thames. Handling coal was, of course, exceptionally dirty and many were the jokes that Londoners made about the men who sailed the colliers and handled the seacoal. It was even said that they never washed or changed their clothes because there would have been no point in doing so. From the mid-nineteenth century the collier trade in seacoal slowly declined because of competition from the railways but it did not die out completely until well after the Second

World War when the last coal-fired power stations closed and domestic use fell away. In earlier times the coal trade had been so lucrative that the duty paid on it when it was landed in London helped to pay for the rebuilding of St Paul's Cathedral after the Great Fire of 1666. London became utterly dependent on coal and there was always a crisis when supplies by sea were disrupted for whatever reason.

As waterborne trade developed on the Thames, there evolved a breed of tough and often truculent men who demanded respect but elicited little affection in return. They demanded respect because their work was vital to the economy and everyday life of London. These were the lightermen, the watermen and the porters. Because the riverside wharves became so congested, large numbers of ships had to anchor in the middle of the river. Their cargoes, whether inward or outward bound, had to be carried in lighters to or from the place where they could be landed or dispatched. Doing this was the job of the lightermen. There was usually a heavy demand and the lightermen were able to charge highly for their services. This obviously made them unpopular. There were licensed watermen entitled to wear a distinctive armband proclaiming their status but as might be expected there were also bogus lightermen touting for business and undercutting those with licences. Turf wars were not unknown with quarter neither given nor expected.

Porters were the men who loaded and unloaded the ships in midstream or at some point on the river side. The quicker they worked, the more they got done and the more they earned. They were not too fussy on how they handled the cargoes even though some were obviously fragile or perishable. They never conceded that any losses were their fault and were constantly in acrimonious confrontation with their paymasters regarding their remuneration. The watermen, who have been mentioned before, were the third group in this triumvirate and as they handled the passenger wherries which plied across and along the river, they were the ones with whom the public had most contact and who were therefore generally the most disliked. Another group of men who demanded a cut of the wealth being generated on the river were the wharf-owners, widely considered to be overcharging for the services they provided. The problem was that all these men who made their living on the river could charge what the market would bear. While most of them remain anonymous and forgotten, collectively they made a vital contribution to the accumulation of wealth on which London's leading position in the world came to be based. The watermen were something of an exclusive fellowship and, for a period, enjoyed considerable power. They formed a guild in 1555 and later admitted lightermen to membership. Members were required to serve an apprenticeship of seven years and they were extremely jealous of their trade. They were vociferous in their opposition to the buildings of new bridges across the Thames in London and had enough power to delay them for decades even though there was a desperate need for additional bridges.

The Thames where it passed through London was densely packed with shipping of every sort and size. Inevitably, there were easy pickings for the light-fingered fraternity and pilfering took place on an industrial scale. Both inward- and outward-going goods were systematically plundered, the booty being taken ashore and emerging, often blatantly, on a thriving black market. Legitimate traders were obviously concerned about this but in the absence of any effective administration of riverine traffic and a police force to back it up, progress was slow. An early measure came in the Elizabethan period when twenty 'legal quays' were set up between London Bridge and the Tower. At these quays, customs duties had to be paid and it was forbidden to land any cargoes or load any vessels at any other point. It was a start but without the machinery to back the new regulations up, little changed. The river became increasingly congested and pilfering even more rampant.

The bustling, teeming port made a great contribution to an essential aspect of London's character which was its cosmopolitanism. It also contributed to the overall wealth of the capital even if much of this wealth found its way into what might be described as an 'alternative economy'. London was full of foreign sailors who were meat and drink for louche figures from London's underworld. Brothels, seedy taverns and alehouses, squalid drinking and gambling clubs and, from at least the eighteenth century, opium dens notably around Limehouse, lured money out of the pockets of sailors who had been paid off and were determined to spend their earnings on the dissipated pleasures so attractive to men who had been a long time at sea. Bug-infested dosshouses were available for those whose money was running out but whose ships were not yet ready to leave the Pool of London. Drunken mariners who were not completely spent-up were at risk from footpads in the streets and the attentions of crimps. These seedy individuals took money for 'recruiting' sailors for ships, both mercantile and naval, which were short of crews. The crimps treated them to drinks until they were insensible, whereupon they were carried off and dumped on board a waiting ship. They were unlikely to regain consciousness until their ship was well its way down the Thames to the open sea.

The congestion on the Thames with its concomitant systematic and costly pilfering was partly relieved by the building of enclosed docks downstream from the Tower. These included the West India Docks in 1802 and the East India Docks 1806. The existence of so much shipping on the Thames encouraged ancillary industries such as shipbuilding and ropemaking, on both sides of the river downstream from the Tower. Although outside the area covered by this book, a host of industries such as sugar-refining clustered along the Thames in what became known as the East End and they depended on shipping for their raw materials and fuel.

The existence of the Thames and the use that was made of it is a necessary but not a sufficient explanation for two closely interrelated issues: the growth of London as a world city and the expansion of the British economy to a situation whereby, for a brief period, perhaps between the mid-1840s and the mid-1870s, Britain was the dominant economic, political and naval force in the world. This situation occurred as the outcome of the interaction of innumerable factors and processes, some going back four or more centuries. The immense wealth generated by the rearing of sheep and the export of wool and woollen cloth has already been mentioned. The fact is that by the end of the fifteenth century some of the preconditions for the development of a modern capitalist-based economy were emerging in England and giving it a head start over many other European countries that could have been potential trading and commercial rivals. England emerged in the seventeenth century as a nation which forged, often through violent upheaval, the form of government and political institutions most suited to encourage the development of capitalism in manufacturing, commercial and financial forms. She came to pursue the development of colonies and international trading arrangements with ruthless energy. She was intent on pursuing commercial profit, by force if necessary, and benefitted by developing a powerful navy and making the most of scientific and technological advances in ship design and building and navigational aids. When the Americas and the Caribbean began to be exploited for the growing of cotton, for example, Britain took a lead in the transportation of African slaves across the Atlantic and the enormously lucrative 'triangular trade'. The processes by which the economy of London and the British Isles developed towards world domination are infinitely more complicated than can be covered here but London and the Thames were at the centre of the process.

London as an Industrial Centre

Between the middle of the eighteenth century and the first quarter of the nineteenth, London's population doubled and it became the largest business centre and market of the world's first modern industrial economy. Crucially, despite the wars with France from 1793 to 1815 and some civil unrest such as the Gordon Riots of 1780, this period was characterized by political stability.

Roy Porter (1994) compared the industrial and business growth of London around 1775 to 1825 with that of provincial cradles of mining and manufacturing industry such as South Wales, the Black Country or Tyneside and Wearside. He concluded: 'the capital hardly lagged in technology and innovation ... As late as the 1850 London's manufacturing output was still unrivalled in Britain ... and the nation's industrial economy was profoundly dependent upon the capital's imports, transport and communications, wholesale and retail networks, finance skills and its service sector more generally.'

London's development was marked by a diversity of economic activity unrivalled elsewhere in the British Isles. In considering how London became the first modern industrial city of over a million people, centred in the world's first industrialized national economy, questions quickly come to mind. How far did the enormous growth of London's accumulated spending power influence its industrial and commercial activity? What goods were required to satisfy the needs of its burgeoning population, and how were they produced? How far was it a market for the manufacture of others, and how far was it a major manufacturing centre in its own right? And how far, say by 1800, had it moved from its earlier characterization as a centre for luxury crafts and trades? How far had London already developed a service economy, and what was its importance within the economy as a whole? How did this huge population actually make a living? These questions require answers which are too complex to be addressed satisfactorily in the current work. All we can do here is to nibble around the edges to provide some relevant points. A leading factor is the sheer diversity of trades. In 1747 one observer estimated nearly 300 separate trades were being pursued in London. In 1843 another survey put the figure at between 1,300 and 1,400.

The growth of the population and the physical size of London from the mid-eighteenth century have to be considered when examining its development as an industrial centre. An observer who had climbed to the dome of St Paul's in 1700 would have been able to see plenty of green countryside. Pastures and scattered farms extended from Lamb's Conduit Fields near Bloomsbury uphill to Highgate and Hampstead. Covent Garden and Lincoln's Inn Fields had only small clusters of buildings surrounding them set as they largely were in fields while St James's and Hyde parks were in an area still largely consisting of open countryside. An observer at St Paul's in 1800, however, would have been hard put to see any open country such was the outward growth of London. The contrast between the fine buildings in the fashionable areas of Mayfair and Marylebone and the squalid overcrowding and jerry-building of working-class districts to the north and east of the City was commented on by foreign visitors. Major public buildings were going up in this period. They included government offices in Whitehall and the impressive, if sinister, Newgate Prison. An infrastructure of street lighting, water supply and sewers was being built from the 1780s which was the envy of other major cities in Europe.

Earlier, in 1756–61, the New Road had been built to provide a means whereby the congested City could be bypassed. Five new bridges across the Thames were built between 1750 and 1819.

To feed London, both its human and livestock, required the produce from London's hinterland. London had specialized markets, some long established, dealing with different commodities. These included Smithfield (meat), Covent Garden and Borough (fruit and vegetables), Billingsgate (fish), Spitalfields (vegetables) and Bermondsey (hides and leather). These in turn attracted businesses associated with the main activity of the adjacent market.

Certain industries came to be associated with specific districts. Clerkenwell by the 1820s was well-known as the centre of London's important clock and watchmaking industry. It housed nearly two-thirds of the industry's firms. However, in a pattern that characterized small businesses at that time, a rich variety of other small workshops clustered in the same area. These included trades as diverse as snuff and tobacco manufacture, confectionery, musical instrument making, book and music selling and bed and mattress making. Around 36 per cent of London's leather-working firms were to be found in Bermondsey but, as with Clerkenwell, a plethora of other trades huddled together in the same area.

Cheapside, in the City, had long been known as a centre of the retailing of a vast range of commodities. As late as the mid-nineteenth century it was still a shopping destination which rivalled the West End although the clientele and its goods were not as fashionable. Typically, of London, however, there was also much industrial activity in Cheapside and its immediate vicinity. Products included fire escapes, guns, umbrellas, toys and metal fanlights. London has always been noted for the visible close juxtaposition of wealth and poverty. Even near the most select residential streets and squares of the West End there was a diversity of small-scale trades, many of which reflected the needs of the area's affluent residents. In 1817 these included wine merchants, booksellers, dealers in foreign ceramics and coffee and spice dealers.

London in the nineteenth century was a major manufacturing centre. It had the disadvantage that, unlike most other manufacturing districts, it had to draw the bulk of its raw materials and fuel from places far away, coal being the obvious example. This factor was not sufficient of a disadvantage, however, to outweigh the momentum which made further economic growth almost inevitable. To London's natural advantages was added a massive demand pull attracting yet more people and new businesses. For example, London's growing population and expanding wealth led to a boom in the construction industry from the middle of the eighteenth century. The demand for new buildings of every sort caused a great increase in the business of suppliers of building materials such as timber merchants and therefore of the carriers who brought suitable timber to the capital. London's housing stock increased by over 120,000 between 1750 and 1831. By that time, it is estimated that around 14 per cent of London's working population was engaged in the construction industry.

It is hard to generalize about London's industries. Some were labour intensive such as shipbuilding and some capital intensive, soap-making being an example. Some industries such as brewing or glass-making came to be dominated by large-scale heavily capitalized concerns while clothing, for example, was invested in a multiplicity of small businesses. There were luxury trades, such as coach-making and gun-making, industries aimed at the widest possible market such as the manufacture of metal household goods, and those satisfying wider trade needs such as shipbuilding. Some trades could be described as finishing trades, especially in the textile sector, but others in the clothing trade, such as hat-making, were involved in every stage of the production process. Most firms in every trade only had a small workforce but then in most trades there were a few who employed very large numbers. This was true, for example of hat-making or wallpaper manufacture.

London had its fair share of noxious industries. A feature of medieval London was the existence cheek by jowl of the houses of the rich and the poor and of various business activities producing a diverse range of frequently repulsive pollutants. Many of these activities moved over the years to peripheral areas such the East End or the Southwark and Bankside areas south of the Thames. Some continued to be a feature of central London although quite what constituted central London changed as the city expanded spatially. Into the nineteenth century there were several large breweries such as Whitbread and Truman in the City. They generated noise and traffic and the strong aroma of brewing would have been on the air although not everyone would have found this objectionable. There was a clutch of tallow-makers around Smithfield Meat Market. They used animal offal as a raw material and the pollution they created would certainly have been objectionable. Bricks were made in Brick Lane on the periphery of the City in Spitalfields.

The use of steam power was a feature of the Industrial Revolution and London was well to the fore in its application as indeed it was in exploiting new technologies yet, paradoxically, large-scale factories and heavy capital equipment existed side by side with small workshops in the same trade, printing being an example. In the emergence of its industries, London, as ever, produced evidence of combined and uneven economic development.

By the 1830s London had acquired the largest urban population the world had ever seen and it was to prove the model for the modern cities of the western world in the later years of the nineteenth century and arguably for the entire globe in the twentieth century. It was a manufacturing centre of international importance, an initiator of consumerism and the hub of a complex national and local transport infrastructure for both passengers and freight. Additionally, it had a sophisticated network of services industries and was at the forefront of developing banking and insurance facilities.

London as a Financial Centre

The capital developed as a financial and commercial centre in the seventeenth century, especially after the restoration of the monarchy in 1660. Among early bankers was Sir Thomas Gresham who also founded the Royal Exchange. Other early banks were Child's, Stones's, Hoare's and Martin's. Business could boom for such enterprises. Child's, which had assets of over £175,000 in 1704 enjoyed an increase to £734,000 in 1754. The banks clustered around Lombard Street and from there being about forty in the 1760s, the number rose to around eighty in 1800.

A sound and secure system of public finance had become a necessity by the end of the seventeenth century and in 1694 it was announced that a Bank of England would be set up. Established first in Poultry, it was not long before its deposits and its influence warranted a move to Threadneedle Street in 1723. Further rapid growth saw a magnificent replacement building later erected on the same site.

A concomitant of banking was insurance. The necessity for insurance had been starkly emphasized by the Great Fire and one early response was the founding of a Fire Office in 1680 charging differential rates on brick buildings and those that were timber-framed. The Fire Office later became the Phoenix whose fireplates indicating that the premises were insured by the company became a common sight on the facades of many houses and other buildings across London and elsewhere.

A famous name from this period was Lloyd's. Edward Lloyd began his insurance business, dealing mostly with marine matters, in a city coffee house in the 1680s and moved to the corner of Lombard Street in 1692. The new premises became the centre of shipping news worldwide and *Lloyd's List & Shopping Gazette* became the bible of international shipping and brought much prestige and business to London over the centuries. 'A1 at Lloyd's' has continued to mean that a ship registered as such at Lloyd's is copper-bottomed from the point of view of insurance.

Markets and Shops

As might be expected, London had England's busiest markets. The medieval markets straddled the City from west to east: they began with the livestock market just outside the City walls at Smithfield and the butchers' shambles and meal market at Newgate, continued along Cheapside to the Stocks and Leadenhall, ran down Gracechurch Street and ended up on Eastcheap and Fish Street Hill. Additionally, large amounts of corn and fish were sold on the quays at Queenhithe and Billingsgate, with numerous other food markets existing throughout the City.

The authorities decided that the City's markets needed reorganization. First, around 1280, they moved the butchers' and fishmongers' stalls from Cheapside to a new timber-covered market called the Stocks. This underwent various enlargements in the fifteenth century and then fell victim to the Great Fire of 1666. A street market existed in front of the mansion known as Leadenhall. This was frequented by country producers, predominantly of poultry and eggs, who came in daily from places around London's periphery to sell their wares. The City authorities had acquired the mansion in 1411 and in 1439 decided to redevelop it as a state-of-the-art, purpose-built market at ground-floor level with storage space upstairs. The gravity with which this august building was regarded was evident in its walls which were topped by battlements. Further market houses were built in the sixteenth century at Newgate, Queenhithe and Southwark. One reason for building them was to remove markets and their associated nuisances from the streets, although tackling this issue took a long time. Eventually the Great Fire did the authorities a service and allowed them to incorporate buildings more suitable for markets in the rebuilding that took place.

There were about twelve principal markets in the City in medieval times but by the 1750s the number had increased to seventeen, several of which were well to the west of the City, showing how the open land between it and Westminster was disappearing. The furthest west of these markets, Shepherd, was close to Piccadilly and provided a largely affluent local population with much of its food.

By the seventeenth century, London's growth as the country's capital was such that there existed a sizeable section of its population that had plenty of money to spend and lots of free time in which to spend it. For them, shopping became a pastime and pleasure as opposed to a simple necessity. Many of the affluent made their way to the Royal Exchange at the junction of Threadneedle Street and Cornhill.

The City contained considerable numbers of shops, often basically the front room of the ground floor with boards on which the wares could be displayed and shutters for security purposes outside opening hours. There would have been great differences between these premises depending on the goods for sale and the clientele at which they were aimed. They impressed a French visitor in 1664 who commented:

> Perhaps there is no town in the world where there are so many and such fine shops. Their displays are not the richest, but their appearance is pleasing: for they are large, and have niches and decorations rivalling those of a theatre. The lay-out of each one is quite different, delighting the gaze and attracting the eyes of passers-by.

Much of what is known about mid-seventeenth century London shops comes from the evergreen diary kept by Samuel Pepys between 1660 and 1669. Pepys (1633–1703) belonged to the emerging professional class, many of whom had enough money to make a pleasure pursuit out of shopping. We know that he spent much time in Cheapside which continued its longstanding role as a major retail centre.

Another popular destination was the shops on London Bridge although these were markedly less fashionable. They included haberdashers, hosiers, glovers, mercers and drapers. Second-hand clothes could be bought in Houndsditch and Long Lane while readymade footwear was sold mainly in Blackfriars and St Martin's. When he decided to buy and then sport a periwig, Pepys visited a number of specialist shops around the Temple.

After the Great Fire, many traders moved west, settling in Covent Garden, the Strand or Holborn. Early in the eighteenth century, the most fashionable shops had gravitated even further west, to the area around St James's where some of London's oldest established and most prestigious shops can still be found. There was a tendency for shops to flaunt increasingly rich, or for some, gaudy and tasteless decoration in order to catch the eye of potential customers. Daniel Defoe pejoratively described what he considered to be excessive decoration as being 'French'.

As London grew so did the number of its residents and visitors who were well off or, if not actually rich, somehow managed to survive on credit. There were some from the aristocracy or those who aspired to that status, who believed it was demeaning even to consider paying bills and impertinent for mere shopkeepers to request them to do so. It was usually only the most prestigious who got away with it. Shopkeepers found that it was good for business if these 'celebrities' were frequently seen on their premises and drew in a crowd.

Frequent changes in clothing fashions meant that those who could afford to do so wanted to be seen in the latest modes, their clothes symbolizing their wealth. Mercers, haberdashers and drapers encouraged such habits and enjoyed good times. As consumer demand increased for luxury goods so growing numbers of manufacturers around London turned to satisfying that demand. Additionally, large quantities of luxury and novelty goods were imported from across the globe to satisfy demand from the London rich. These goods were invariably imported through London.

Retailers went out of their way to exploit the market provided by the London rich. A feature of West End shopping became the showrooms in which some of the firms displayed the full range of their products. Prominent among these was the shop of Josiah Wedgwood, the Staffordshire potter, who added showrooms to his York Street premises in 1767. Other retailers who were also manufacturers followed suit. This was all about flattering the customer and making them more likely to make a purchase if they were enjoying a 'leisure occasion'. To encourage this, some emporia offered comfortable furniture for relaxation and free refreshments. However, there were cads who unashamedly drank the wine and tea and worked their way through the comestibles without the slightest intention of actually purchasing anything.

The rich were keen to do their shopping in places which had an exclusive ambience. They had no wish to hobnob with the common herd. This helps to explain the development of arcades of expensive shops where patrons could move about with no concern about the elements or the other hazards experienced on London's streets. Only select trades were allowed to rent the shops and automatically excluded were any businesses that were noisy, noxious or offensive. One of the earliest was Burlington Arcade in Piccadilly, opened around 1820. To ensure decorous behaviour, beadles were on patrol to enforce the rules. No one in the arcade was allowed to run, whistle or sing, carry a large parcel or wheel a pram.

Perhaps a logical development of the showrooms mentioned above were the bazaars. These were huge roofed, open-plan spaces with traders renting counters on the one or two floors of grandiose buildings designed for the purpose. They exploited the technological potential of iron and glass to create vast spaces lit from above and to add to the experience of the patrons, entertainments and services of various sorts were also available. Probably the first was the Soho Bazaar which opened in February 1816. Several rooms on two floors were laid out with mahogany-topped counters that were rented out on a daily basis to 200 female traders. The Soho Bazaar was famously caricatured by George Cruikshank as a place populated by flirts and dandies. This spurred the owner to employ porters to turn away anyone 'calculated to lessen the respectability of the place'. To cater for the respectable clientele the proprietor wanted, conservatories, exhibitions and picture galleries provided additional attractions. Perhaps the best known of London's bazaars was the Royal or Queen's Bazaar at 73 Oxford Street. In its original form this had a short life. It opened in 1828 and burnt down in 1829, ironically when displaying a diorama called 'The Destruction of York Minster by Fire'.

Other London bazaars included the huge Baker Street Bazaar and the London Crystal Palace built in 1858 with entrances on Oxford Street and Great Portland Street. This drew on the technological innovations incorporated in the building affectionately known as the Crystal Palace in Hyde Park which had housed the Great Exhibition of 1851. These bazaars all had a retail function but they were much more than glorified shops: they aimed to create an experience for their customers where they could relax, be stimulated and entertained and, above all, stay around spending money.

Chapter 4

London 1500–1700

From Medieval City to Modern Metropolis

The sixteenth and seventeenth centuries proved to be momentous times for the capital. It witnessed a tenfold increase in population (from about 50,000 to one nearing 500,000), a growth of trade and a significant suburban expansion. More people meant overcrowding, poor sanitation, disease and high death rates. In the century between the Spanish Armada (1588) and the 'Glorious Revolution' (1688) there was religious extremism, sedition, instability, royal collapse, civil war, plague and fire. Little wonder, that England was seen by foreign observers as 'Devil Land'. Nonetheless, despite the upheavals and catastrophe the period also brought creativity. Entertainment produced Shakespearian and Jacobean theatre whilst popular but violent forms continued, like bear baiting, public punishments and executions. London's trading community provided an important engine in the growth of the capital. For example, around 1400 London was smaller and a lightweight commercial performer compared to many of the great cities of Europe – Paris, Venice, Milan and Amsterdam. At the beginning of this period, most of London's population lived within the medieval walls but by 1700 only a minority did. London became one of Europe's largest cities, attracting the admiration of foreign visitors and ready to become the principal commercial centre of Europe.

Religious Changes

The accession of Henry VIII in 1509, the second Tudor monarch, who succeeded his father Henry VII, heralded changes that transformed much of London's religious landscape. It was a townscape dominated by the spires and towers of over a hundred churches as well as some thirty monastic houses and hospitals. A religious Reformation (changes from Catholic to Protestant belief) had been set in motion in Europe but Henry VIII remained a staunch Catholic. It was his desire to divorce his first wife, Catherine of Aragon, and marry Ann Boleyn, rather than any strong religious beliefs, which meant Henry had to break with the Roman Catholic Church. Henry proceeded to do so and duly established himself as Head of the Church of England, thus replacing the authority of the Pope. This break heralded in changes between 1530 and 1570 that not only reshaped the physical appearance of parts of London but also had an impact on events and its people. London had been fertile ground for dissent before the Reformation and this continued throughout the next two centuries with Protestantism finding an influential voice in the City, Parliament and pulpit.

Citizens were forced to choose between the new or old religion, or more appropriately between private faith and public conformity. Anything that smacked of Catholicism had to be destroyed – religious icons, painted windows, shrines, and tabernacles. In addition, religious houses, priories, chapels, shrines, hospitals and properties changed hands. In 1532, the monastery of Holy Trinity at Aldgate, was forced to surrender itself and its lands to the King. At Charterhouse the Prior and six Carthusian monks refused to take an oath recognizing Henry as head of the church and were hanged, drawn and quartered, most of them at Tyburn. The priory church of Elsing Spital Cripplegate, was one of the first to close in London and the larger monasteries followed from 1538, including Bermondsey Abbey, Blackfriars, Whitefriars at Fleet Street, and St Bartholomew's Priory at Smithfield. A few religious houses survived this asset stripping. St Mary of Bethlehem became Bethlem Hospital (Bedlam) and Greyfriars became Christ's Hospital orphanage and school. However, most of the religious houses were demolished and plundered. The Dissolution had provided an opportunity for those of rank and property to buy up even more land. For example, Thomas Audley, 1st Baron Audley of Walden, acquired Holy Trinity Priory, Aldgate, whilst the site of the Charterhouse in Smithfield was bought by Sir Edward (later Lord) North and then purchased by Thomas Howard, 4th Duke of Norfolk.

Accompanying this destruction of property were the regular and brutal executions of both Protestants and Catholics. Smithfield saw more heretics go to the flames in the 1550s than in any other place in England. Executions during the reign of Henry were especially numerous and provided crowds with a regular feast of gruesome entertainment. Such was the scale of executions during Henry's reign that Thomas More in 1516 recorded that twenty were sometimes hanged at one gallows. Such gruesome activity wasn't confined to Henry's reign. Henry Machyn, diarist and undertaker, wrote that in the space of one month in 1557 he saw eight felons hanged at Tyburn, three men and two women burnt at Smithfield for heresy, and seven pirates hanged at Wapping. Like many Londoners, Machyn witnessed executions as part of the popular calendar ritual attended by large crowds.

The religious changes during the reign of Henry VIII (1509–47) and Edward VI (1547–53) were to be briefly undone by Henry's daughter Mary, a devout Catholic. Mary succeeded to the throne in 1553 but only reigned for five years. During her reign 283 Protestants were burned, seventy-eight in London and fifty-six at Smithfield. The first Protestant to be publicly burned at Smithfield in Mary's reign was John Rogers, vicar of St Sepulchre's at Newgate, on 4 February 1555. Among the mass of people who came to see the execution were his eleven children and his wife who was holding their baby at her breast. Rogers was 'burnt to ashes, washing his hands in the flame as he was burning'. Many others followed. A marble monument now stands in Smithfield to the Protestant martyrs who were executed there.

A few years later in Elizabeth's reign (1558–1603) Tyburn (near Marble Arch) would become the designated place for the execution of Catholics who in their turn would be celebrated as martyrs. Between 1581 and 1603, 180 Catholics were executed for treason, most of these at Tyburn. However, the Elizabethan regime insisted that Catholics be executed as traitors and not for their religious opinions. As traitors this meant they would be hanged, drawn and quartered. On one particular execution day in 1584 George Haydock, John Nutter, Thomas Hemerford, James Fenn and John Munden were drawn on hurdles with five other priests to Tyburn. The cart was then driven away, and the officer was said to have pulled the rope several times before Haydock fell. He was then disemboweled while alive. A similar fate awaited the other priests. Nothing remains of this infamous site except a stone plaque at the intersection of Edgware Road and Marble Arch. The present Tyburn Convent on Bayswater Road, built in 1903, contains a number of relics including linen and straw stained with the blood of five Jesuit martyrs.

Whilst many buildings were destroyed during Henry VIII's reign he was the most prolific of British monarchs in the building of palaces, many of which were in London although few remain today with the exception of Hampton Court, St James's and Eltham. At the beginning of his reign the seat of royal power was Westminster Palace. However, part of this burned down in 1521 and a new palace was built at Bridewell near Fleet Street. It was here that Henry began his attempt to divorce Catherine. Later Henry's son, Edward VI, gave up the residence which was then turned into a prison where the poor were put to work with the name Bridewell becoming a generic term for prisons. Elizabeth I's preferred residences were Greenwich,

Whitehall and Hampton Court. However, John Stow (1525–1605) recorded in 1570 that 'the queen came from her house at the Strand, called Somerset House, to Sir Thomas Gresham's house in Bishopsgate Street where she dined'.

A View of London

Our knowledge of what London was like in the sixteenth and seventeenth centuries has been greatly enhanced by the work of chronicler John Stow and illustrator Wenceslaus Hollar (1607–77), best known for his topographical works and maps, notably the *Long View of London from Bankside* (1647). Hollar's 'Long View' involved a six-sheet engraving initially drawn from St Mary Overy's tower, later to become Southwark Cathedral in 1905. The panoramic view takes in the countryside west of Parliament to the tidal waters east of the City. Individual buildings are portrayed including, on the north bank from left to right, the Palace of Whitehall, Covent Garden, Baynard's Castle, the old Gothic St Paul's Cathedral, the Guildhall, the Royal Exchange, old London Bridge lined with buildings, Billingsgate and the Tower of London. In the foreground is Bankside with its theatres, the Globe and Hope. Different seagoing vessels including the small boats that ferried people can be seen on the Thames. With the growth of trade by the mid-seventeenth century collisions on the Thames were common.

John Stow described in detail in *A Survey of London* (1598), topography, buildings, monuments, people, life, and customs as well as an account of the City's origins and growth. A measure of how much London dramatically changed over the next century from Stow's account can be seen in John Strype's (1643–1737) *A Survey of the Cities of London and Westminster* (1720) which is an expanded version of Stow's book. Strype's account reflects the huge changes brought by population growth and the rebuilding of the City as a result of the Great Fire.

Stow, who lived at Aldgate, noted with some concern the growth of tenements, cramped courts, slums and alleys 'pestered with people'. He was clearly anxious when the Bailiff of Romford was executed 'upon the pavement of my door where I then kept house'.

By 1600 the population of London had grown to around 200,000, boosted by large numbers of migrants seeking work in London. Quick to exploit this movement of people was a thriving and rapacious landlord economy that put business before beauty and contributed to the dreadful overcrowding which made disease, filth and burials inevitable. Added to this problem was the volume of animals kept for slaughter and the regular flow of cattle that passed through the streets on their way to market. The livestock market at Smithfield supplied half of the meat consumed in London. Thomas Platter, a Swiss visitor, wrote in 1599 that London 'was so populous … that one simply cannot walk along the street for the crowd. Animal droppings, especially from the large number of dogs, fouled the streets although the faeces provided a useful ingredient in the processing of leather tanning.'

Noise, Night-time and Nuisances

A population living cheek by jowl also had the regular delights of the stench from a multitude of small industries and the smells emanating from dunghills, carcasses, privies, festering matter, stagnant gutters as well as body odour.

There was also the problem of noise to contend with, especially in houses that were ill equipped to minimize sounds, in particular ground floors without windows. By-laws were made to deal with nuisances although they were not very effective. In 1595 a law required Londoners to observe certain noise restrictions after nine at night including any man 'making affray, or beating his wife, or servant, or singing or revelling in his house'. The same law ordered that 'hammer men (smiths, pewterers, and founders) shall not work after the hours of nine in the night'.

Regular intrusions of noise included bells (church, traders, curfew etc.), traffic, hawkers, animals (barking, grunting, screeching), alehouses and drunks, houses that doubled as workshops, street musicians and cries of pain through lack of medicine. Thomas Dekker (1572–1632) described the pain of plague victims echoing through the streets in 1603 (*The Wonderfull Yeare*). He wrote of how the narrow London streets at night filled with the groans of the sick and dying. In an environment where there was little privacy the sounds of sexual activity were difficult to suppress. The infidelities of Samuel Pepys are well documented. In the nine-year period of his diary (1660–9) he had sexual contact with at least fifty women, many of which were at night including his visit to a Mrs Bagwell where 'we did go up in the dark … and upon the bed', and on another occasion he 'walked up and down in the fields till it was dark night' before continuing with his pleasures. As Shakespeare noted, 'Light and lust are deadly enemies.'

The hours of night, apart from when a full moon shone, were almost devoid of illumination. In the absence of street lighting, other than candles, all sorts of dangers presented themselves. Darkness was a nursery for rogues, thieves, streetwalkers and beggars. It was left to the watchmen, or 'bellmen', to patrol the streets. Apart from the threat of criminal activity, other dangers prevailed, including the emptying of chamber pots full of urine and excrement slung from windows into the street on any poor passer-by. Open cellar doors, dunghills, broken pavements, unfenced stairs, rubbish, construction material and wells were a regular hazard. It must have been perilous for anyone walking home after a drunken night. A linkboy could be hired, from Temple Bar and London Bridge, to help navigate people around the streets and alleys.

Adequate street lighting in London would have to wait another couple of centuries. In 1417 the Mayor of London ordered that all homes must hang lanterns outdoors after nightfall during the winter months. However, as with other European countries, it wasn't until the late seventeenth century that London became more regularly illuminated at night. By the end of the seventeenth century the French writer and traveller Francis Maximilian Misson noted, 'They set up [at every tenth house] in the streets of London, lamps, which, by means of a very thick convex glass, throw out great rays of light which illuminate the path.' This was thanks to inventor and entrepreneur Edward Hemmings who patented his 'Lamps with Convex Glasses' and first used them on Kensington Road. London would have to wait until the nineteenth century before the introduction of gas lighting (1807) and electric street lighting (1878 – along the Thames Embankment and near Holborn Viaduct).

Publishing and Pubs

Cities do not exist in isolation and London's trading position was ideally placed. England's main export was cloth, which increased by over 90 per cent by the mid-sixteenth century, helped greatly by the role of Merchant Adventurers. Merchants like Thomas Gresham contributed to London's prominence in European trade. In Gresham's case he established the Royal Exchange in 1570 as a commercial headquarters and modelled it on the Antwerp Bourse. The Exchange was built as a gathering place for international merchants in London. However, what was novel about the building was that on the upper floor he also added retail shops and one of the first to visit was Queen Elizabeth who opened the Exchange. Elizabeth was so pleased with the shops that she allowed Gresham to name the building the Royal Exchange. During the reigns of Elizabeth I and James I (1603–25) the City prospered and emerged as a financial capital whilst also maintaining a multitude of small trades and workshops.

Amongst those trades was the abundance of bookshops in the City. The invention and spread of the printing press from the fifteenth century contributed to a prolific output of all manner of books as well as to the spread of literacy in the Elizabethan period. Indicative of this boom was that about three-quarters of tradesmen could sign their name and almost half of those sentenced to death in the early seventeenth century pleaded benefit of clergy (giving proof of literacy).

William Caxton (c. 1422–92) had learnt the recently invented technique of printing in Cologne. He returned to England in 1476 and set up a press by Westminster Abbey and the output of books flowed. His apprentice, Wynkyn de Worde, was more commercially minded and took his goods to the buyer. The first printing press in England with moveable type was set up alongside St Bride's Church on Fleet Street where there was a flourishing demand for printed literature from the many clergy and lawyers who lived around the area.

St Paul's Cathedral precinct and Fleet Street were appropriate locations given their importance as a major thoroughfare between the commercial centre of the City of London and the Court and Abbey at Westminster. In addition, Fleet Street had already established itself as first a monastic location and then a legal one. The Inns of Court and a growing number of legal professions transformed Fleet Street and Holborn. Given such a concentration of literary professions there would inevitably be a demand for scriveners to write out copies of religious and legal documents.

De Worde produced over 700 publications in a period of forty years. It was de Worde who began the commercialization of the production of printed books in England and laid the foundations for commercial publishing by popularizing a great variety of literature: children's books, short histories, poetry, romances, instructions for pilgrims, marriage, household practice, animal husbandry and the lurid and sensational material that would prove popular for the next few centuries. De Worde and those who came after him were not only printers but also booksellers selling their products from the premises where they had their presses. The development and spread of printing had an enormous impact as books, bookshops and censorship flourished.

One of the biggest threats to law and order as well as political stability for Tudor governments was the problem of vagrancy (which often equated with villainy). In light of the religious changes during the sixteenth century rumours of conspiracy, real and imagined, were rife. This fear was reflected in a series of royal proclamations. In 1596 the Court of Aldermen appointed a marshal for Southwark with the task of arresting rogues, beggars, idle and vagrant persons.

Such people inhabited various rookeries and in 1580 a proclamation attempted to check the extent of building within three miles of the City. By 1603 demands went further when a proclamation called for the destruction of houses in the suburbs for fear that they were breeding grounds for plague as well as for criminals and idle beggars. Much of this was true with regard to Southwark and was borne out with periodic outbreaks of plague between 1577 and 1641 (plague deaths in 1603 and 1625 killed up to 20 per cent of London's population). Given the social composition of those living in Southwark, it was no surprise that the City authorities viewed it as a dangerous and lawless place, rife with thieves and rogues of every type.

Another dangerous and social problem in this period was the alehouse. The alehouse witnessed a growth between 1550 and 1650, with numbers more than doubling from around 25,000 to 55,000. This growth was facilitated by the transition from ale to beer making. In the City alone there were 400 taverns and 1,000 alehouses in the early seventeenth century. Writer Robert Burton lamented that Londoners 'flocked to taverns as if they were born to no other end but to eat and drink'.

As well as the alehouse and tavern, the coffee house added a new culture to drinking and socializing. It is believed that the first coffee house opened in Constantinople in 1554/5, and a century later the first one to open in London was in 1652 at St Michael's Alley, Cornhill. Other houses followed in the City and on the fringes of the developing West End. By the early 1680s there were approximately 2,000 in London. For many years they remained the haunt of an educated, commercial and mainly male clientele. A foreign visitor, Henri Misson, noted in 1698:

> These Houses, which are very numerous in London, are extremely convenient. You have all manner of news there: you have a good Fire, which you may sit by as long as you please; you have a Dish of Coffee; you meet your Friends for the transaction of Business, and all for a penny, if you do not care to spend more.

The legacy of the Tudor dynasty has continued to provide a lasting fascination and popularity in literature, film and TV, but the dynasty proved to be weak in the ability to continue a line of succession. Despite Henry's six marriages he only produced three legitimate heirs – Mary, Edward and Elizabeth – who in turn produced no heirs. When Elizabeth died in 1603, it fell to the Stuart line from the marriage of Henry VIII's sister Margaret to the Scottish King James IV whose great-grandson, James I (and VI of

Scotland) succeeded to the thrones of England and Ireland in the Union of the Crowns in 1603 at the age of 36. His journey to London to celebrate his kingship was delayed because of the plague but his eventual arrival was marked with an extravagant pageant of street theatre and music.

1600–60: The Road to Civil War

Describing the funeral of Elizabeth I in March 1603, chronicler John Stow wrote: 'there was such a general sighing and groaning, and weeping, and the like hath not been seen or known in the memory of man.' Her successor James I, who was often referred to as the 'wisest fool in Christendom', reigned until 1625 when his son Charles succeeded him. James held a firm belief in the Divine Right of Kings, believing he was not accountable to anyone but God. Prior to him becoming king, Catholics had pleaded with James for more tolerance; after all, his mother, Mary Queen of Scots, had been a fervent Catholic. When he became king, he proceeded to ban Jesuits from entering the country and imposed a £20 fine on those not attending a Church of England service. The case for tolerance was undermined in 1605 when a Catholic plan, the 'Gunpowder Plot', to blow up king and parliament was uncovered. Six years later James commissioned the King James Authorized Version of the Bible.

Soon after his arrival in London James adopted the Palace of Whitehall as his residence. The Palace was the residence of English monarchs between 1530 and 1698 and the Banqueting House was the only major part of Whitehall Palace to survive a devastating fire in 1698. Inigo Jones, the famous architect, designed the Banqueting House, which was built between 1619 and 1622. Years later it would witness the execution of Charles I in 1649.

Whereas Elizabeth had forbade building in the suburbs, James's reign was marked by an expansion of buildings north of the Strand around Leicester Square, Covent Garden and Lincoln's Inn Fields. This development was a result of James selling licences to landowners like the Earl of Salisbury, Viscount Cranborne and later the Earl of Bedford. Street names still bear extensive testimony to the families of the landed aristocracy.

During Elizabeth's reign London's religious sympathies were with Protestantism and towards a growing anti-Catholicism. By the 1620s Puritans, those who wished to purify the Church from all traces of Catholicism, were in a small vocal minority but they found a receptive audience among some of the merchants and artisans. Anti-Catholicism was made worse when King Charles I married a French Catholic, Henrietta Maria, in 1625. The ceremony was marked by an elaborate procession along the Thames accompanied by thousands of boats, crowds waving and a discharge of cannon from fifty ships. Bells rang until late into the night and bonfires were lit. Suspicions were aroused or confirmed when Henrietta refused a Protestant ceremony and to enter Westminster Abbey the following year for the coronation. Many of those in the cheering crowds would, in seventeen years' time, be at war with their king.

Four years after his accession Charles dissolved Parliament, believing he could rule without it. Protests followed during the 1630s and reprisals against Puritan preachers were harsh as witnessed by the punishment meted out to Prynne, Bastwick and Burton for criticizing Church practice. All three were sentenced to stand in the pillory at the Palace Yard, Westminster, to be branded on the cheek, have their ears cropped and imprisoned for life.

Charles's extravagant use of money on art and masques (entertainment that revolved around elaborate costumes and sets), his perceived tolerance of Catholic or high church practices, attempts to raise taxes without Parliamentary approval and his ill-judged attempt to impose the *Common Prayer Book* on Protestant Scotland, which led the Scots to rebel, were a recipe for disaster. All this proved too much and hostile feelings towards Charles's policies were vented when he recalled Parliament in 1640. Charles gambled and lost in January 1642 when he walked into Parliament supported by 500 soldiers and attempted to arrest five MPs who he suspected of plotting against him. Unfortunately for him the five members had fled and within days Charles had to leave London and would not return until his trial and execution in 1649. Such pent-up grievances opened the road to civil war in 1642. The City, which had been a vital source of borrowing for the Crown, dealt a major blow to Charles when it declared to finance the Parliamentary war effort. Royalists attempted to seize the City but were repelled at Turnham Green. London prepared for war by building a defensive system of ditches and fortifications, stretching from Hyde Park to the Tower and establishing a river patrol on the Thames.

In 1643 a royalist pamphlet speculated that when the country was eventually ruined and monarchy dissolved the blame would lay squarely on the 'rebellious, bloody city of London'. As the war progressed displaced people from the provinces sought refuge in London and those wounded in conflict were tended in the hospitals whilst others begged on the streets. Small workshops as well as the arms industry produced weapons and uniforms. London's economy suffered during the years as a result of

Royalist blockades on trade. The capital's population was controlled by a combination of curfews and the Parliamentary army.

For such a relatively small area the financial impact the City of London had on the course of the civil wars was hugely significant. It would be no exaggeration to say that London was England's greatest asset during this conflict. Not only did it have money, resources and manpower but also over a hundred churches where worshipers listened to Protestant sermons. London's zealous Lord Mayor, Isaac Pennington (1584–1661), championed Parliament's cause in the City. His role was influential as he, along with his supporters and agitators, promoted Parliament's efforts and attempted to silence the opposition.

Throughout the four-year period of the first civil war London remained relatively unscathed but Parliament played an important role during this period. Preachers found fertile ground as radical groups, the Levellers, Quakers, Fifth Monarchists and Ranters, spread their ideas through pamphlets free from censorship. From 1646 London was divided between those who wanted a tougher stance taken against Charles and those who wanted a speedy end to the war by making peace with Charles whatever the terms.

However, the army's main political support in London came from artisans and tradesmen. A brief second civil war in 1648 was followed in December 1648 with Parliament being purged of anyone supporting Charles. The King was charged with treason and put on trial at Westminster Hall in January 1649 where he was condemned to death as a traitor. He was led to a makeshift scaffold outside the Banqueting House in Whitehall where he was beheaded. His reign had been largely disastrous but he went to his death with dignity.

London, during the period of the Commonwealth (1649–60) witnessed both gains and losses for its citizens. There were improvements in poor relief and London's sick and elderly were sheltered in charitable institutions, widows and orphans of soldiers were supported, the education of children was a priority and there were improvements to roads and the postal service. Despite the dour image of Puritanism many entertainments in London continued such as fairs, tennis courts, alehouses, bowling, dancing, music and coffee houses. Although theatres were closed, many plays continued in taverns, houses and fairs. Naval power increased thus bringing more employment and shipbuilding on the Thames. The move towards a limited religious toleration saw Jews allowed back into England in 1657, who built their first synagogue in Creechurch Lane in the City.

As part of Oliver Cromwell's moral reforms, alehouses were more tightly controlled, theatres were closed, the celebration of Christmas was considered too Popish, brothels and prostitutes were suppressed and the presence of the army on the streets was felt to be intrusive in the daily lives of the people. Censorship crept back in after a fruitful period of freedom. John Milton (1608–74), who was born in Bread Street in the City, had supported Parliament and had advocated freedom of the press in the 1640s, arguing that it should be left to the individual to decide if their reading material was a corrupting influence or not.

Amidst the tensions and conflicts of these decades there were other developments, for example, the establishment of the first 'post office' in Bishopsgate Street in 1635. Thomas Witherings, an English merchant and MP, was a postal administrator who opened the post office, where members of the public could take mail for posting and collect mail sent to them. By 1660 the General Letter Office, which later became the General Post Office (GPO) was established. The GPO bought slums east of St Martin's Le Grand, which became Britain's first mail facility.

Between 1640 and 1660 Britain and Ireland had been at war and tens of thousands had died, the Archbishop of Canterbury and the king had been publicly executed, the monarchy and the House of Lords abolished, a republic created, Oliver Cromwell had been made Lord Protector, Quakers had given women the right to speak freely in meetings and, for a brief period, many radical voices had been given the freedom to express their ideas. Royalist and historian of the civil wars, Edward Hyde, 1st Earl of Lord Clarendon (1609–74), bemoaned that 'a more inferior sort of common people' had taken over. In 1660 it all came to an end. Despite the Restoration of monarchy, things could not go back to how they were as the French Ambassador to the court of Charles II noted, 'It has a monarchical appearance, and there is a king, but it is very far from being a monarchy.' Embryonic political parties – the Tories and the Whigs – began to emerge and the power of monarchy and church would, after the 'Glorious Revolution of 1688', be overshadowed by the rule of Parliament and the law.

Monarchy Restored

After eleven years of republican governments the country returned to monarchy in 1660 – the Restoration – when Charles II (r. 1660–85) returned from exile in Europe and became king. He was greeted to the pealing of bells and cheering crowds before proceeding to Whitehall Palace. He wanted to make peace with London and no doubt the City, which had been instrumental in contributing to the defeat of his father and in restoring monarchy. Such was the importance of the City of London. Charles's restoration was followed by his coronation in 1661 and his marriage to Catherine of Braganza in 1662, a Portuguese Catholic. These occasions provided an opportunity for a market in commemorative goods: jugs, rings, thimbles and the first coronation mug.

However, revenge was taken on the regicides that had signed Charles I's death warrant. Twelve were executed at Charing Cross and Tyburn. As if to send out a reminder of the deed, a statue of Charles I on horseback was erected in Charing Cross in 1674. Samuel Pepys recorded the execution of one of the regicides: 'I went out to Charing Cross, to see Major-General Harrison, hanged, drawn, and quartered ... he looked as cheerful as any man could do in that condition. He was presently cut down, and his head and heart shown to the people.' Three key signatories to the death warrant, Oliver Cromwell, John Bradshaw (the presiding judge) and Henry Ireton (Cromwell's son-in-law and a general in the Parliamentarian army) were exhumed and ritually executed. Pepys recoded the event on 30 January 1661: 'This morning the carcasses of Cromwell, Ireton, and Bradshaw were drawn upon a sledge to Tyburn, and then taken out of their coffins, and in their shrouds hanged by the neck, until the going down of the sun. They were cut then down, their heads taken off, and their bodies buried in a grave made under the gallows.' Their heads were skewered on poles and displayed at Westminster Hall. Cromwell's stayed there for some twenty years until it was blown down by a storm. Retrieved by a passerby, the head gained a long and fascinating history until it was interred in the walls of the antechapel of Sidney Sussex College, Cambridge (Cromwell's old college) in 1960.

Among the raft of legislation passed by the Cavalier Parliament (1661–79) was the first licensing of hackney carriages (1662). The name is believed to be derived from the former village of Hackney, which supplied horses from its meadows for the horse-drawn carriages. A list of 400 licences was published and regulations were drawn up concerning the coaches, charges, height of horses, areas to be covered, rent, and that priority be given for the issuing of licences to 'ancient coachmen and their widows'.

Our knowledge of Restoration London, its people, topography and the momentous events, has been greatly enhanced by the diarists Samuel Pepys and John Evelyn (1620–1706). In 1661 Evelyn published his pamphlet *Fumifugium, or the Inconveniencie of the Aer and Smoak of London Dissipated* in which he criticized the polluting smoke and noxious waste poured out from industries, especially lime-burning and soap-boiling. London had a reputation from the thirteenth century for its blackened coal-smoke skies resulting from the large concentration of coal stoves and the stocks of coal piles resulting from the sea trade. Evelyn was not alone in bemoaning the state of the air and the smoke that pervaded London. He wrote: 'this horrid Smoake obscures our Churches, and makes our Palaces look old, fouls our Clothes, and corrupts the waters ... and contaminates whatsoever is expos'd to it.' He added that the inhabitants 'breathe nothing but an impure and thick mist ... such coughing and snuffling to be heard as in the London churches where the barking and spitting is incessant and importunate'.

For most of the year the prevailing wind blew from the west so little wonder that the wealthier sort started to migrate in that direction.

The persistence of the 'pea-souper' was expressed over three centuries later in a Sherlock Holmes story where Watson comments: 'In the third week of November, in the year 1895, a dense yellow fog settled down upon London. From the Monday to the Thursday I doubt whether it was ever possible from our windows in Baker Street to see the loom of the opposite houses.' This air pollution would come back with a vengeance in the Great Smog of 1952.

If smoke and polluted air was one problem then the cold winters of the late seventeenth century were another. The freezing of the River Thames was a common occurrence and provided an opportunity for frost fairs as well as other popular activities. During the 'Great Winter' of 1684/5 John Evelyn wrote that people were 'sliding with skeetes and there was bull-baiting, horse and coach races, puppet plays ... it seemed a bacchanalian triumph or carnival on the water'. That winter was so severe that the seas off the southern coast froze for two miles from the shore. Evelyn thought it a 'severe judgement on the land ... men and cattle perishing in divers[e] places, and the very seas so lock'd up with ice, that no vessels could stir out or come in'. Whilst frost fairs brought great frivolity, conditions also brought hardship for the thousands of workers and their families whose livelihoods depended on the river. An estimated quarter of London's population relied on the Thames for their source of income, which during times of severe freezing was threatened.

Plague, Fire and Rebuilding

Twenty years before the 'Great Winter' London encountered a series of devastating events. On 30 April 1665 Pepys wrote ominously in his diary: 'Great fears of the Sickenesse here in the City ... it being said that two or three houses are already shut up. God preserve us all.' London had experienced outbreaks of plague during the sixteenth and seventeenth centuries but not on this scale and not helped by a strong easterly wind. The earliest cases of disease occurred in the spring of 1665 in St Giles-in-the-Fields. By mid-August, Pepys wrote of deserted streets and citizens 'walking like people that had taken leave of the world'. Evelyn also noted the extent of the plague when, on 13 September 1665, he wrote, 'there were perishing now near ten-thousand poore Creatures weekly.' Those who could afford it fled the City.

By September 1666, the Great Plague had peaked and started to decline. It had claimed about 15 per cent of London's population. Although 68,596 deaths were recorded the actual number was probably over 100,000. Many if not hundreds of plague pits were scattered across the City and the surrounding countryside. The majority were in the grounds of churches, but hastily constructed pits were dug around the fields surrounding London notably to the north of the City but also in the St Giles graveyard, Golden Square in Soho and Aldgate. Daniel Defoe described a visit to Aldgate in his *Journal of the Plague Year* (1722): 'A terrible pit it was ... about forty feet in length, and about fifteen or sixteen feet broad, and ... nine feet deep ... there was no parish in or about London where it raged with such violence as in the two parishes of Aldgate and Whitechappel.'

As one tragedy came to an end another began. London was a tinderbox and fires were a common occurrence. The one that broke out in 1666 started on Sunday, 3 September at Thomas Farrinor's baker's shop in Pudding Lane when he failed to put out a fire under his oven. W. G. Bell described Pudding Lane in his book on the Great Fire (1920) as 'a line of tottering houses [which] ran unevenly down the steep hill to the Thames'. Conspiracy theories abounded as to the cause and the usual suspects were blamed: Catholics, Jews and foreigners, with one unfortunate Frenchman, Robert Hubert, executed despite his innocence. The fire raged for four days destroying four-fifths of the City, including over 1,300 houses, eighty-seven churches, and many buildings including the Guildhall, the Royal Exchange and St Paul's Cathedral. It left tens of thousands homeless.

By the third day of the fire Pepys saw the flames running down to Fleet Street:

> Up by five o'clock; Walked thence, and saw all the town burned; and a miserable sight of Paul's church, with all the roof fallen, and the body of the quire fallen into St Fayth's; Paul's School also, Ludgate and Fleet Street, my father's house [in Salisbury Court] and the church [St Bride's] ... Fenchurch Street, Gracious (Gracechurch) Street, Lombard Street all in dust.

There has been a general belief that the Great Fire took few lives but this is disputed. John Evelyn commented that he noticed in the heat the stench of the bodies of many people. In Shoe Lane 80-year-old Paul Lowell, a watchmaker, refused to leave his home: his remains were found in the ruins. Contemporaries claimed that the old, sick, homeless and helpless were burned in their beds. In order to cope with those affected by the fire the City authorities rented out plots of land on fields so that the homeless could build temporary homes in places like Moorfields. People were still living in these shantytowns up to eight years later. Not to lose an opportunity to make money out of unfortunate circumstances, many landlords raised their rents. Pepys noted, 'Strange to hear what is bid for houses all up and down here.'

As with any crisis – hurricanes or plagues – the rich know when to head for higher ground and many clergy followed them. Daniel Defoe, in his *A Journal of The Plague Year*, commented that the wealthiest people and those 'unencumbered with trades and business' departed, whilst 'the rest stayed, and seemed to abide the worst'. In an earlier outbreak Benjamin Spencer wrote in a pamphlet (1625) that fleeing Londoners revealed their 'unkindness, un-charitableness and distrustfulness' whilst Thomas Dekker, expressed his anger at the 'run-aways' from London, 'How shall the lame, and blind, and half-starved be fed? ... it is not Christian.' Londoners who were left behind fell prey to a raft of quack doctors who exploited their plight.

A third disaster, which came a year later, in June 1667, was the embarrassing and dreadful loss of the English navy to the Dutch in the Second Anglo-Dutch War. This was a conflict partly over control of the seas and trade routes in which England tried to end the domination of the Dutch during a period of commercial rivalry. The humiliation damaged the personal reputation of Charles II as Dutch ships sailed down the Medway destroying thirteen Royal Navy ships. It created such panic in London that people sent their most valued possessions out of the City, fearing imminent occupation by Dutch forces. An anxious Pepys wrote, 'I do fear so much that the whole kingdom is undone.' Many Londoners were angry with Charles, blaming him for spending more time on his pleasures. Rioters broke windows, destroyed his recently planted trees, with disorder and protests continuing for some time after.

These disastrous few years were followed by a sense of purpose. The Great Fire had destroyed more than 13,000 medieval, Tudor and early seventeenth-century buildings. However, it precipitated a great rebuilding. Plans were submitted from various individuals including Sir Christopher Wren (1632–1723, knighted 1675), although his plans, inspired by the streets and buildings of Paris, were not taken up. In October 1666, commissioners were tasked with regulating the rebuilding and the Building Acts that followed ensured that a better city would emerge, one more orderly and less flammable. Regulations determined street widths and building dimensions, and that houses were to be of brick and stone. By 1670 6,000 houses had been built and fifty-one parish churches rebuilt under the direction of Wren. Within a decade the area destroyed by the fire was completed with many of the new streets resembling those in Westminster. However, a more ambitious grand rebuilding of the City was limited and would not follow the designs of those in France or Italy. London's ground plan of narrow streets and alleys survived despite plans to the contrary because it was difficult to impose a new scheme on a city that was owned by many private individuals. Nonetheless the rebuilt City was more attractive thanks to the work of Wren.

Wren's main project was the rebuilding of St Paul's Cathedral where the first foundations were laid in 1675. The dome was finished in 1708 and the cathedral completed in 1711, making it the first cathedral to be built after the English Reformation of the sixteenth century. Just over half a mile to the east of St Paul's is the 202-feet-high Monument designed by Wren's friend Robert Hooke commemorating the Fire. London's development wasn't confined to the City: the suburbs expanded in every direction; there was also a growth in fashionable squares west of the City between 1665 and 1700, including Bloomsbury Square, Leicester Square, Grosvenor Square and Red Lion Square.

One of the country's most well-known residences is Downing Street which is synonymous with the British prime minister. The street was built in the 1680s and named after Irishman Sir George Downing whose various roles included statesman, soldier, diplomat, spymaster and preacher. Downing, whom Pepys called a 'perfidious rogue', was rewarded with a valuable piece of land now known as Downing Street. Downing had the cul-de-sac built between 1682 and 1684 with two-storey townhouses, coach houses and stables. Unfortunately, the buildings were constructed quickly and cheaply: over 250 years later Winston Churchill remarked that Number 10 was 'shaky and lightly built by the profiteering contractor whose name they bear'. Number 10 has been the official residence of British prime ministers since 1735.

People's Pains and Pleasures

The poet John Dryden (1631–1700) described London as a 'Phoenix rising from her ashes' but the problems of health, disease and lack of sanitation persisted. A regular source for the causes of death in London was the Bills of Mortality, which were published weekly. They were intended to monitor burials from 1592 to 1595 but as from 1629 the cause of death was given. Apart from old age, infant mortality, stillborn and the plague, the following ailments accounted for a substantial number of deaths each year: 'Rising of the Lights' (inflammation of the liver or alternatively, croup), 'Surfet' or surfeit (vomiting from over-eating or gluttony), thrush and sore mouth, measles, jaundice (condition caused by blockage of intestines), 'Livergrown' (possibly rickets), 'Impostume' (abscess), 'Kil'd by several accidents', ague (intermittent fever), 'Colick, Stone or Strangury' (convulsive pain in the abdomen or bowels), worms, 'Tissick' (cough), drowned, 'Purples and spotted Feaver' (purples – rash due to spontaneous bleeding in to the skin), 'Pleurisie and Spleen', palsy (paralysis or difficulty with muscle control), 'breakbone fever' (mosquito-borne disease caused by a virus), 'King's Evil' or 'Evil' (scrofula, tuberculosis of neck and lymph glands), sores and ulcers, 'Apoplexy, & planet struck' (sudden severe affliction or paralysis), 'Mortification' (gangrene) and cancer.

In 1662 the demographer John Graunt (1620–74) estimated that in London for every hundred live children born thirty-six died in their first six years and twenty-four in their first ten years. He also noted, 'That Autumn, or the Fall is the most unhealthfull season … That in London there have been twelve burials for eleven Christnings … That about 6,000 per Annum come up to London out of the Country … Physicians have two Women Patients to one Man, and yet more Men die than Women.' Graunt attributed such a low life expectancy to the 'Fumes, Steams and Stenches'.

The pox was widespread in London with its ability to disfigure and impoverish. Syphilis, one of the deadliest of all venereal diseases, spread rapidly throughout Europe. Elizabethans had many names for this foul malady including the French pox which became a convenient term among political propagandists, as it was easier to blame the spread of the disease on foreigners. William Clowes (1544–1604), an Elizabethan surgeon, reported in 1585 that the victims of syphilis were so great the London hospitals had no room for them. So alarmed by the extent of sexual vice the City, authorities issued a proclamation against 'the Stynkynge and Horrible Synne of Lecherie'. Clowes was clear as to where the blame lay for the spread of the pox:

> The cause lies with the licentiousness, and beastly disorder
> of a great number of rogues, and vagabonds: the filthy life of
> many lewd and idle persons, both men, and women, about

the city of London, and the great number of lewd alehouses,
which are the very nests and harborers of such filthy creatures.

People were vulnerable to infection and contamination. Cesspits and mounds of human and animal waste polluted the streets. London had a primitive and basic system of sewerage, which only carried surface water. Excrement went into the cesspit under the house or in the garden. Leaking toilets were not uncommon as Pepys noted: '20 October 1660: ... going down my cellar to look, I put my foot into a heap of turds, by which I find that Mr Turner's house of office is full and comes into my cellar.' He had no further luck on a visit when finding that a chamber pot was not available; he noted that 'I was forced in this strange house to rise and shit in the chimney twice'. Pepys's experience was not uncommon for urban dwellers where solid and liquid waste ran frequently from houses into open gutters. Various carters and dustmen set up businesses to carry away large amounts of waste including privy waste (or night-soil collectors as they became known).

The Thames tributaries, especially the Fleet River or the Fleet Ditch, were open sewers and contributed to the spread of infection. During the 1670s the river was widened and canalized from Holborn to the Thames. By the end of the seventeenth century the satirist Jonathan Swift (1667–1745) gave a vivid picture of how the Fleet was a depository for all types of filth: 'Seapings from butcher's stalls, dung, guts and blood, Drowned puppies, stinking sprats, all drenched in mud, Dead cats and turnip-tops come tumbling down into the flood.' One such flood in 1679 broke through the back of several wholesale butchers and carried off cattle. By 1766 the Fleet was covered over between Fleet Street and the Thames.

Medicines were concocted from a wide and weird collection of ingredients. Leading herbalist Nicholas Culpeper (1615–54) who was supplied with herbs from Finsbury Fields, Hampstead and Bow, put great faith in the use of millipedes for pains in the ear. The *London Pharmacopoeia* that appeared in 1618, initially for London apothecaries, covered the use of drugs including roots, leaves and animal parts such as 'horn of a rhinoceros, elephant tusk ... frog spawn, penis of a bull, flesh of vipers ... oil of foxes'. Most people would visit a barber for regular treatment as barbers and surgeons were members of the same organization until 1745. Although there were advances in the seventeenth century and London was very much the birthplace of new ideas in science and medicine, effective healthcare was some way off and quacks continued to prosper.

The theatre of the crowd was a familiar part of London's history and the capital teemed with the pleasures of sex, eating, drinking and bawdy entertainment including public executions. Thousands of people gathered for the execution of the Babington conspirators (an assumed plot to remove Elizabeth from the throne and replace her with Mary Queen of Scots) in 1586 where there was 'no lane, street, alley, or house in the suburbs of London or in the hamlets bordering the city out of which there issued not some of each sex and age'.

In 1676 when four men and one woman took their final journey to Tyburn 'vast numbers of people [followed] the carts to behold the last sad scene'. Pepys, attending an execution in 1664 along with over 14,000 others, spent a 'shilling to stand upon the wheel of a cart, in great pain, above an hour before the execution was done'. Those who were not fortunate enough to see the execution crammed into the fields to watch the burning of the victim's entrails.

Men playing football in the street was a common sight along with itinerant puppeteers, or 'motion men', jugglers, tumblers and musicians. London was particularly rich in fairs held at Southwark, Paddington, Hampstead, Highgate, Tottenham Court, Bow, Mile End, Pinner, and Mayfair along with many smaller ones. Shows included animals, 'mermaids', bearded ladies, prize fighters, fairies, giants, bizarre acts, exotic entertainers, minstrels, fortune tellers and itinerant beggars. Bartholomew Fair held each August in Smithfield became London's largest fair and had achieved international importance by the mid-seventeenth century. The poet and Jesuit priest, Robert Southwell, wrote in the 1590s of the 'fools, the drunkards, the madmen, the monsters, the pickpockets' and the various areas of 'lewdness and impurity, at Bartholomew Fair'. However, fairs often conflicted with a growing residential London and some of those in polite society and authority viewed fairs as dangerous and tending to disorder.

More sedate types of leisure pursuits developed. The first classical square introduced into Britain was by Inigo Jones at Covent Garden in the 1630s, inspired by his visits to Europe. This square became the prototype for many others after the Restoration: Bloomsbury Square (1661) and St James's Square (1660s). Public concerts were pioneered in the 1670s and other forms of entertainment that began by the late seventeenth century would come into their own in the next century, notably the pleasure gardens, which provide an example of the commercialization of leisure.

During the 1690s there was a craze for buying lottery tickets. Tickets were advertised in newspapers and sold in over 120 outlets in London, including Jonathan's Coffee House in Exchange Alley, the Grey Hound Inn in Southwark, and various shops, booths and taverns. Prizes included consumer goods, property, land, shares and cash. The cost of some tickets was as low as a penny; lotteries provided most people, as they do now, with the chance to indulge their dreams of being rich. In 1693 Thomas Neale, a groom porter, organized a lottery that offered a cash prize of £3,000. Such schemes encouraged a variety of entrepreneurs to launch similar projects and proved to be more popular and successful than England's first lottery in 1568.

Religious Crisis (Again), Diversity and Expansion

An image of the Restoration is that of Charles II as the 'Merry Monarch', which is assumed to stand in contrast to the staid and solemn Puritan morality that preceded his reign. It is an image that stands in contrast to the everyday experiences of most people. Artist Sir Peter Lely portrayed the extravagance and licentiousness of court life. There was an easy-going morality at court, but also a cultural flourishing of literature, art, music, comedy and poetry. The theatre, which had been banned during the Commonwealth period, thrived and was complemented by the humorous dramas of playwrights like Dryden. Women appeared on stage for the first time. Satire found a rich vein of material in politicians, clergy and the law – subjects that would become even greater targets in the next century.

Charles II's time in exile had taught him the value of compromise, hence he preferred not to get too involved in the affairs of state. As long as he could pursue his interests (sports, gossip, philandering) he was sufficiently content. However, problems surfaced when he died in February 1685. Although Charles had many illegitimate children by various mistresses, he left no legitimate heir and the throne passed to his Catholic brother, James II. James's attempts to promote Catholicism only confirmed the fears of many.

In November 1688 London was in state of tension as news filtered through that William of Orange had landed at Brixham in the south-west with a Dutch army and was marching towards the capital to claim 'the liberties of England and the Protestant religion'. When James decided to leave London in December and eventually fled to France to join his family, rioting broke out, aimed at houses of wealthy Catholics, chapels, embassies and anything and anyone suspected of being Catholic. Mobs tore down the chapel in St James's and killed a soldier at Charing Cross.

With the support of rich London merchants, Protestant nobles and James's daughters Mary and Anne, William of Orange entered London in December and went straight to St James's Palace. Those rich merchants via the Corporation of London continued to assert the City's rights when, in 1690, it was declared

> That the mayor, commonalty and citizens of London shall for ever hereafter remain, continue and be, and prescribe to be, a body politic ... and shall have and enjoy all their rights, gifts, charters, grants, liberties, privileges, franchises, customs, usages, constitutions, prescriptions, immunities, markets, duties, tolls, lands, tenements, estates and hereditaments whatsoever.

The so-called 'Glorious Revolution' of 1688 was followed in April 1689 when William III and his wife Mary II were crowned joint monarchs. However, Mary's share of the reign was short as she died at the age of 32 in 1694 as a result of a smallpox outbreak in London.

During the sixteenth and early seventeenth centuries the population of London and its immediate suburbs grew more rapidly than the population of the country as a whole. By the end of the seventeenth century London was the largest city in Europe with a population in excess of half a million. London's diverse population reflected a growing cosmopolitan capital city. Apart from large numbers of domestic migrants, were Huguenot (French Protestants) and Flemish refugees. Hundreds of Huguenots settled in Soho and also in Spitalfields, Lambeth and Battersea. By 1690 they made up nearly 10 per cent of London's population. There were also many Asian and African seamen. Jews were allowed back into Britain in the mid-seventeenth century and could be found around Whitechapel and Soho, whilst Irish settlers came to dominate the area around St Giles. Parish records from St Botolph's, Aldgate, record French and Dutch immigrants, a Persian, several Indians and one 'East Indian' (a Bengali). Early maps show the rapid urban growth particularly in places along the South Bank of the Thames. The population of Southwark grew threefold in the century after 1550 and the area of Borough and Bankside was, by the later seventeenth century, more densely populated than the growing suburbs of East London.

Although the City of London and the City of Westminster began to embrace each other by the early seventeenth century, they never merged into a single municipality. The City, as defined by its boundaries, developed a unique form of government as it grew as an international financial centre. At particular moments of crisis, such as the civil war, it wielded power over Parliaments and the Crown. Its financial status was further enhanced in the last decade of the seventeenth century when the Bank of England was established in 1694 to act as a banker to the government, making loan capital available on a greater scale and allowing merchants autonomy from the Crown.

By the end of the seventeenth century much of London was newly built. Westminster developed its political significance with the Houses of Parliament as well as religious (Westminster Abbey) and legal (the law courts) influence. With the courtly and stylish St James's area it would later see the growth of the fashionable 'West End'. From the 1670s there was an expansion around Leicester Fields, Haymarket, Soho, St Giles and Bloomsbury. On the southern side of the Thames away from City regulation, Bankside continued with its reputation as a 'sanctuary', attracting all manner of fugitives from the law and offering raffish recreations with its cockpits, theatres, brothels, bear gardens, bawdy taverns and alehouses. Theatres such as the Swan, Globe and Rose flourished in these unregulated liberties. Southwark also had a strong manufacturing presence, notably those industries banished from the City: tanneries, dyes, soap and tallow, timber yards and vinegar. The Thames was of great importance in providing trade, shipbuilding and employment for thousands. Divisions between, the City, Westminster and Southwark – political, financial, religious, cultural and social – were distinct and often extreme. Many of the old problems – crime, poverty, disease and pollution – persisted. For all the upheaval, London was, by the end the seventeenth century, on the brink of becoming a modern metropolis.

Chapter 5

Eighteenth-century London

'Full of Wonders and Wickedness'

After the upheavals of the seventeenth century, London could look forward to some degree of stability and growth. It would not always be stable and growth often brought disruption and displacement for many. Commerce saw refinements in banking, insurance and trade. New financial institutions emerged, which marked new ways of doing business. Industrialization and urbanization both nationally and in London had profound social effects. The capital experienced growth in geographical area and in its population with the latter increasing from around half a million to nearly one million by 1800. London accounted for about 16 per cent of the population of England as well as being the largest city in the world.

A century later, but relevant to the eighteenth century, David Copperfield commented that London was 'fuller of wonders and wickedness than all the cities of the earth'. This great city was, and is, one of contrasts and extremes in wealth. A free market in people, trade, services and goods created fortunes, which were visible in the building of grand houses, palaces and squares. In addition, the century witnessed a new metropolitan elegance with the growth of the West End, which, as Roy Porter wrote, 'decisively shaped the capital's future'. It was a place where people could shop, be entertained and where the gentry and grandees chose to live. On the other side of the coin there were parts of London that witnessed overcrowding, squalor, disease, poverty and feral children roaming the streets. Crime flourished and was met with a severe code of punishment. Politically, there were changes, but there was also a greater lampooning of politicians and aristocracy by satirists who found outlets in a widespread and uncontrolled print culture. From the death of Queen Anne in 1714 until at least 1830 the age is referred to as the Georgian period after the successive Hanoverian kings, George I, George II, George III and George IV.

Georgian London: Houses and Estates

The new century did not get off to the best start when a cyclone hit central and southern England causing much damage and loss of life. What became known as the 'Great Storm of 1703' uprooted thousands of trees, blew down over 2,000 chimney stacks in London, and removed the lead roofing from a hundred churches including Westminster Abbey, as well as blowing fish out of the ponds in St James's Park. On the Thames 700 ships were torn from their moorings whilst others were destroyed. Daniel Defoe placed an advertisement in the *London Gazette* appealing for witnesses to send in their accounts of the gale, which he published as *The Storm* the following year.

Many thought the storm was a divine punishment from God or a portent of things to come. Nonetheless, the eighteenth century saw a continued development of trade as merchants, bankers and ship owners benefitted from overseas expansion in the Indian Ocean, Africa, and the West Indies, particularly the transatlantic slave trade. Other rich pickings were to be found in investments in insurance, overseas holdings, stock and property speculation. Such financial opportunities led to a rise in a wealthy middle class who found residences in Marylebone and Mayfair, with aristocrats settling in St James's and later Belgravia, migrating westwards from the increasingly overcrowded City and its surrounds. A measure of how socially fashionable the West End had become by the mid-eighteenth century is reflected in the fact that every major aristocratic and gentrified family in the country maintained a house there largely to participate in the influential London Season. Thus, a relatively small group of rich people had a significant influence on the prosperity of London through their spending and the employment they created. Domestic service, the most common employment for women, was required in the large houses as well as a multitude of other types of work. Defoe, reflecting on the extent of building and expansion in the 1720s, wrote that west London was a 'world full of bricklayers and labourers'. This expansion also brought with it public spaces, shops, clubs theatres and arcades.

Around Mayfair and north of Oxford Street occurred a significant building boom as squares and terraces were laid out. The Cavendish-Harley family developed their estates here and many streets and squares bear the names of aristocratic families: Curzon, Grosvenor and Berkeley estates to the north of Piccadilly and the Portman and Portland estates of Marylebone. At the end of the seventeenth century Marylebone was a small village with little more than a hundred houses but growth was taking place as reflected in the *Daily Journal* which commented in 1728 that people were arriving in Marylebone from their country estates. Real transformation came in the late Georgian and Regency years with the fashionable squares built in the century following 1717, alongside the elegant residential streets such as Portland Place. Developments during the Georgian era marked out the distinctive urban and classical identity of Marylebone with its fashionable squares and the surrounding estates. The first of these squares was Cavendish (1719) followed by Portman (1764–84), Manchester (1776–8), and Dorset (from 1787 to 1811, the site of Thomas Lord's first cricket ground). These squares and the residential areas that surrounded them were fine examples of Georgian town planning.

The planning and building of residential districts in the West End was one of the most remarkable changes in London during the eighteenth century. Inevitably, such developments clashed with older traditions. For example, Tyburn, located near Marble Arch, was the most infamous execution venue in the country and often drew large crowds. Its demise in 1783 had little to do with humane or enlightened attitudes towards penal policy: executions at Tyburn ceased because of the disorder and disruption they engendered, notably along the route from Newgate via Oxford Street. Wealthy citizens taking up residence in the highly fashionable streets and squares of Marylebone and Mayfair objected to the presence of unruly and irreverent crowds on hanging days, hence executions were moved to Newgate.

Soho had developed by the late seventeenth century when several aristocratic families moved into the area, accompanied by the development of fashionable houses and Soho Square (1720). However, the aim of turning Soho into an upper-class estate similar to Mayfair or Marylebone never came to fruition. It became a haunt for foreign communities, particularly French Huguenots, and literary notables. Dr Johnson established his Literary Club on Gerrard Street; included among its members were the artist Joshua Reynolds, actor David Garrick and novelist Oliver Goldsmith. Most of the shops were those of craftsmen. Thomas Chippendale had a workshop in St Martin's Lane. It was also on the corner of St Martin's Lane and Newport Street that Josiah Wedgwood established his London warehouse in 1767. The colourful character Chevalier d'Éon (1728–1810) lived on Brewer Street for over thirty years as a woman. He had also been a writer, spy, diplomat, transvestite and an exceptional swordsperson. At nearby High Holborn, William Hamley, a Cornishman, set up his Noah's Ark toy shop in 1760 where he stocked tin soldiers, hoops, wooden horses and rag dolls. His shop attracted well-heeled families, nobility and royalty and was so successful that a new branch opened in Regent's Street in 1881.

Museums and significant palaces were built during this century including the British Museum in 1759, and Buckingham House (the future palace) in 1703. A classical architectural style typical of many of the 'new buildings became a feature of the Georgian period and owed a debt to the leading architects of the day, notably the Adam brothers, Robert and James. However, the straight lines were not to everyone's taste. Poet Robert Southey (1744–1843) bemoaned that

> this metropolis of fashion ... has the most monotonous appearance imaginable. The streets are perfectly parallel and uniformly extended brick walls, about forty feet high, with equally extended ranges of windows and doors, all precisely alike, and without any appearance of being distinct houses.

One development that proved to be a blunder for the Adam brothers was the Adelphi (Greek for brothers). In 1768 the brothers leased the site of Durham House on the Strand near the river and laid out a number of streets culminating in a magnificent terrace of eleven palatial houses. However, their attempt to transform an unfashionable into a fashionable quarter turned into a commercial disaster. The project was in the wrong area and too near a working river. They had difficulty selling the houses and appealed to King George III to organize a lottery to sell the estate and avoid bankruptcy. Nonetheless, the influence of the Adam brothers provided a stylish and classy array of townhouses.

Public Buildings

The proliferation of private houses benefitted speculators, landlords and entrepreneurial builders. They left a legacy of fine houses, shops, terraces, inns and mansions. This period also saw a growth or rebuilding of public projects in the form of prisons, churches, museums, alms-houses, hospitals, schools, government offices and bridges. Until 1750 the only bridge in the capital across the Thames was London Bridge. Two additional bridges were added, Westminster Bridge (1750), after a troubled construction, and Blackfriars Bridge (1769), both of which contributed to a southward residential expansion, as did the removal of buildings on London Bridge in 1759.

Health care was rudimentary with only four main hospitals, which had their origins in the monastic hospices – Christ's, St Bartholomew's, St Thomas's and Bethlem. During the eighteenth century there were over twenty hospitals for the sick and poor, many of which were voluntary institutions based on subscriptions from wealthy benefactors. These included Guy's (1725), St George's (1733) and Westminster Infirmary (1719). In addition, there emerged dispensaries, apothecaries, physicians, asylums and a raft of quack doctors. The London Lock Hospital, founded in 1747 in Grosvenor Place, Belgravia, was the first voluntary hospital for venereal diseases. However, health care still left a lot to be desired and most people had to rely on a mixture of old remedies, potions and powders, making do, family support or simply putting up with the pain.

Many churches replaced those destroyed in the Great Fire but the Church Building Act of 1711 led to the construction of twelve new churches (fifty had been intended), including six designed by Nicholas Hawksmoor (1661–1736), an English architect who had worked with Sir Christopher Wren. Some of the other churches built included St John's, Smith Square and St Mary Le Strand.

Although there were a number of prisons in London, they were not long-term penal establishments. They served as holding, correctional or debtor facilities. More prisoners died from 'goal fever' (typhus) spread by fleas and lice than from execution. The main London prisons were built in the nineteenth century with Millbank being the first in 1812. Newgate Prison, which stood near the site of the present Central Criminal Court, the Old Bailey, was built in the twelfth century and demolished in 1904. It was extended and rebuilt many times. In 1770 it was enlarged and a new sessions house was added. This new prison was designed with the intention of discouraging law-breaking. However, just as construction was almost finished, it was attacked by a mob during the anti-Catholic Gordon Riots in June 1780. Gutted by fire, the walls were badly damaged and repairs were estimated at £30,000. Eventually, the new prison was finally completed in 1782, in time for it to become the main site of execution in London. The first execution took place on 9 December 1783 when executioner Edward Dennis ended the lives of ten felons. In 1785 the gallows bore even more fruit when twenty men were hanged in just one morning. Old Bailey (the street) was narrow, hence the new execution site lacked the large amount of open space that was available at Tyburn. Opposite the site of the Newgate gallows at 18 Old Bailey stands the Magpie and Stump. On execution days, successive landlords offered, for a substantial fee, hospitality to rich patrons who enjoyed a good hanging.

The perennial problem of traffic congestion plagued London in the eighteenth century as much as it does now. Winter was particularly bad with old sunken roads filled with mud after heavy rain. A multitude of narrow alleys and lanes proved increasingly inconvenient to horse-drawn vehicles. To overcome this problem Parliament enacted a series of significant Building Acts in the eighteenth and nineteenth centuries, which initiated important infrastructure projects and improved the fabric of the city. In 1762 the Westminster Paving Acts was introduced and was followed by other Acts for the City and elsewhere. The purpose was to keep local trade flowing but they also provided for regular street cleaning, clear passageways for traffic, widening of certain streets and lanes, gutters and underground drains. Obstructions such as coalholes and protruding shop signs were removed so people could walk along pavements unhindered by traffic, carriages and animals.

Improvements brought about by the Street Acts were dramatic. They also signalled the end of the old City gates – Ludgate, Newgate, Aldersgate, Cripplegate, Moorgate, Bishopsgate and Aldgate – which had been a defining part of the City's history for centuries. They were now deemed a hindrance and finally removed. Nothing remains of the gates as most of them were sold for building materials. However, a statue of Queen Elizabeth I from Ludgate was relocated to the outer wall of St Dunstan-in-the-West Church where it remains. At Moorgate the stone was used to support the newly widened centre arch of London Bridge whilst a section of Aldgate was bought by Ebenezer Mussell of Bethnal Green who then rebuilt it on the north side of his mansion, Aldgate House, which was pulled down in 1809.

In the townscape of the capital a word of mention must go to the London plane tree, which accounts for over half of the city's tree population and is in evidence in many of the squares. Berkeley Square, which has around thirty planted in 1789 is a particularly good place to view them.

The Poor

In his poem about London, William Blake (1757–1827) raged, on behalf of the poor and enslaved, against wealth, the church, the establishment and privilege, Whilst the rich had shifted to comfortable and stylish residences in the west, the poor crowded into St Giles, Spitalfields, Southwark, Whitechapel and the East End. The living conditions in these places were breeding grounds for disease. One doctor, George Cheyne (1671–1743), commented in 1733 on the number of fires, the clouds of 'stinking breaths and perspiration', the foul smells, 'the putrefying bodies', 'dunghills, animal droppings, and disease'. A large number of parish workhouses were created in the 1720s, and by 1760, 2 per cent of London's population were housed in these institutions.

It was probably no coincidence that the Great Plague started in St Giles in the spring of 1665 and the first victims of the plague were buried in St Giles churchyard. The district was reckoned to have the highest recorded rate of petty offences in the eighteenth century. In the 1740s St Giles was described as full of common lodging houses and gin shops and it was here that the artist William Hogarth (1697–1764) found a rich vein of material for some of his great prints. Hogarth worked from nearby St Martin's Lane and used St Giles as the nearest sketching ground for his themes related to poverty or violence, notably his famous Gin Lane illustration which portrays the evils of gin-drinking. Hogarth's depiction was part of a campaign against the uncontrolled production and sale of cheap gin which culminated in the Gin Act of 1751.

St Giles was one of a number of migration points in London, a location on the edge of town providing convenient access to a stream of people arriving on foot. The slums or rookery of St Giles had a high concentration of Irish Catholic immigrants by the mid-eighteenth century and was often referred to as 'Little Dublin', or 'Little Ireland'.

Many of the poor were homeless including large numbers of children. It was not uncommon for them to die, especially in the cold weather like the 'poor boy' found dead on a dunghill in a stable in Holborn in 1771. In his excellent book on the eighteenth century, Jerry White tells of a Dr Robert Willan who found up to eight family members to a bed or the two old women who, in 1763, died of starvation in a ruinous house in Stonecutter Street, Fleet Market.

A high number of children understandably resorted to crime quite often in order to survive. Records of young people sentenced to transportation to Australia on the First Fleet in the 1780s reflect the harsh treatment they received, such as 13-year-old Elizabeth Hayward, a clog maker who had stolen a silk bonnet. A month after her arrival in Australia, in February 1788, she received thirty lashes for insolence. The youngest on the Fleet was 13-year-old John Hudson, a chimney sweep, who had been tried and convicted at the Old Bailey. Londoners William Edwards (14) and Phoebe Flarty (15) were sentenced to seven years each for stealing clothes. Young boys awaiting transportation makes for sad reading. James Holmes, aged 13 from Southwark, had run away from a brutal father and found shelter in a house of criminals. His account in Home Office records in the National Archives is almost straight out of Charles Dickens:

> Two of the boys took me to a house kept by a Jew and he agreed to board and house me for 2/6d. a week provided I brought and sold to him all I might steal. He has about 13 boys in the house on the same terms and there are four housebreakers living in the same house ... they are all grown men ... A coat is hung in the kitchen and boys practise how to pick the pockets.

Markets and Eating

The poor could always look to the many markets in London for cheap food and goods. Markets have a long history and by the eighteenth century they were catering for a growing and diverse population. Those among the very poor who could not afford the fresh produce resorted to street sellers and hawkers who sold inferior produce. Street sellers had traded for centuries and would cry out their wares, which included puddings and pies, sausages, and hot gingerbreads, all sold from a heated brazier.

Many working-class people frequented markets in the evening, especially Saturdays when goods were sold cheaply. Spitalfields was London's largest potato market and its cheapness appealed to the poor. Poverty and potatoes often went together. In Farringdon the Fleet provided refuge for the poor and homeless where they would shelter in the buildings. It was described in 1715 as 'an harbour for rogues and vagabond persons at night'. Fleet market became so dilapidated by the 1820s and an obstacle to traffic that it was closed down.

A wide variety of markets existed, which ranged from retail and wholesale, as well as those that specialized in certain goods, particularly fish or meat, and general markets which sold different types of products. During the eighteenth century there was a rise in the very large markets. In 1751 the Corn Exchange was built in Mark Lane near the Tower and by the end of the century it was, according to corn merchants, 'the greatest market in the world'. Smithfield was London's oldest and only lasting cattle market throughout this century. Billingsgate was London's only wholesale fish market where fishermen landed and sold their catches. Borough market in Southwark changed after its relocation in 1756 and became known for its vegetables. The most celebrated market in Georgian and Victorian London was Covent Garden, which was well placed between the commercial City and the gentrified West End, and, with its spacious piazza, it proved to be popular among artists. In 1670 the Duke of Bedford obtained a royal licence to establish a market that sold flowers, fruit and vegetables. By the eighteenth century it was the city's main provider of these products, most of which were grown in market gardens near the city. It was also by this time noted for the abundance of brothels and prostitutes. Descriptions of prostitutes in the area could be found in *Harris's List of Covent Garden Ladies,* which was the 'essential guide and accessory for any serious gentleman of leisure'. Published in 1757, the small pocket book (price two shillings and sixpence) described, often in lurid detail, the sexual specialities of around 200 prostitutes in the area of Covent Garden. The phrase 'old Drury', after nearby Drury Lane, became a synonym for prostitutes throughout the eighteenth century. Prostitution could be found throughout London, although it was not until the Vagrancy Act of 1824 that the term 'common prostitute' was used and became criminalized.

Food could be found in great variety and abundance at many London fairs. Bartholomew Fair in Smithfield was particularly famous for its hot food stalls. On one of his visits to the fair the satirical writer Ned Ward (1667–1731) commented on the fumes of tobacco and over-roasted pork. On ordering some cooked meat, Ward soon became disappointed as the man in charge of turning the roast swine 'rubbed his ears, breast, neck and arm pits with the same cloth which he applied to his pigs'. The enormous sale of roast pork at Bartholomew Fair gave way to beef sausages, for which the fair became famous for. Gingerbread was another favourite of the London crowds that gathered there to take advantage of the cheap bread, pies and puddings. Cookshops also provided cheaper foods, especially cuts of meat, and were popular in the slum area between St Martin's Street and the Strand. Hot food and drink were also served in taverns, alehouses, pleasure gardens and coffee shops. Chophouses, which had developed in the seventeenth century, served customers seated on benches or wooden boxes with a curtain partition around. A famous chophouse known for cuts of beefsteaks was Dolly's in Paternoster Row. It was described as a well-appointed chophouse and tavern, which also had a coffee room, with projecting fireplaces. James Boswell often went to Dolly's and in December 1762 wrote that he had 'a large, fat, beef-steak and a beer' for a shilling.

An expanding overseas trade and empire brought such imports as coffee, tea, sugar and tobacco. Economic prosperity and the growth of a middle-class consumer saw an increase in spending on fashion, leisure and eating. Inns offered accommodation as well as food and drink for visitors to London. The Saracen's Head in Friday Street in the City had over thirty guest rooms as well as serving hot meals that included roast meat, pasties, pies and toasted cheese. The famous Cheshire Cheese on Fleet Street took pride in its puddings accompanied by large brown creamy ale, which were both served within minutes. Malted beer was popular as was porter, a product of London brewers from the 1720s. The term 'restaurant', meaning a place serving food in a respectable environment, did not emerge until the nineteenth century.

Shopping

Food and manufactured goods had been sold in small shops and markets since medieval times, but large high-street markets and high-class shops took off in the Georgian period. Shops with luxury goods displayed in large shop windows became fashionable and appealed to the wealthier shopper as well as those who wished to browse – the window shopper. A huge variety of trades catered for a wide range of tastes.

Grand shopping arcades had opened in Paris in the eighteenth century, which provided comfortable and stylish shopping away from the openness of the streets and the rain. London followed later with the Burlington Arcade (1819) in Piccadilly. Fortnum & Mason was established in 1707 in St James's Market, Piccadilly, and supplied wealthy residents in Mayfair and St James's with their groceries and wine.

London offered the largest and most diverse shopping in the country. It was a magnet for those who had money to spend and were prepared to travel from far and wide. In the 1720s Cesar de Saussure, a French Protestant from Switzerland, described London's four main shopping streets, the Strand, Fleet Street, Cheapside and Cornhill, as 'the finest in Europe'. Later in the eighteenth century the focus for shopping moved west to Oxford Street and later Regent Street.

Europe's busiest shopping street today is Oxford Street. Until the mid-eighteenth century it had been variously called the Tyburn, Uxbridge, Oxford or Worcester Road. From 1721 the road was administered by a turnpike trust, which set up a gate at the junction with Park Lane (then Tyburn Lane). Images of the street in the 1730s show it as still very rural. Oxford Street was a major route between the City and the west where livestock was brought to market and travellers moved to and fro. With the removal of the Tyburn gallows in 1783 and developments around Park

Lane, including the demise of the May Fair, Oxford Street could begin life as a fashionable promenade for shopping. Sophie von La Roche, a German novelist, recorded her impression in 1786:

> Just imagine … a street taking half an hour to cover from end to end, with double rows of brightly shining lamps, in the middle of which stands an equally long row of beautifully lacquered coaches … Up to eleven o'clock at night there are as many people along this street as at Frankfurt during the fair.

Among those shops were furriers (Sneider's established in 1785 and Nicholay's Fur and Feather Manufactory in 1780), furniture suppliers to the nobility (Robert Gillow, 1760), linen drapers, boot- and shoe-makers, perfumiers, hosiers and glovers. Larger stores, like Clark and Debenham's, who had opened a small shop around the corner in Wigmore Street in 1778, would have to wait before they made their appearance on Oxford Street. Nonetheless, by the reign of George III, Oxford Street and its immediate area was well placed to take advantage of London's westward expansion, Georgian architectural elegance, wealthy inhabitants, particularly around Marylebone and Mayfair, and the products of an expanding industrial economy. All of which found an outlet in the shops and consumers attracted to this fashionable street.

Cheapside had been the principal commercial hub and one of busiest shopping streets for centuries. It was known for selling a diverse range of goods, many of which were made and sold on the premises. In the eighteenth century a number of women had businesses there and were also members of the livery companies. They traded as furniture makers, printers, fan-makers, silversmiths, goldsmiths and milliners. William Hogarth's sisters, Mary and Ann, sold fabrics and readymade clothes. The three Sleepe sisters, Martha, Esther and Mary, made and sold fans from their shop in Cheapside. Other businesswomen included Elizabeth Bowen who sold whalebones and Hannah Jones, a wax chandler. To the west in St James's Street was one of the London's oldest shops, Berry Bros. and Rudd, started in 1698 by a woman. We only know her surname as Bourne and as a widow and a mother, with at least two daughters, she is referred to as Widow Bourne. The shop supplied the newly fashionable coffee houses of St James's before later specializing in wines. Over 300 years later Berry Bros. still trades under the Sign of the Coffee Mill.

A new type of shopping space was the Georgian 'warehouse' where large numbers of goods could be sold within one, big, retailing space.

A number of these included the sale of quack medicines. In 1772 'The True Antidote Against Bugs' could be bought from the Printing Office and Picture Warehouse in Bow, or the bestselling ' Balsam for Life' was sold at the medicinal warehouse in Cheapside. In 1724 The Hungary Water Warehouse was a comb-maker's shop in Ludgate Hill whilst Ann Young owned the Snuff Warehouse. In 1786 Fillagree Pearce advertised his Perfumery and Toy Warehouse, which sold goods varying from card boxes to chimney ornaments. Toyshops were popular although Bromstead's Toy Warehouse in Jermyn Street sold other goods including the 'Female Elixir', which promised to 'procure natural evacuations'.

Entertainment

Roy Porter wrote that Georgian London had a 'well-mapped topography of pleasure'. The area around Fleet Street, the Strand, Covent Garden and Charing Cross were being taken over by inns and taverns, shops, shows and street performers. In *The Spectator* of 1711, essayist and politician Joseph Addison (1672–1719) commented on

> the great Trouble and Inconvenience which Ladies were at, in travelling up and down to the several Shows that are exhibited in different Quarters of the Town. The dancing Monkeys are in one place; the Puppet-Show in another; the Opera in a third; not to mention the Lions.

A lion from Barbary was shown at the Duke of Marlborough's Head in Fleet Street.

Exhibitions of curiosities drew large crowds of sightseers. Along the Strand and Fleet Street were exotic animals, which could be seen in taverns and assembly rooms: birds and monkeys from Africa, or even tigers and zebras. *The Manners and Customs of London During the Eighteenth Century* (1810) records for 1718 on Fleet Street a juggling exhibition of a fire-eater by the name of De Hightrehight, who 'ate burning coals, chewed flaming brimstone and swallowed it … ate brimstone, bees-wax, sealing wax, and rosin, with a spoon'. Other entertainers included 'giants' like the seven-foot Essex woman, named Gordon, dwarf exhibits like Buckinger who was twenty-nine-inches tall and had no legs or hands but could write, thread a needle and shuffle a pack of cards. *Rackstraw's Museum of Anatomy and Natural Curiosities*, located between Temple Bar and Chancery Lane, had an eclectic mix of waxworks including the death masks of Oliver Cromwell and Isaac Newton and a mummy said to be Pharaoh's daughter.

In 1710 the *Tatler* reported on an exhibition at the Duke of Marlborough's Head showing a moving picture, which involved a number of cutout figures activated by hidden clockwork that made them perform repetitive motions. Mrs Salmon's (1650–1740) waxworks were established long before those of Madame Tussaud. Mrs Salmon, a toymaker and something of an eccentric, moved her collection of waxworks from St Martin-Le-Grand to the Horn tavern on the north side of Fleet Street in 1711. Her collection consisted of historical, mythical, horrific, comical and fantastical personalities and events. In 1795 her waxworks were moved again to more spacious apartments at the corner of the Inner Temple Gate.

Theatres

In 1700 the only two venues in the city allowed to perform spoken drama were the Theatre Royal, Drury Lane, and the Lincoln's Inn Fields Theatre. They were called 'patent theatres' because they had to be licensed by the king in order to perform serious drama. However, from the 1720s more were built in London and the eighteenth century would become the great age of the theatre. A setback came when in 1737 Robert Walpole's government attempted to impose censorship by renewing the monopoly of the patent theatres and insisting that every script had to be approved by the Lord Chamberlain, who was also given the powers to close down shows. Walpole's personal vendetta against theatres stemmed from a satirical farce, *The Golden Rump*, which mocked him and the royal family. This did not stop theatre managers who proved to be creative in finding legal loopholes and offered melodrama, pantomime, ballet, opera and music instead of 'serious' drama.

New theatres of the Georgian period were built to accommodate large crowds who went to nightly performances of plays, ballets and various types of entertainment. The first of these was the Queen's Theatre, in the Haymarket (1705) where operas were performed and the name of the theatre changing with the gender of the monarch. Originally named in honour of Queen Anne (r. 1702–14) it became the King's Theatre on the accession of George I in 1714 and was renamed Her Majesty's Theatre in 1837 for Queen Victoria.

Theatre audiences were often a riotous lot who could be rude and noisy. Food and alcohol were consumed in great quantity, and actors were often pelted with rotten fruit and vegetables. At the famous Theatre Royal, Drury Lane, riots brought disruption and damage on a number of occasions and there was even an assassination attempt on King George III in 1800. A person's social rank and class dictated their place in the theatre. The wealthier classes were seated in boxes alongside the stage, while working-class men and women were squeezed into hot and dirty galleries. Theatres attracted pickpockets, and in the 'pit' in front of the stage, young men would drink, eat nuts and mingle with prostitutes.

Pleasure Gardens

It was men who frequented most of the eating establishments in the eighteenth century. However, women could enjoy eating out in the growing number of tea and pleasure gardens. The pleasure garden was one of the most significant innovations in entertainment and leisure during the eighteenth century. They had developed from the parks and outdoor spaces where the cost of a ticket was required for entry. Investors and entrepreneurs developed gardens into popular and commercial spaces like 21-year-old Jonathan Tyers who transformed a small country house into Vauxhall Gardens.

The largest of the pleasure gardens were those at Vauxhall (the most famous) and Ranelagh in Chelsea (the most fashionable). Both of these were located on the side of the Thames where the river was often used for spectacles including the Lord Mayor's procession and royal flotillas. Smaller pleasure gardens were established at Marylebone, Hampstead and Sadler's Wells.

Laid out in the style of formal gardens with shrubberies and miniature waterways, they variously provided music, dancing, eating and drinking, operas, masquerades and illuminations. Although they were designed for wealthier and the more respectable customers, they soon became popular with all. Marylebone Gardens were opened in 1650 near Marylebone High Street but it was not until the first half of the eighteenth century that they offered the same sort of facilities that made the Vauxhall and Ranelagh Gardens so popular. Two bowling greens provided a nucleus around which the gardens developed. For an admission fee of a shilling theatrical performances, balls, concerts and magnificent firework displays could be enjoyed.

At Vauxhall Gardens George Frederic Handel became something of a composer-in-residence during the 1730s and 1740s whilst visitors to

Ranelagh admired the Chinese Pavilion, or watched the fountain of mirrors. As with other London pleasure gardens, those in Marylebone tended to cater originally for a rich and fashionable clientele only to find that they could make more money by providing more disreputable entertainments, which attracted rakes, rogues and prostitutes. The glory days of Marylebone Gardens seem to have been in their last thirty or so years before they closed in 1778. Vauxhall continued for longer, finally closing in 1859 and thus marking the end of an era.

Blood Sports

Less sedate and refined was the continuity of blood sports particularly cock fighting, dog fighting and boxing in which the gentry and elite played an influential role in encouraging a variety of these sports. From bull baiting to prize fighting, many sports were associated with gambling. Bankside had a long reputation for bear gardens and bull baiting but it was not alone. In 1772, at Tothill Fields, Westminster, over seventy bulldogs were released in a bull-baiting spectacle with over 10,000 people cheering them on. A popular bear garden venue was in Clerkenwell at Hockley-in-the-Hole whilst Covent Garden not only had bear baiting but also held cockfights and bare-knuckle prize fights including women's matches.

Between 1719 and 1730 James Figg was the first recognized bare-knuckle champion of England. He only lost once in over 270 fights (claiming he was ill when he lost). Such was his reputation that he was painted by Hogarth and newspapers reported his death in 1734 at the age of 40. Figg opened an 'academy of arms' off the east end of Oxford Street. Regular prize fights were held there in the 1720s and contests took place every Wednesday with challengers coming from far and wide. Large crowds attended; fights were not limited to men as women fighters were also popular. For additional entertainment animals were baited to fight each other.

The lack of sensitivity towards animals is depicted in William Hogarth's series *The Four Stages of Cruelty* (1751). In *The First Stage of Cruelty*, a group of children and bystanders are enjoying the sight of a dog mauling a cat. Another part of the illustration shows two cats hanging by their tales from a street sign; two other young men are sticking an arrow into a dog. The popularity of many blood sports began to disappear, at least publicly, by the end of the century with changing attitudes to animal rights and subsequently animal baiting was made illegal in the early 1800s.

Punishments

London's association with crime is as long as that of brutal public punishments. Whippings, brandings, mutilations, transportation, public executions and humiliation in the stocks and the pillory, which all ended in the nineteenth century, existed for a range of offences. Before 1868 many of these were part of the public spectacle. Significant changes were taking place in the Georgian period and there was a growing concern, especially from those in positions of authority, that public hangings were not having the desired effect of deterring people from committing crimes.

In the middle of the eighteenth century, three major institutions of confinement can be identified in London. These were the debtors' prisons, the jails and the houses of correction, commonly known as bridewells (from Henry VIII's Bridewell Palace converted to a correctional facility). In London, debtors were confined particularly in Ludgate, King's Bench, the Fleet and the Marshalsea in Southwark. The regimes within the various houses of correction varied widely. All were dirty and pest-ridden but an inmate who underwent a brief stay in the Clerkenwell House of Correction in 1757 made it clear that many of its prisoners spent their time lounging around gaming, drinking and fornicating.

The famous triangular gallows at Tyburn provided a day out for crowds who would walk or ride into the suburbs to take air, eat, drink and play games in the fields. Two of the largest crowds assembled to witness an execution at Tyburn were those for Jack Sheppard and Jonathan Wild but for very different reasons. Twenty-two-year-old Sheppard (1702–24), a thief and escapologist, became part of London's folklore when he was executed in November 1724. Tens of thousands turned out to cheer him. An attempted plan to rescue his body after the execution failed in a melee that followed which saw blows exchanged between the crowd who were trying to protect him from and what they thought were the surgeon's agents.

Six months later the notorious thief-taker Jonathan Wild prompted thousands of people to turn out for his execution. However, in Wild's case the crowd came to express their absolute contempt. Wild had built a corrupt business on the exploitation of others' vulnerabilities. The lack of an effective police system led to the emergence of the 'thief-taker', men and, on occasion, women who caught and delivered wrong-doers (and the innocent) for whom rewards had been offered. Wild was booed and pelted with a wide variety of missiles, including excrement and the festering corpses of cats and dogs. The crowd rejoiced to see the once powerful Wild brought down. His skeleton can be seen in the Hunterian Museum, at the Royal College of Surgeons in Lincoln Inn Fields, Holborn.

Prisons were run for profit and inevitably this led to corruption. Reformers like John Howard saw that the drunken crowds at Tyburn and Newgate were ineffective as a deterrent to crime. Pressure for penal reform grew stronger in the late eighteenth century although there would still be a long wait for the end of public punishments. Further developments such as custodial sentences, the right to a defence, the abolition of many capital offences, the introduction of juvenile institutions and a national police force (the Metropolitan Police Act of 1829 established a full-time, professional and centrally organized police force for the Greater London area). The London City Police was formed in 1832.

Sex – Vice – Drink and Moral Reformers

Daniel Defoe noted in 1728 that 'you'll see no such impudence as in the streets of London'. The capital had a long and well-established reputation for the extent of its vice. Radical and social reformer Francis Place described prostitutes in Catherine's Street near the Strand in the 1780s as wearing clean stockings and shoes because it was fashionable to be flashy around the heels but their gowns were low, revealing their breasts, their hair was often full of lice and drunkenness was common. It was a description that almost bears out James Boswell's (1740–95), experience in 1769 when he searched for a woman in St James's Park who he said was 'ugly, lean and had a breath that smelt of spirits'. Little wonder that Boswell's diary records up to nineteen episodes of venereal disease between 1760 and 1786, mostly contracted from prostitutes.

The Strand was the most notorious stretch for streetwalkers as well as the many alleys that ran off from there, notably Catherine Street. In his poem, 'Trivia, or the Art of Walking the Streets of London' (1716) John Gay wrote:

> *may thy virtue guard thee through the roads*
> *Of Drury's mazy courts, and dark abodes,*
> *The harlots guileful paths, who nightly stand,*
> *Where Katherine-street descends into the Strand*

Estimates of how many prostitutes there were in London vary wildly from 5,000 to 50,000. There were certainly proportionately more streetwalkers

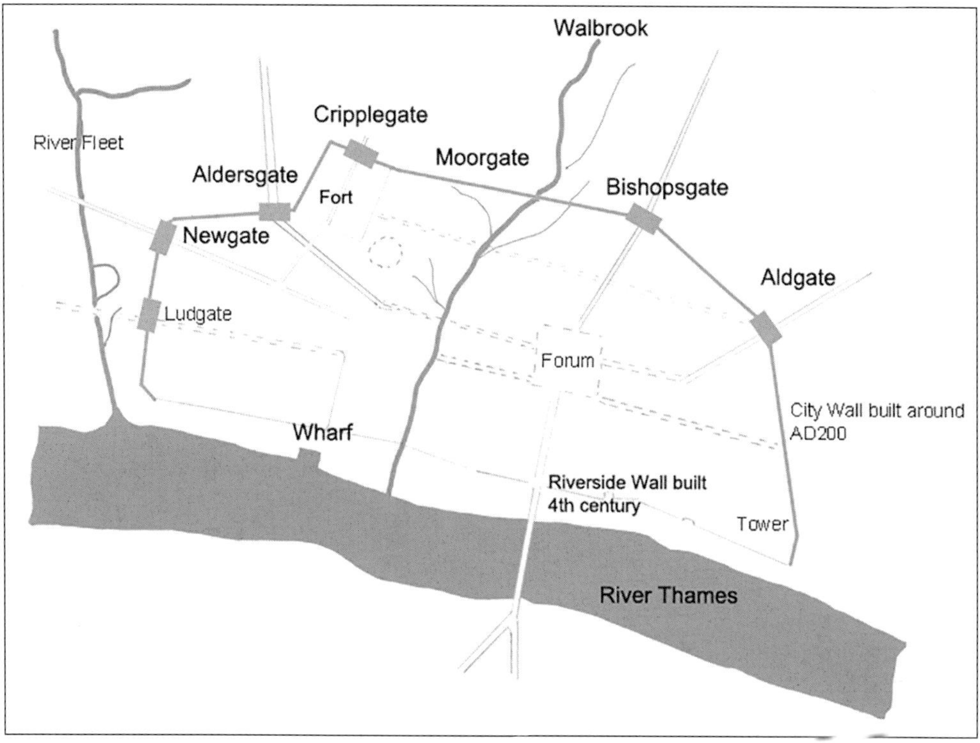

Map of the Roman City with wall and location of gates. Moorgate was expanded from a postern or smaller gate in the early fifteenth century.

Part of the city wall bastion at the Barbican.

Left: Statue believed to be of Roman Emperor Trajan at Tower Hill.

Below: Part of the old city wall in a carpark near the Museum of London.

Above: Reminders of the
importance of trade. North
side of the River Thames.

Right: Ferryman's Seat
located in the side of a
restaurant on Bankside at the
junction of Bear Gardens.

Left: Plaque to the Hanseatic League celebrating 600 years of trade. Located on the east wall of Cannon Street Station.

Below: The burning of John Rogers at Smithfield, 1555.

Above: Decapitated heads above London Bridge Gate, southern side.

Right: Statue of Oliver Cromwell outside Westminster Hall.

Above left: Statue of Queen Elizabeth I outside the church of St Dunstan-in-the-West, Fleet Street. It stood on the western side of Ludgate until the gate was taken down in 1760.

Above right: Monument of John Stow in St Andrew Undershaft off Leadenhall Street. The quill is changed in a memorial service every three years.

Long View of London from Bankside by Wenceslaus Hollar, 1647.

Adelphi, London's first neoclassical building by the Adam Brothers, built on the Thames near the Strand.

Above: Courtyard of the Royal Exchange in the eighteenth century.

Right: *Gin Lane* (1751) by William Hogarth depicting the evils of gin drinking.

Aldgate House with a section of the old gate on the northern side (far left). Aldgate House was pulled down in 1809.

The pillory at Charing Cross.

The Idle 'Prentice Executed at Tyburn (1747) by William Hogarth.

Gordon Riots, 1780 – attacking Newgate Prison.

Above left: *Ludgate Hill: A Block in the Street*, Gustave Dore, from *London, A Pilgrimage*, 1872.

Above right: Victorian grandeur, Russell Hotel, 1898.

Surgery before anesthetics: the Old Operating Theatre, St Thomas Street. The theatre dates from 1822 and is the oldest surviving surgical theatre in Europe.

Above: Digging up
Marylebone Road in
the nineteenth century.

Right: Victorian street
cleaners.

Above: The Central
Criminal Court or
the Old Bailey. Also
the site of Newgate
Prison (1188–1902)
and the City
gate of Newgate
(demolished 1777).

Left: Steps at
Bethnal Green
Station. A
plaque to the left
commemorates
'173 Men, Women
and Children who
lost their lives on …
3 March 1943'.

Above: *The Evening News* reporting the Blitz on London.

Right: Plaque at Stainer Street dedicated to sixty-eight people who lost their lives on 17 February 1940.

Below: Examples of wartime posters displayed in the disused Strand Underground Station.

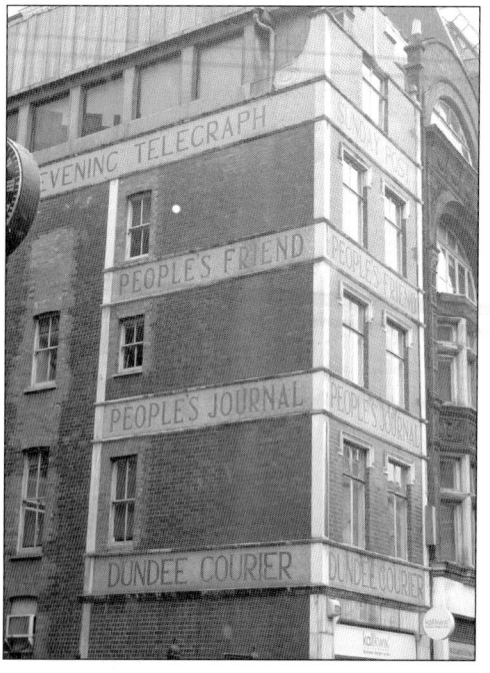

Above left: A reminder of what Fleet Street was famous for.

Above right: Sir Christopher Wren's Temple Bar marked the gateway to the City of London via Fleet Street for 200 years, often bearing the heads and limbs of those executed for high treason. It is now located in Paternoster Square opposite St Paul's Cathedral.

Left: Strand Underground Station, discontinued in 1994. It had served as a wartime shelter for people as well as the Elgin Marbles.

St Paul's from the Millennium Bridge.

The City and the 'Gherkin' from Bankside.

Above left: St Pancras
International railway
terminus.

Above right: A deserted
Tower Bridge during the
Coronavirus pandemic
lockdown.

Left: The old and the new:
the Tower of London
with the Shard in the
background.

in London than elsewhere in Britain, many who were female migrants. Likewise, many men came to London to seek out prostitutes.

Anti-vice societies were formed in the capital mainly to clamp down on prostitutes and brothels and later the proliferation of pornography sold in bookshops. The Society for the Reformation of Manners was set up in the 1691 and campaigned against what they saw as all types of debauchery and lewd activities, especially sodomy, which remained a capital offence until 1861. By establishing a system of 'guardians', the Society tried to root out the flourishing gay sub-culture in London, particularly in the areas around the Royal Exchange, Moorfields, Seven Dials, Covent Garden and the southern side of St James's Park, which was a popular cruising ground frequented by soldiers from the nearby barracks. 'Molly houses' sprang up, catering for gay men who could drink, eat, dress up as women, socialize and have sex. Journalist Ned Ward, in *The Secret History of London Clubs* (1709) described the houses as a place where a 'curious band of fellows' met and held parties'. One particular raid in 1726 was on Margaret 'Mother' Clap's House in Holborn, which resulted in the arrest of forty men. She was sentenced to stand in the pillory in Smithfield, fined and imprisoned for two years for keeping a disorderly house for the entertainment of sodomites whilst three of the men were executed.

Prostitution was not illegal and punishments were only given for disorderly offences. Institutions were founded including the Magdalen Hospital for Penitent Prostitutes in 1758, and more indirectly, foundling hospitals which attempted to prevent young girls from falling into prostitution. Thomas Coram (1668–1751) opened the first Foundling Hospital in Hatton Garden in 1741; four years later it moved to Lamb's Conduit Fields, Bloomsbury, where destitute mothers would leave their children outside the doors.

Sexual infections, or the 'clap' or 'pox' as they were referred to, were rife in London and prostitutes were blamed for spreading the disease. Venereal disease was dangerous and, as yet, incurable. In Hogarth's *The Harlot's Progress* (plate 5, 1732) Moll, the harlot in question, is shown dying of syphilis with her pock-marked face covered with fake beauty spots whilst several opiates and 'cures' litter the floor. The Lock Hospital in Grosvenor Place, opened in 1746, was an attempt to deal with venereal disease where, six years later, some 1500 patients were being cured including married women, children and many destitute people. In St Martin's Lane in the 1740s condoms, made from animal membrane and tied to the penis by a ribbon, could be bought. Campaigners continued their moral crusade and, despite the attempts of various hospitals, prostitution, disease and the associated issues of crime and poverty escalated in the Victorian period.

Another vice that campaigners fought against was drink. Teetotal societies would emerge in the next century but religious figures like John Wesley were already proclaiming in 1743 'that buying, selling, and drinking of liquor, unless absolutely necessary, were evils to be avoided'. Between 1700 and 1760 Londoners developed a passion for gin in what became known as the 'Gin Craze'. It was estimated that at least 7,000 gin shops were selling the spirit by 1730 for as little as a few pennies. Originally imported from Holland in the late seventeenth century, gin only became popular in England when William of Orange took the throne in 1688. By the end of the century Britain was at war with France and in order to protect the economy the government put a heavy duty on the import of spirits and lifted restrictions on domestic spirit production, which created a market for poor-quality grain. The gin distilled in London was much stronger than that imported from Holland and often adulterated with awful, even toxic, impurities with disastrous consequences, leading to a rise in crime, prostitution, high death rates and falling birth rates. In 1736 the Gin Act taxed retail sales and made selling gin without an annual licence illegal. This led to illicit sales of gin with names that included 'Ladies Delight' and 'Cuckold's Comfort'. Propaganda against gin drinking and a further Act in 1751 proved more successful and were also helped by a series of bad harvests, which forced grain prices up. By 1760 the Gin Craze had just about run its course.

London was never short of moralists both secular and religious. Religion's role in daily life during the eighteenth century was no longer the dominant force it had once been, especially in urban areas. As London expanded beyond the City walls, churches were less in evidence and the alehouse and tavern provided an alternative where communities could gather.

There was a greater degree of religious tolerance (but not for Roman Catholics) compared to other European countries. The Toleration Act (1689) had granted freedom of worship to Nonconformists (e.g. Baptists, Presbyterians, Independents) although they were denied holding any political office. London had a large proportion of Dissenters (Protestants who were not Anglicans/Church of England) who met in meeting houses, livery halls and taverns. Protestant chapels did grow with over 250 by the end of the century. Much of this was due to the rise of Methodism from 1740 when John Wesley experienced a conversion after attending a meeting at St Mary, Aldersgate, in 1738.

There was still a continuing hostility towards Catholics particularly in the first half of the century. This was largely associated with the fear of Jacobitism (those who supported the restoration of the exiled king James II and his descendants after the Glorious Revolution of 1688), especially after a number of failed attempts to restore the exiled Stuarts. Reminders of Catholic 'treason' were etched into the base of the Monument and the anti-Catholic processions which included Guy Fawkes Night and the anniversary of Queen Elizabeth I's birthday on 17 November. In the 1730s there had been anti-Irish riots as well as attacks against London Catholics and their properties in Suffolk Street where the Foot Guards had to be called upon. Anti-Catholicism found its most violent expression in the Gordon Riots of 1780.

The themes of morality, prudery and hypocrisy provided a rich seam for satirists in Georgian London. Between 1770 and 1830 some 20,000 satirical prints were produced, enjoyed and consumed in the capital. Crowds gathered outside print-shop windows of the fashionable West End to look at the latest outrageous illustrations. A French visitor noted in 1772 that the area around Westminster Hall was populated with a 'prodigious number of little shops ... every day lined with prints in which the chief persons [in ministry and Parliament] are handled without mercy'. About 50 per cent of prints dealt with political issues, especially corruption, with others focusing on personal matters like scandals among the ruling class. Bare breasts and backsides were a regular staple as well as urinating, vomiting, defecating and farting.

Caricatures had their origins in the 1720s but the satirical prints really flourished after the 1760s with the likes of brilliant satirists, James Gillray (1756–1815) and Thomas Rowlandson (1756–1827). Late Georgian London was depicted through their anarchic images. Other satirical artist-engravers and print sellers included Samuel William Fores with his Caricature Warehouse on the corner of Sackville Street, Piccadilly, and William Holland of Oxford Street who boasted of having the largest collection of humorous prints in Europe. People could buy prints for sixpence (plain) or one shilling (coloured) or they could pay an entry fee of one shilling to view. So popular was the fashion for these cartoons the industry employed thousands of tradesmen and artists.

The grim, downcast and criminal sides of London were portrayed in Hogarth's illustrations. *Four Times a Day* (1738) set in Soho, Charing Cross and Covent Garden whereas later images, for example those by Rowlandson and George Cruikshank, showed a less judgemental image of the capital. Isaac Cruikshank's *The Origins of Cockney* (1798) pokes fun at a flourishing but vulgar-looking family on a country walk a mile from the City, pointing to animals and commenting on their noises including that of a cock.

As Pepys and Evelyn gave us insights into seventeenth century London life the eighteenth century provided us with rich observations from novelists, diarists, guidebooks (which developed in the Georgian period) and illustrators. Writers and critics such as James Boswell, Samuel Johnson, Henry Fielding and William Hogarth saw both the dark side of London, its disease, crime and poverty but also its diversity, vibrancy and its beauty. William Wordsworth's (1770–1850) poem 'Composed upon Westminster Bridge' (1802) depicts the city's serene splendour in the early morning:

Earth has not anything to show more fair:
Dull would he be of soul who could pass by
A sight so touching in its majesty ...
This City now doth, like a garment, wear
The beauty of the morning; silent, bare,
Ships, towers, domes, theatres, and temples lie
Open unto the fields, and to the sky

London, then as now, has many faces. In a letter to Wordsworth in 1801 Charles Lamb paid homage to London:

I have passed all my days in London ... The lighted shops of the Strand and Fleet Street; the innumerable trades, tradesmen and customers, coaches, wagons, playhouses; all the bustle and wickedness round about Covent Garden; the very women of the town; the watchmen, drunken scenes, rattles ... the crowds, the very dirt and mud, the sun shining upon houses and pavements, the print shops, the old bookstalls ... coffeehouses, steams of soups from kitchens, the pantomimes – London itself a pantomime and a masquerade – all these things work themselves into my mind and feed me ... The wonder of these sights impels me into night walks about her crowded streets, and I often shed tears in the motley Strand from fullness of joy at so much life.

The works of the great figures in English literature were published and sold in Fleet Street. Indeed, some of the authors actually lived there. In Salisbury Court, Samuel Richardson, author of the first English novel, *Pamela*, lived, printed, published and wrote his books; Oliver Goldsmith passed the closing years of his life in Brick Court off Middle Temple Lane; Samuel Pepys was born in Salisbury Court and essayist Charles Lamb (1775–1834) lived variously in Chancery Lane, Mitre Court and close to Inner Temple. In 1748 Samuel Johnson came to 17 Gough Square where, after years of toil and dogged persistence and with the help of six amanuenses, he compiled his great work *A Dictionary of the English Language* in 1755. Across the square facing the house is a statue of Dr Johnson's favourite cat, Hodge (unveiled in 1997).

Writer and poet Oliver Goldsmith (1730–74) wrote his best-known work, *The Vicar of Wakefield*, when he lived in Wine Office Court. A more tragic figure was the poet Thomas Chatterton (1752–70) who committed suicide at the young age of 17. Chatterton influenced the Romantics Keats, Wordsworth and Coleridge. On 24 August 1770 he ended his life by arsenic poisoning and was buried in the Shoe Lane Workhouse Cemetery.

The eighteenth century was an exciting time for publishing. In 1702 Elizabeth Mallett launched the first successful and regular English daily newspaper, *The Daily Courant*, based next to the King's Arms tavern. With the emergence of newspapers came the rise of the journalist and Grub Street became associated with this practice. Grub Street was a real street near Moorgate and it was here that the foundations of Fleet Street and the modern newspaper were laid. In 1830, the street's name was changed to Milton Street after a local builder. Grub Street was an area of poverty, vice, disreputable tenements, brothels and alleys. It was also a place associated with writers and publishers. By the early nineteenth century there were fifty-two London papers and over a hundred other titles. London newspapers were delivered to the provinces courtesy of the night mail coaches. William Henry Smith and his brother owned a 'Stationers and Newsmen' business in Duke Street and the Strand. Their father started the business in 1792 at Little Grosvenor Street.

By the end of the eighteenth century London was the largest city in Europe and was becoming the new Rome with its architecture, leisure, trade, ports, politics and a growing imperial status.

Chapter 6

Unruly London

'If you do not want to live among wicked people, do not live in London'

It is commonplace that we view the past through the prism of our own times and its mores but we must avoid attempts to distort or tailor the past in order to serve present political purposes. Much of Britain's history and that of London in particular is punctuated by violence, crime, corruption and 'anti-social behaviour'. Historian Harold Perkin (1969) described the English before 1780 as 'one of the most aggressive, brutal, rowdy, outspoken, riotous cruel and bloodthirsty nations in the world'. Roy Porter in his magisterial *London: A Social History* (1994), argued that in the eighteenth century 'violence was as English as plum pudding'. If these observations are true, it is inevitable that such behaviour was likely to have been manifested most intensely in the unique conditions of London. Many Londoners were inured to images of death. Public executions as well as the display of rotting bodies on gibbets and city gates and spiked heads on poles were common sights.

London in the eighteenth century housed more than a tenth of the population of England and Wales and the decisions made there dominated the whole country. They were made by a self-perpetuating elite which was unaccountable and unrepresentative whilst the majority of people had no say in the making of public policy. Vast numbers dwelt in insanitary hovels with only a minimal provision for the old, the ill and the incapable.

In this chapter, selected aspects of London's more riotous history will be considered. Such behaviour had of course been a feature of earlier periods in London's history, but it perhaps peaked in the period from the late seventeenth century to the early nineteenth century. Certainly, many social and political practices of this period contrast starkly with the mores of the Victorian era during which, as Perkin again observes, the English 'became one of the most inhibited, polite orderly, tender-minded, prudish and hypocritical' of European people. In the eighteenth century the

English commonalty had a Europe-wide reputation for its turbulence and volatility and foreign visitors were struck by the lack of deference which it extended to its supposed 'betters'.

Riots

Under legislation passed in 1715 largely to counter possible political subversion, a riot was held to have taken place if three or more people assembled to do an unlawful act, usually committed a breach of the peace, and then performed it. Only the most serious riots were prosecuted at the Old Bailey.

A capital felony occurred if, when ordered by a magistrate to disperse, they had not done so within one hour. Damage to property included types of malicious damage that were considered crimes against the public and some of these offences became subject to capital punishment under the Black Act of 1723 (named in response to poaching committed by men who disguised themselves by 'blacking' their faces). Many offenders received other punishments. For example, in 1687, John Moor, Obedia Bow, and Richard Baston were all tried at the Old Bailey for 'Riotously and Tumulteously assembling with divers others to pull down the house of Thomas Griffith of St Andrews Holbourn'. They were variously sentenced to public whipping, fines, imprisonment and hard labour. From the late seventeenth century many appeared at the Old Bailey on charges of breaking the peace and rioting.

Over twenty people were arrested in 1725 for being armed with guns, pistols, swords, broomsticks and staves 'and having their Faces black'd, or being otherwise disguised' in the Parish of St Paul's Shadwell. They were attempting to free some prisoners. Another interpretation of riot involved James Beaver and four others who were fined in 1716 for assembling along with some 'Hundreds of People who were very rude, violent, and tumultuous' in Salisbury Court. They acted in a 'Riotous Manner under a Pretence of celebrating in a publick and insulting Manner the Death of Thomas Bean, a Malefactor convicted and executed'.

In the absence of a regular police force, the magistrate could deploy troops to back his diktat with force including the use of firearms if necessary. The Riot Act was immensely unpopular not least with the soldiery who did not relish the policing role they might find themselves being ordered to undertake. Soldiers at this time were billeted with civilians, and being close to the people, might sympathize with the cause of the rioters. The authorities were aware of this and the possibility that troops might fraternize with rioters was one of the reasons why barracks came to be used at a later stage. It is significant that John Fielding who was the Bow Street magistrate from the 1750s to the late 1770s only ever brought the military in to deal with riotous disorder as a last resort, firmly believing that their presence could easily inflame an already volatile situation.

In the eighteenth and early nineteenth centuries, London witnessed riots spurred on by anger over a wide range of issues: the price of food, opposition to turnpikes and their associated tolls, taxes, press gangs, conditions in workhouses and prisons, excessive fares demanded by chairmen (men who touted for business for their sedan chairs), Roman Catholics, the Irish, religious dissenters, Jews and foreigners working as servants in London, theatre prices, political elections and their outcomes, the execution of popular felons, the activities of body snatchers and their partners in crime, the surgeon-anatomists, and the sadistic practices inflicted by schoolmasters on their pupils.

Central London contained distinct patterns of settlement. Many in the City were involved in mercantile and commercial activities whilst the gentry and aristocracy dominated the West End. The East End had a significantly poorer population. Joseph Addison writing in *The Spectator* in 1712 noted that 'the inhabitants of St James's, live under the same laws, and speak the same language, and are a distinct people from those of Cheapside, who are likewise removed from those of the Temple on the one side, and those of Smithfield on the other, by several climates and degrees in their way of thinking and conversing'.

The common people of London formed the bulk of London's population, and were excluded from participation in the political processes. The irony was that many of London's impoverished masses regarded themselves as 'free' by comparison with their counterparts in many more authoritarian European states. Political philosopher Edmund Burke (1729–97), not known as a friend of the masses, was astute enough to identify the dilemma in which they found themselves. The rioting in which Londoners engaged was often in defence of what the ordinary people regarded as their inalienable rights and interests from incursion by arbitrary and often corrupt authority.

The London mob contained many regularly employed labourers, skilled artisans, tradesmen and shopkeepers with a sprinkling of the intellectually inclined middle class. Only occasionally did these mobs gather in sufficient numbers and with sufficient determination to constitute a serious threat to public order. There was also an element of entertainment in a good riot. People spent much of their time on the streets and even a small riot could provide some free knockabout entertainment.

Whenever possible, life was lived on the teeming streets and by common agreement that is where individual and communal grievances were aired and, sometimes, acted on. These seem to have taken on a more edgy character from the beginning of the eighteenth century perhaps because London was spreading out from the area previously controlled quite closely by the City of London. The citizenry felt a new freedom to express their grievances of which there were many. Court reports indicate a change with far more women being involved, increased violence and petty nastiness such as spitting and throwing mud and stones.

Groups of workers such as weavers and tailors became increasingly likely to take to the streets in pursuit of increased wages or to protect jobs threatened by labour-saving machinery and cheap imports. In 1719 London calico weavers led crowds to attack women wearing this imported cloth. 'Down with the Calicos!' was the rallying call in this case; 'Down with Irish!' rang out in riots in 1736 against Irish workers prepared to accept low wages and 'Wilkes and Liberty!' in the riots of 1768 supporting the maverick radical politician John Wilkes and his criticism of George III. A common practice was to display lighted candles in premises indicating support for a particular cause and to use coercion if there was a refusal to do so. This might involve pelting the building with stones or even arson.

In 1738 there was anger when French actors were employed at the Little Haymarket Theatre to replace native players and mobs seized potatoes and apples from vendors' street barrows and bombarded the theatre, breaking all its windows. In 1749 sailors violently attacked brothels to exact revenge for some of their number who had been robbed in these places. Loafers and others joined in, before the riotous mob proceeded to attack other brothels.

Drums, bells, trumpets and tin cans were often sounded or beaten to call up a crowd and people would often join in for the excitement and entertainment that a riot could provide without necessarily being interested in the issue involved. Flags were often carried by demonstrators bearing a colour associated with a particular cause. The followers of John Wilkes, for example, carried blue flags and sported blue cockades. Sometimes bonfires were lit in the streets. In 1761, for example, after a hated tax was imposed on porter, a strong beer popular with working people, effigies of the MP who introduced the relevant bill and of publicans who quickly imposed the resulting higher prices, were burned in public places. Houses were often 'pulled down' in riots. They were not literally pulled down: mobs would carry away windows, doors, interior fittings and furnishings and burn them in the streets. Often the premises concerned were attacked because they were the centre of religious activity of a sort that was disapproved of.

So Catholic chapels were on the receiving end in 1688, dissenting meeting houses during the Sacheverell Riots of 1710, a Presbyterian meeting house in 1715 and Catholic premises again in the Gordon Riots of 1780.

In 1794 the houses of 'crimps', men who got others drunk and, when they were insensible, offered them 'for sale' to the military or naval authorities to bolster recruitment, were attacked and destroyed. The crimps, with no homes to go to, had been ritually 'purged' from the community. Riots were generally, although not always, well disciplined and where violence was employed, it was usually against property rather than persons. People who were the object of hatred were more often burnt in effigy than directly attacked.

There existed in London and elsewhere a hard-headed sense of outrage which has sometimes been described as the 'moral economy'. The common people felt that it was highly immoral when the price of food and other necessities increased as the result of profiteering. There was a strong sense of what was a fair price and fair practice. The gigantic Albion Flour Mills, Southwark burnt down on two occasions. The first time, arson was suspected and acclaimed by the populace who believed that the owners were practising adulteration and got what they deserved. On the second occasion the buildings caught fire and were almost destroyed. Huge crowds turned out to watch the conflagration, dancing and singing by way of celebration. In 1800 and 1801 there were food riots occasioned by scarcity and the resultant rising prices. Officialdom explained these phenomena as the result of Napoleon's continental blockade but popular opinion put the problems down to speculation by government insiders. Feelings ran high and a monster meeting was planned for Kennington Common. The authorities put on a show of military strength and the demonstration did not take place.

By the end of the eighteenth century, riots were becoming less frequent but more violent. The mobs had more recourse to firearms and purpose-made weapons to which the authorities responded by increasing their repressive measures. The likelihood of violence and of personal injury or even death is likely to have deterred many of those who previously had enjoyed a good rumpus. As crime rose seemingly out of control and before the age of effective policing, the main recourse of the authorities was to increase the number of crimes that carried a capital sentence. Frequently the punishment was 'commuted' to transportation, a fate some regarded as worse than death. The gratuitous violence and destruction of the Gordon Riots had made the authorities determined to use any means necessary to prevent a recurrence.

The Gordon Riots

Without doubt, the Gordon Riots provided the most outstanding example of public disorder in London in the eighteenth century. The riots occurred in the summer of 1780 and lasted a week, during which the hated Newgate Prison was destroyed and a serious attack launched on the Bank of England. The crowd ran amok and the events scared London's rich so much that as with other crises affecting the capital, many of them decamped for the duration. The experience etched itself into the collective memory of London and provided the theme for the novel *Barnaby Rudge* by Dickens, published in 1841.

The riots were named after Lord George Gordon, an unstable, possibly insane Scottish Protestant with a manic hatred of all things to do with Roman Catholicism. He had put himself at the head of a movement demanding repeal of the Catholic Relief Act. This had been passed in 1778 as an attempt to address two or more centuries of bitter religious conflict and which was aimed at reducing some of the systematic discrimination suffered by the Catholic community. Most of the Protestant population believed that the Catholic minority wanted to return the country to the thrall of Popery and were prepared to use every means at their disposal, including foreign military intervention, to achieve that end.

A few days before, Gordon had given some intimation of his intentions when speaking in Parliament and these manifested themselves in a huge meeting in St George's Fields, Southwark. There Gordon made many inflammatory statements which were rapturously greeted by the crowd and he called on them to sign a mass petition to be presented to Parliament demanding repeal of the Relief Act. With enthusiasm those present rushed to put their mark or their signatures on the petition which was then taken across the Thames to Westminster. Up to this point the crowd, though highly excited and noisy, was under control and it was only when they reached Parliament that violence broke out. Gordon harangued any politicians he came across but it quickly became obvious that the House of Commons was not even going to consider the petition. The mood then turned angry and the crowd, rapidly transformed into a mob, streamed off in an easterly direction, totally out of control. Witnesses said that it no longer consisted largely of people who were simply anti-Catholic. The mob went on the rampage, venting their collective resentment at the raw deal life had served up to them. Homes and business premises of Catholics and known sympathizers were attacked and in some cases torched. People in Moorfields, with its large Irish Catholic population, were randomly set upon. However, as if by some unspoked consensus, the main objective of the mob's hatred turned from Catholicism to the notorious Newgate Prison. Conditions in the prison were appalling even by the standards of the time. The law was regarded as the rich man's law; most of the prison inmates were viewed as being punished for their crimes because they were poor. Newgate somehow symbolized the inequalities and injustices of contemporary society. The prison was destroyed and its inmates released in something like an act of collective catharsis. Other prisons were likewise attacked and burned. The house of the hated Lord Chief Justice in Bloomsbury was attacked and destroyed. An unsuccessful attempt was made to destroy the Bank of England. An attack was launched on the tollbooths at Blackfriars Bridge. This had been opened in 1769 and the tolls had always been a source of resentment. The tollgates were broken down and all the toll money appropriated by the attackers. A Catholic gin distiller had rather foolishly tried to bribe the mob to go away by giving them money and liquor. Initially the mob moved on but returned later and set fire to the distillery. Large quantities of spirits escaped to flow down the gutters and many people lay down and drank their fill until they were immolated in the flames when the gin ignited.

There were distinct phases during the riots. The initial meeting and march organized by the Protestant Association consisted largely of progressive elements of a respectable nature who saw in Catholicism reactionary and foreign-inspired elements they disliked. The appearance of 'hate figures' at Westminster and the realization that Parliament was not going to respond favourably to the petition was another factor. Many of the more law-abiding section of petitioners left, from disappointment or perhaps sensing impending trouble. A mob with a rather different social mix containing apprentices, servants, some criminals, professional troublemakers and others looking for some exciting action, turned it into a more violent phase. They searched out Catholic individuals and buildings which then widened to include other unpopular figures of authority such as Sir John Fielding, whose home in Bow Street was destroyed. The authorities seemed to regard this action as tolerable protest up to a point, but that perception changed when attacks were aimed at the Bank of England and a number of prestigious businesses.

The military was brought in, employing violence to quell the riots and then the majesty of the law to bring a selection of the perpetrators to justice. Some 20,000 troops were used and estimates of between 300 and 1,000 rioters died, not all at the hands of the soldiers. Twenty-five rioters were hanged. Issues around Catholic emancipation became entirely subsidiary to the safeguarding of property.

Lord George Gordon (1751–93) was born in Upper Grosvenor Street, a younger son of the Duke of Gordon. After a none too successful stint in the Royal Navy he became a Member of Parliament and in 1779 accepted the presidency of the Protestant Association, a militant body that wanted the repeal of the Catholic Relief Act of 1778. Gordon's anti-Catholic speeches always drew large crowds. He led the march on Parliament and was later tried for high treason. He was acquitted when the court was unable to prove he had taken any part in the riots themselves.

Later he flirted with Quakerism and then embraced Judaism. Eschewing obscurity, he then lost several libel cases and was sent to prison where he annoyed the other inmates by playing the bagpipes. He lived in some style in prison, entertaining members of high society before dying of goal fever. His effigy was later displayed in Madame Tussaud's.

Violence

Violence was never far away from showing itself on London's streets. Murder was probably rarer than in most European capitals but foreign visitors certainly perceived actual or threatened violence as a prominent feature of London life. Killers were tried for premeditated murder although there were some distinctions, such as duellists, who were convicted of the lesser offence of manslaughter. The Murder Act stated that the bodies of those executed for murder should be delivered to surgeons for dissection or hung in chains for display.

Fighting, among individuals and gangs, was common. In 1761, for example, a group of butchers' boys from Leadenhall Market set on and routed a press gang. Had they been asked, they would have justified their action on the grounds that everyone hated what the press gangs did. On an earlier occasion, a similar gang seeking any fit-looking men in a Southwark tavern, was set upon by drinkers and passersby armed with improvised weapons and, after a battle royal, was forced to withdraw. Press gangs were universally despised.

It is perhaps easy to gain a misleading impression of the degree of violence on London's streets because those who wrote about what they saw and experienced were more likely to record things that made a strong impression. It may well be that one observer who, in 1718, wrote that Londoners were afraid to walk the streets or visit drinking places, coffee houses or theatres, for example, was exaggerating. He claimed that they went in fear that their hats and wigs might be snatched, their swords stolen or in the course of being robbed, they might be knocked down, slashed or stabbed. However, the risk was high. For example, in 1717, Richard Yeoman and William Dehew of St Clement Danes received the death sentence for assaulting Daniel Oldridge on the highway, and stealing his hat and wig worth five shillings. In 1730 Roger Johnson was arrested for assault on the highway at Chancery Lane when he threw a handful of snuff into the face of the victim and then stole his 'Periwig, value 30 shillings and a Hat, Value 10 shillings' before proceeding to beat him. There are certainly numerous reports of gangs of robbers who usually had specialized modi operandi. Some sat in upstairs rooms holding a device like a fishing rod and a hook with which they removed wigs – there was a good market in secondhand wigs. Others stopped the carriages of rich folk and quickly cut through the straps which attached the compartment to the chassis. In the ensuing chaos, the rich passengers were easy targets. The robbers themselves and their booty would vanish instantly into the nearest rookery.

Highwaymen were criminals who somehow captured the imagination at the time and have continued to do so since. Stories are legion about dashing, handsome and courteous highwaymen such as Claude Duval who won the hearts of attractive young women while lightening their purses. However, for any such highway robber there were dozens who dispensed with the pleasantries and used the threat or actuality of violence when relieving their victims of their valuables. Susan Perry of Clerkenwell was sentenced to death for robbing 4-year-old John Pace of his clothes on the highway in 1713. She then strangled him to death and dumped his body in a ditch. Elizabeth Hardis was also sentenced to death for assaulting Joseph Archer on the highway in Lincolns Inn Fields and stealing from him money, belongings and his clothes. Basically, they were vicious mounted thugs but their place in popular mythology might have something to do with the fact that they naturally preferred robbing the better-off from which ordinary folk gained some vicarious satisfaction. No such romantic myths were attached to those who carried out their depredations on foot and were derisively dismissed as mere footpads. For much of the eighteenth century, there was still open country between the City and Westminster and there were rich pickings to be had from many of those passing from one district to the other.

A major factor in crime, poverty and despair was drink. In his illustrations *Beer Street* and *Gin Lane* William Hogarth contrasted the robust but simple pleasures to be obtained from quaffing good English ale with the despair, destitution and debauchery associated with drinking gin. Alcoholism was widespread, especially among the poor. By the time of the 'Gin Craze' there were over 6,000 houses in London selling gin. Hogarth regarded gin as an insidious foreign import that was undermining the collective character and morale of the English people even though it gave them temporary distraction from the misery and squalor which was the lot of so many. Gin was introduced into Britain from the Netherlands in the 1690s. Being dirt cheap and very potent, it soon became extremely popular and gin-drinking assumed epidemic proportions.

The worst addicts virtually lived on gin and were completely debilitated by it, losing the ability to do anything with their lives and usually dying prematurely and painfully. Gin was available not only in drinking dens but in prisons, brothels, barber shops and even from itinerant street vendors. The children of gin-soaked parents sadly became victims of the craze. Judith Defour had placed her 2-year-old daughter Mary Defour in a workhouse in 1734. One particular day she took her child out of the workhouse for a short while and met up with a friend called Sukey. The 36-year-old Judith Defour told a tragic tale to the court: 'On Sunday night we took the child into the fields and stripped [her], and tied a linen handkerchief about her neck to keep her from crying.' They proceeded to murder the girl, laid her in a ditch near Bethnal Green then sold all her clothes. 'We parted [with] the money for a quarter of Gin.' The two murderers were sentenced to death.

Various measures were taken by government to reduce consumption but gin-drinking, particularly in London, was almost out of control. However, in 1751 heavy duties on gin finally effected a drastic fall in consumption but not before violent protest riots on London's streets.

Ingenious ways to partake in secretive gin drinking were found. In 1738 Captain Dudley Bradstreet (1711–63), author, spy, criminal and entrepreneur, is credited to have invented what became known as the 'Puss and Mew Shop' establishment where drinkers could get their ration of gin. He rented a small house near Aldersgate and hung a sign of a cat outside. Intriguingly the sign had a hole in the cat's mouth and a protruding lead pipe under the cat's paw where the gin could be poured out. The customer would request a dram of gin and then place a coin in the cat's mouth. Puss and Mew shops soon caught on elsewhere. A replica of the Puss and Mew sign can be seen at the Beefeater Gin Distillery in Kennington.

The English had a fear of the idea of a professional and official police force. They thought that such a force would somehow conflict with their liberties as 'free-born Englishmen' although for most people it is unclear what these liberties actually were. The ill-lit streets were patrolled after dark by night watchmen who were usually aged, often infirm and drunk and virtually useless for law enforcement. Consequently, the authorities, knowing that they had limited resources to apprehend criminals, decided to make an example of those who were brought before the courts. Punishment was often savage and involved large numbers of capital offences and transportation. Despite this, records from the Old Bailey show that many perpetrators were not given the death sentence.

Some districts were known as criminal rookeries in which virtually the entire population lived on the proceeds of crime or begging. These rookeries constituted a 'no-go' area for the authorities and the rudimentary law-enforcement bodies of the time. Any stranger penetrating such areas would be lucky to emerge alive, particularly if he looked prosperous. The most notorious rookery was almost certainly St Giles, mockingly called the 'Holy Land'. Covering about eight acres of squalor, it was ideally positioned for underworld activities. Its thieves and beggars only had a short distance before they entered affluent districts in which rich pickings were readily available. Other dangerous areas included Alsatia and Southwark. Alsatia, which ran south off Fleet Street and the notorious Ram Alley, now Hare Place, epitomized all that was dreadful about such rookeries with its reeking dens, unlicensed dram shops, broken gutters and dilapidated house fronts. It was a district known for its brothels and criminal hideouts where a fugitive was safe from pursuit once he or she vanished into the maze of dark alleys and passageways.

London saw a considerable increase in poverty and overcrowding in the eighteenth century, partly because of unprecedented migration from the countryside. This made for a highly volatile social mix and a rootlessness among the majority of the population who shared poverty and squalor but little else except contempt for authority. The perception of London's better-off citizens, except those debauchees who liked slumming it, was that London was a dangerous and anarchic place in which they went in fear of their persons, property and commercial interests.

This view is clear in some of the best-known works of William Hogarth such as *Industry and Idleness*, *Gin Lane*, *Beer Street* and *The Four Stages of Cruelty*. While these have a satirical content, they provide hard-hitting graphic propaganda in which Hogarth presents contemporary London as a city of divided and alienated communities. In drawing on disorder and crime and punishment, he adeptly juxtaposes opposing values and social conditions – of virtue and vice, diligence and indolence, prosperity and poverty, the clash of which he believed was undermining and endangering prosperity and security. Hogarth sought to influence London opinion in favour of probity, hard work and respectability and perhaps thought that diligence and the creation of wealth pointed the way towards greater morality. His work provides a penetrating insight particularly into the criminal life of London in the first half of the eighteenth century.

Hogarth's prints often display cruelty to animals. Many cruel and sadistic practices involving betting on animals, such as dog fights or ratting (dogs killing rats), continued in the back room of pubs or some other organized venue. A pub in Compton Street, Soho, advertised, 'Ratting for the Million', which involved dogs being placed in a large wire pit and killing as many rats in the shortest time possible. Rats were usually caught from the sewers of which there was always an abundant supply and it was a case of the bigger the better. One landlord told Henry Mayhew (*London Labour and the London Poor* Volume 3, 1851) that 'I should think I buy in the course of the year, on the average, from 300 to 700 rats a week'. In the fights rules stipulated that any man touching rats or dogs or acting in an unfair way would have his dog disqualified. Officials included a referee and a timekeeper. In Cambridge Circus at the intersection of Shaftesbury Avenue and Charing Cross Road there existed a small dirty place where people would bet at the rat pit. The dogs, usually terrier breeds, were efficient, gripping and tossing the rats through the air.

Notable London Rogues and Villains

Colonel Francis Charteris has been described as 'the rake to end all rakes. He was born in 1676 into a family of Scottish gentry, he launched himself at an early age into two professions – one was soldiering where he was court-martialled; the other at which he excelled was gambling. He mixed in elevated social circles and it was widely alleged that he owed his success at cards to cheating. He was also notorious for his sexual licentiousness.

Early in the eighteenth century, Charteris came to London and set up a fashionable establishment in Poland Street after having made a socially and financially advantageous marriage. Although discharged dishonourably from the army, he now began to style himself 'Colonel Charteris'. He set out with determination to even further enrich himself and by 1713 he owned three country estates and even became a magistrate!

His sexual exploits were legendary and he was happy to pander to the sexual proclivities of others. His London homes, first Poland Street and then another in George Street, were brothels catering for some of the most exotic sexual practices. They doubled as gambling dens for the rich fools who were easily parted from their money. In the early nineteenth century brothels varied from the high-class ones in Mayfair to those in the lowest slums of St Giles and Covent Garden. As with the exclusive male clubs around St James, brothels catered for the pleasures of the aristocracy and the well-to-do. So well organized were some of these 'Nunneries' that they employed surgeons, as in the case of Mrs. Hayes's brothel in King Street, to inspect the prostitutes.

Charteris was convicted of rape which was a capital offence but he had influential friends and was reprieved. Nonetheless, he was now finished in London and retired to Edinburgh where he died in 1732. His reputation followed him because at his funeral his coffin was pelted with garbage and excrement and dead dogs and cats were thrown into his grave.

Clergy, by virtue of their profession, are imbued with moral authority. This makes them easy targets when they transgress. The Reverend William Dodd was a man of many parts, most of them deeply flawed. He was a dandy and fop derided by his detractors as the 'Macaroni Parson'. His efforts raised laudable amounts for charity but he lived totally beyond his means and often had recourse to begging charity from his acquaintances.

Dodd became involved with the Magdalen Hospital which set out to reform and rehabilitate 'fallen women'. He laid on successful fund-raising events at which he made impassioned and moving appeals for cash which sometimes brought his audience to tears. However, his own lack of cash meant that he had several spells in debtors' prison. In 1765 Dodd became personal tutor to a youth who became Lord Chesterfield. He proved a staunch friend and found Dodd a new living after scandal forced him to resign and flee abroad until things cooled down. However, Dodd continued to spend money which he did not possess. Forgery was a capital offence and it was Dodd's undoing. His case excited immense public interest and hundreds had to be turned away from the Old Bailey. He was found guilty and sentenced to death by hanging at Tyburn which attracted one of the largest crowds ever seen there.

One of the most high-profile murders of the nineteenth century was the stabbing of Lord John Russell (1767–1840) by his 23-year-old valet, Francois Benjamin Courvoisier, in Mayfair. It was a frenzied attack during which Russell's head was almost severed from his neck. Russell was a member of the British aristocracy and longtime MP for Tavistock. On 5 May he returned home from his club and had dinner at seven o clock before eventually retiring. Next morning the housemaid saw his pillow saturated with blood, and Russell lying in bed, dead, his throat cut. Articles had been stolen which were later found hidden behind the skirting board in the valet's room.

Courvoisier's execution caused great attraction with people paying good money to obtain a decent view. William Makepeace Thackeray (1811–63), who attended the execution, wrote, 'The character of the crowd was ... quite festive – jokes bandying about here and there, and jolly laughs breaking out.' Charles Dickens, who was also there, found the scene absolutely sickening and concluded that public executions were cruel and barbaric and demeaning for the spectators. He believed that executions were necessary but should be carried out behind closed walls.

The whole ritual surrounding a public execution, the procession to the gallows, the selling of food, drink and broadsheets, the opportunities for pickpockets, the drunken revelry and fights, the last dying speech followed by the agonizing death throes of the condemned, the undignified scramble for the corpse by agents of the anatomists and the family of the deceased, were all part of what resembled a carnival performance, carnivals combined with humour and savagery.

Henry Fauntleroy was an intelligent and resourceful man of great charm who enjoyed an extravagant and vibrant life style which included a succession of highly attractive mistresses. Driven by his libido, Fauntleroy found himself threatened by insolvency and so he drifted into crime. He had worked for seven years as a clerk at the London bank of Marsh, Stracey, Fauntleroy & Graham, in Berners Street of which his father was one of the co-founders. Fauntleroy was taken into partnership and the whole business of the firm was left in his hands. In 1824 the bank suspended its dealings and on 10 September Fauntleroy was taken into custody and charged with appropriating trust funds by forging the trustees' signatures. Given his reputation, rumours began to spread that he had squandered £250,000 in debauchery.

His trial took place at the Old Bailey on 30 October 1824. The most extraordinary part of the case concerned the damning evidence found among Fauntleroy's private papers, which left him no option but to admit his guilt. He pleaded that he had used the misappropriated funds to pay his firm's debts but it was not enough to save him from the death sentence. His execution took place at Newgate in November 1824 and it was estimated that nearly 100,000 people turned out. Every window and roof, which could command a view of the dreadful ceremony, was occupied. One curiosity arising from this execution was that an Italian, Edmund Angelini, offered to be executed in Fauntleroy's place on the grounds that he himself was much less a useful member of society, not being a married man and father like Fauntleroy.

From the early eighteenth century there was a thriving market in tabloid-style journalism where cheap literature supplied an insatiable popular appetite for sensation and titillation. This early literature marked out the beginnings of a genre consisting of tales of sex, blood and gore. Wilful murder captured the imagination of Victorians who would read the lurid details of such crimes in newspapers, broadsheets, novels and illustrated papers such as *The Illustrated Police News*. Such a popular demand for crime would later feed an audience who avidly read the stories of the greatest of all fictional detectives and resident of the West End, Sherlock Holmes, in *The Strand Magazine*. Although crime and criminals, both real and fictional, fascinate us they also repulse us.

Perhaps a footnote to two riotous fictional characters should be made, the original Tom and Jerry. Pierce Egan (1772–1849) was a writer who created Tom and Jerry Hawthorne in 1821 and like their latter-day cartoon namesakes the pair were often associated with fighting, causing trouble and getting into various scrapes. Their activities spanned across a great deal of London, particularly the West End. The characters became very popular in Egan's monthly journal, *Life in London*. His tales tell of the rough and tumble of street life through the adventures of rich young Regency men. They ride in the parks, box and fence, visit the opera, take part in heavy drinking, rioting, bet on cock fights and the dogs, gamble, go slumming, keep mistresses, indulge in many forms of debauchery and visit brothels. Insights into brothels are revealed in Egan's observations when he notes that 'in the Metropolis … prostitution is so profitable a business, and conducted so openly, that hundreds of persons keep houses of ill-fame, for the reception of girls not more than twelve or thirteen years of age, without a blush upon their cheeks'.

Chapter 7

Victorian London

'The dust and din and steam of town'

The nineteenth century saw Britain's rise as the dominant world power. London contributed enormously to that process and benefitted from it, becoming the leading city in the world. Modern London can be said to date from the Victorian period.

Change hit London with seemingly unstoppable force. There was no precedent for London's growth in area and in population. A total of around half a million people in 1861 grew to over two million in 1901 in what is now described as 'Greater London'. The eve of the First World War saw London home to over seven million people. This growth was proportionately far greater than that of the UK's population as a whole and ensured London's unquestionable dominance of, and influence on, the life of the British Isles.

Observers were fascinated by London's growth. Some saw it as remorseless and malignant. One writer in 1901 described it as 'like a great, hungry sea, which flows on and on, filling up every creek, and then overspreads its borders, flooding the plains beyond'. London was the world's largest and most prosperous city in the nineteenth century and foreign visitors were awestruck by its size, its diversity and level of activity. However, it had grown largely unplanned, uncoordinated and making it up as it went along. Extraordinary wealth and opulence lived cheek by jowl with destitution and utter despair. This chapter attempts to probe aspects of this dual nature of nineteenth-century London.

The Two Worlds of London

Commentators came to the London phenomenon from many angles. One of these focused on the social impact of its growth and the poverty that seemed to be a paradoxical and undesirable concomitant. Investigations resulted in a flood of pamphlets and books exemplified by *The Bitter Cry of Outcast London* (1883) by Andrew Mearns, a nonconformist minister. Most such researchers wanted to influence public opinion and bring about social change.

Parallels were drawn with the contemporary exploration of 'darkest Africa' and identified the 'darkest London' inhabited by the 30 per cent of its population which lived in poverty in a city marked by much conspicuous affluence. Contrasts were made between the East End and the West End and how, certainly by the 1880s and 1890s, there was a version of 'social distancing'. Residential districts were distinguished from each other by the income of their occupants. Several investigators commented to the effect that the respective inhabitants of the East End and the West End knew virtually nothing about each other. One clergyman in 1856 observed that 'they differ in external appearance, clothes, pursuits and pleasures'.

Contrasts between rich and poor were perhaps more concentrated and evident in London than anywhere else in Britain. London was the epitome of the 'Two Englands' identified in literature by writers as diverse as Thomas Carlyle and Benjamin Disraeli. Henry Mayhew and J. Binny neatly captured this dual character of London in their introduction to *The Criminal Prisons of London*, published in 1862:

> Viewing the great Metropolis as an absolute world, Belgravia and Bethnal Green become the opposite poles of the London sphere – the frigid zones as it were, of the Capital, the one icy from its exceeding fashion, form and ceremony; and the other wrapped in a perpetual winter of withering poverty. Of such a world, Temple Bar is the unmistakable equator, dividing the City hemisphere from that of the West End.

This theme of counterpoint and division is taken up by Friedrich Engels in *The Condition of the Working Class in England* (1845):

> Hundreds and thousands of men and women drawn from all classes and ranks of society pack the streets of London. Are they not all human beings with the same innate characteristics and personalities? Are they not all equally interested in the pursuit of happiness? And do they not all aim at happiness by following similar methods? Yet they rush past each other as if they had nothing in common … The more that Londoners are packed into a tiny space, the more repulsive and disgraceful becomes the brutal indifference with which they ignore their

neighbours and selfishly concentrate upon their private affairs. We know well enough that this isolation is everywhere the fundamental principle of modern society. But nowhere is this selfish egotism as blatantly evident as in the frantic bustle of the great city.

It was from about 1880s that the term 'East End' came into regular use. Arthur Morrison in *Tales of Mean Streets* described the East End as 'An evil plexus of slums that hide human creeping things; where filthy men and women live on penn'orths of gin, where collars and clean shirts are decencies unknown, where every citizen wears a black eye, and none ever combs his hair'. T. H. Huxley, the eminent scientist, said that 'Polynesian savages' were 'not half so savage, so unclean, so irreclaimable as the dweller of a tenement in the East End'. Poverty was not unknown even in the West End but it was largely hidden from view. In the East End it was everywhere to be seen.

To observers with a social conscience, the East End was visible evidence of the deeply flawed priorities of contemporary society. Ironically, many residents of the opulent West End had problems of their own. To their horror, parts of Mayfair were being invaded by plutocrats, some of them American, who had made their fortunes overseas and, having taken up residence, were trying to buy their way into the elite of London society.

So, London was composed of two worlds. One was dark, dirty and menacing; the other opulent, dazzling and ostentatious. This juxtaposition became the subject of much discussion as London grew to be recognized as a world city above all others.

It became a matter of fascination, not least to the increasing number of foreign visitors, including investigative journalists, because London was not only the capital of the most powerful nation in the world but also the hub of an empire that straddled the globe. The Great Exhibition in Hyde Park in 1851 had attracted many from overseas but their number palled by comparison with those attracted by the Queen's Jubilees later in the century. Some visitors took the trouble to investigate London's dual character. Was London the prototype of the modern world city? Was it inevitable that such a city would contain these striking differences in wealth and power and the opportunities that went with them? It was said that the sun never set on the British Empire but an apt retort to this came from the man who remarked about the same sun which never set on the Empire also never rose on the dark alleys of the East End. There was an indissoluble connection between poverty and imperialism.

The spatial growth involved required new forms of public transport. Access to these facilities depended on ability to pay. This led to distinct social segregation. The less well-off had to live near their places of work, ideally within walking distance. Enclaves of the housing of the very rich continued to be found in parts of central London but many of the middle classes 'fled' with great determination to the expanding suburbs around the periphery. These districts were marked by being socially delineated, sometimes down to adjacent streets. A person's address, now more than ever, indicated their wealth and social standing in the circles that cared about such things. White-collar workers particularly aspired to upward social mobility. This is the mindset so gently and affectionately examined through the person of Mr Pooter in George and Weedon Grossmith's minor classic, *The Diary of a Nobody*. The hero of this epic, a junior city clerk, is immensely proud of his achievement of moving up the social scale and being able to rent 'The Laurels', Brickfield Terrace, Holloway. He manages to get a reduction in the rent because the railway nearby caused vibrations.

Those least able to move away the from the grimy areas, where housing and industry were in proximity, included large numbers of casually employed, largely unskilled men in such occupations as building, but particularly on the docks. Many of them did not know from day to day whether there would be work and, if so, how much. For skilled and semi-skilled manual workers in regular work, and many lower middle-class people, extensive inner suburbs developed in the last part of the century. The earlier, more affluent residents moved out of such places as West Ham and these districts disappeared under street after street of monotonous but solidly built terraced housing. When the railways started to provide cheap 'workmen's fares' and electric trams began running, workers from these districts could move out of central London and afford to commute to and from the infinite range of employment opportunities that central London provided.

Although it was still possible in London to move only a short distance from a prestigious address into an area of utter poverty and dilapidation, many of the well-to-do and the middle classes moved around the metropolis in such a way that they could largely avoid entering those areas of substandard and slum housing. The 'no-go' district for supposedly respectable Londoners was the East End. Life in this district was described with stark clarity by Jack London in *The People of the Abyss* after he lived there for a few months in 1901. An American writer and socialist, he wanted to draw attention to the iniquity that such a place could exist in a city of great wealth and adjacent to the busiest seaport in the world. The perception of many people was that the East End was even worse than the description London gave in his book. It was a hive of filth, squalor, despair, desperation, crime and violence, inhabited by base and amoral subspecies of humanity. The sensational murders associated with 'Jack the Ripper' only heightened the jaundiced perception of the East End. The burgeoning popular press of the later nineteenth century took great delight in publishing sensational material which scared the middle class into believing that the slum-dwellers were about to emerge from the abyss bringing incest, disease and lawlessness with them.

The East End contained teeming yards, courts, alleys and streets of largely jerry-built damp and insanitary housing and some now older and dilapidated, once grand houses whose previous tenants had escaped from the area. These were usually subdivided into what are now called multi-occupied dwellings and it was not uncommon for two or more families to occupy just one room within these rotting slums. The unfortunate occupants would be engaged in the sweated trades in workshops in the middle of an otherwise largely residential district or casually employed in loading and unloading ships at the Pool of London, the riverside wharves and the enclosed docks. The latter work was sporadic, the sweated trade poorly paid and those involved lived for much of the time in great poverty. It is not surprising that many of the area's residents turned to crime simply to survive and in doing so fulfilled the stereotype which characterized the districts and its people.

The social researcher Charles Booth estimated that 30 per cent of Londoners lived in poverty in 1890. Although sympathetic to the lack of public health provision, the low wages and the unemployment and underemployment, he blamed the poor for much that was miserable in their lives. He recognized that irregular earnings accounted for widespread poverty but he singled out the vast number of drinking places as providing the poor with a relatively cheap and quick road to oblivion which undermined their moral fibre and rendered them incapable of challenging the circumstances in which they found themselves. His survey of the living conditions and culture of London's poor was extraordinarily detailed. The *Life and Labour of the People of London* ran to no fewer than seventeen volumes and included sections on 'Industry', 'Religious Influences' and 'Poverty'. It was a monumental piece of social research.

He produced maps and diagrams to support his findings. They included 'poverty maps'. In these he demonstrated that in many districts close to the City, such as Clerkenwell, Hoxton, Whitechapel and Southwark, more than 40 per cent of families fell into the 'poor' category. These were poorly paid workers or those who experienced irregular employment. For the indigent, child-rearers or elderly, incapacity or prolonged unemployment could plunge them from being poor into real poverty. The worst deprivation Booth revealed in his maps was in central London and close to the Thames. He advocated old age pensions and housing reform to tackle the intimate connection between overcrowding and poverty. He and his assistants concluded, rather gloomily, that London was breeding an unskilled, unhealthy and morally degenerate race.

Much of the worst housing in London consisted of the former homes of the well-heeled and could be found in enclaves across most localities. There is a fascination for the historian in following the pattern of the rise and fall of the housing stock and its occupants in particular districts. The process has never been static and today's readers will be well aware of the process of gentrification that has turned some formerly dingy districts into highly sought-after and desirable neighbourhoods. Where this has happened, it is almost an iron law that the poorer residents are just ruthlessly displaced and forced to try their luck in a market where there has always been a shortage of affordable housing.

All around that central part of what later became known as 'Greater London' were aged buildings, sometimes timber-framed, some of them grand and others quite humble, which survived as living accommodation into the nineteenth century. A few had survived the Great Fire but they tended to be run down and were likely to be demolished for redevelopment. Perhaps the most characteristic homes erected in the eighteenth and nineteenth centuries were variations on the terrace theme. These could be grand buildings, stuccoed and of several storeys and occupied by the very rich. They then descended in size and grandeur to dwellings designed for the middle class and the skilled upper-working class. Many of the larger terraces in affluent areas like Kensington, Bayswater and Bloomsbury were built around a communal garden to which only the residents had access. Purpose-built blocks of flats aimed at middle-class occupation appeared from the mid-nineteenth century. The key to understanding the housing of nineteenth-century London was class. This could be reduced in simple terms to 'ability to pay'.

There was a marked tendency among comfortably off, well-housed Londoners to blame the poor for the squalor and degradation in which they lived. The Victorian period saw something of a change in attitudes. Growing scientific knowledge increased awareness about the intimate relationship between dirt and disease. While poverty remained very evident right up to 1914, significant moves had been made by public and private agencies to tackle public health and environmental issues. Bodies such as the

Metropolitan Association for Improving the Dwellings of the Industrious Classes, the East End Dwellings Company and the Peabody Trust erected very distinctive blocks of tenements, often where clearance of notorious slum rookeries had taken place. Of barrack-like appearance, the flats in these blocks were a vast improvement on the earlier slums although some facilities, often including toilets, were shared between several flats. They did something to tackle the housing crisis of London but the problem was that the rents charged, while not extortionate, were affordable only to those in regular employment. Many of these tenement blocks were very solidly built and are still in occupancy in various parts of central London.

The most extensive slum-clearance scheme was that of the notorious rookery known as 'Old Nichol', just outside the City. The Boundary Street scheme in Shoreditch, dated from 1900 and was developed by the LCC under the Housing Act of 1890. It was a model but one which was not necessarily replicated in later schemes. It was distinguished by wide streets and impressively handsome blocks of flats focused around a central garden.

Social meeting places and facilities such as pubs, theatres, places of worship and even cemeteries reflected the Victorian obsession with segregating people along the lines of their perceived class. Cemetery companies were scrupulous in selling space for interments the size and placing of which were carefully graded around financial considerations. Although there were masses of tiny drinking places in impoverished areas of rundown housing that also contained small and often very polluting industrial premises, there were also some gigantic drinking establishments scattered across the metropolis. The largest were divided up into distinct areas like tap room, bar, smoke room, commercial room, saloon and lounge and each was likely to cater for a different clientele with prices to correspond. There were huge theatres like the Britannia in Hoxton which had seats for 3,450 patrons and many tiers all protected by differential pricing.

Public Works

By the middle of the nineteenth century, it was clear that London lacked a local government structure that could deliver the public services required by its size and the needs of its people. Outside the City of London, there was a mass of parish vestries. Some were self-perpetuating and largely inactive, others relatively democratic and conscientious in the performance of their duties. All jealously guarded their individual fiefdoms. Additional bodies had responsibilities for street lighting and sewage, for example, but all seemed resistant to the idea of change. The so-called square mile known as the City retained its ancient form of government by Lord Mayor and Corporation. It was described as an institution defying the 'march of improvement'. It was immensely powerful and especially impervious to the idea of change. No body existed to take responsibility for London as a whole. It was quite difficult to define exactly what was meant by London. Although it was by far the largest city in Britain, it had been excluded from the series of local government reforms passed in 1835 and the terms of important Public Health Act of 1848.

This situation was tackled by the Metropolitan Management Act of 1855 which set up the Metropolitan Board of Works (MBW). The most urgent problem was that of sewage. Before the mid-1850s sewers dealt only with surface water which was discharged directly into the Thames from which the water companies were extracting the drinking water they sold to their subscribers. Human waste was deposited into cesspits whose contents frequently leaked into wells and obviously polluted the water supply. Little was known about microscopic disease-bearing organisms such as those which caused epidemics of cholera, for example. Rich and poor alike took their water from polluted sources, often with fatal consequences.

Crisis point was reached in 1858 with what became known as the 'Great Stink'. Not only human but every sort of rejectamenta from industry and abattoirs, for example, found its way into the tributaries of, and the Thames itself. That summer was very warm, the tidal flow sluggish, the river full of the foulest detritus imaginable. With black humour it was said that there was so much solid and semi-solid matter in the Thames that if a person wanted to cross it, they did not need a bridge. Needless to say, the stench was indescribable. People believed that the smell itself could have fatal effects. The authorities were jolted into taking remedial action: the Chief Engineer of the MBW, Sir Joseph Bazalgette, designed an ingenious system of what were called 'intercepting sewers'. At long last the existing ramshackle and inadequate system of existing sewers that drained into the Thames was reorganized, enlarged and extended so that effluent was discharged further downstream beyond London's boundaries. Huge sewage works were built at the outfall points of Beckton and Crossness.

The MBW followed up this ambitions scheme with the building of new roads and improvement of others which helped considerably to tackle the chronic congestion to found in parts of central London. The opportunity was taken when building some of the new roads such as Shaftesbury Avenue for them to be driven through rookeries or slums which were districts notorious for their insanitary conditions, their poverty, vice and crime. These districts were at least partly cleared and redeveloped. In doing this, London gained some streets and public structures such as Holborn Viaduct, of which it could justly be proud.

Despite positive work done by the MBW, London remained poorly provided with the kind of services it needed. Water supply was provided by a handful of companies who overcharged for services of poor quality while gas was provided by a cartel of three companies. William Gladstone told the House of Commons in 1884: 'The local government of London is not what it certainly ought to be, the crown of all our local and municipal institutions.' In local government terms, London lagged severely behind Birmingham, for example.

The MBW always had powerful enemies who claimed that it was undemocratic and corrupt. A coalition of opponents succeeded in having it replaced by a newly created London County Council (LCC) in 1888. This, it was alleged, would be able to divert resources then being concentrated in the generally affluent West End to the more needy East End. The LCC, in turn, found itself under criticism and some of its powers were redistributed in 1899 to twenty-eight new metropolitan borough councils in a pattern of local government which was to last until the 1960s. Meanwhile the City of London rolled on.

Public Health

At the beginning of the nineteenth century the concept of public health would have had little resonance. However, as London grew almost exponentially and its filth, pollution and disease increased, so issues of health forced themselves onto the public agenda.

The Poor Law system was formalized in 1834 and the workhouses for which it made provision found themselves taking on wider functions than originally envisaged. Those who were physically incapacitated constituted a large proportion of workhouse inmates and it is not surprising that workhouses assumed some of the functions of infirmaries. Those who ran the workhouses were always keen to minimize costs. It became clear that the poor were more prone to various epidemic diseases than the better-off. Workhouses found themselves having to minister to the needs of people suffering from, for example, smallpox and measles and their various complications. Among the most serious epidemic diseases was cholera, with major outbreaks in 1832 and 1848/9. Cholera was waterborne and did not distinguish between the social class of those it affected. Rich and poor alike shared an interest in tackling cholera and the various other conditions which ravaged London's population.

Until this time theories about the nature of diseases and how they were transmitted had scarcely moved on from primitive times. The accepted view was that whatever caused disease was given off by miasmas which were poisonous gases produced by rotting organic matter. Disease was therefore the product of dirt. Remove the offensive material and a cleaner environment would create less disease.

It is ironic that technological progress exacerbated public health issues. The invention of flushing water closets meant that those who could afford these innovative devices were flushing their excretory matter into sewers and then into the Thames from which the water companies extracted the water which they provided for London's citizens. Nothing was known in the 1830s and 1840s about microscopic disease-bearing organisms. Empirically, however, it became evident that there were areas in London of particularly high mortality from cholera and that the inhabitants of these areas shared the same sources of water. If there was something apparently lethal in the water supplies then surely the priority was to provide clean water. It followed that legal bodies ultimately responsible to the public were required to tackle an issue which was of burning importance to London's populace. This initial groping towards a solution of the problem may seem blindingly obvious to us today but was in sharp conflict with the prevailing political economy of laissez-faire which advocated the absolute minimum of government intervention in the economic and social life of the nation. Additionally, any attempt to implement an effective public health system in London was likely to find itself opposed by the labyrinthine collection of bodies who, not very effectively, carried out the functions of local government.

Various national acts were passed including the major Public Health Act of 1848. This wide-ranging act dealt with drainage, water supplies and, importantly, the appointment of local medical officers of health. They had powers to regulate 'offensive trades', remove 'nuisances', identify dwellings no longer fit for habitation and provide burial grounds, public baths and parks. This was widely resented as government interference in matters best dealt with on a local basis proved particularly difficult to apply in London. Ironically, the City Corporation, usually immovable in its opposition to any change that it did not like, pre-empted the 1848 Act by appointing John Simon as Medical Officer. It was an inspired choice. He was energetic, committed and, just as important, highly skilled in the persuasive way in which he dealt with the hidebound fogeys who made up the Corporation.

His efforts meant that for many years, the City was a healthier place than the surrounding parts of the metropolis.

The work done by the Metropolitan Board of Works and its Chief Engineer, Joseph Bazalgette, has already been briefly mentioned. His grand scheme of interconnected sewers also included such works as the building of the Victoria Embankment. This involved reclaiming land by extending into the Thames. The Thames therefore became narrower and, being constricted, flowed faster, thereby helping to shift the undesirable detritus which it accumulated in its journey from the Cotswolds. The Circle and District Underground railways were routed beneath the Embankment which became a handsome thoroughfare, a popular resort and object of pride for Londoners.

The private water companies were hostile to any form of regulation, proving dilatory or negligent in implementing measures required by legislation. Their opposition effectively ended in 1902 when they were brought under local government control. By this time London's sanitary provision had improved considerably. Waterborne diseases were in marked decline. Whereas Whitechapel, for example, had a typhoid death rate of 116 per 100,000 in 1850–60, by 1890–1900 the rate was down to thirteen per 100,000. The streets were cleaner and better paved.

Another official intervention was the compulsory purchase of unfit dwellings which was strongly resented by those who believed that the economy should be left alone to regulate itself. However, poor housing became a major public health issue in which the 1841 census revealed the case of seventeen dwellings which were occupied by 485 people. The average number of occupants per room was eighteen but one room housed no fewer than thirty-two woebegone souls. What we would now describe as 'multi-occupied' dwellings lacked adequate water supplies, proper sanitation or means of refuse disposal. Dozens of people might have to share a single privy. Absentee landlords largely refused to carry out any repairs and it was not unknown for the most decrepit of dwellings suddenly to collapse without warning. Some of the worst slum properties were owned by titled plutocrats, City livery companies and the Church of England, although they usually put a barrier between themselves and their unfortunate tenants by employing agents to 'manage' the renting business and the premises themselves.

Slum-clearance programmes theoretically became easier under various acts passed in the 1850s, 1860s and 1870s but they often proved to be something of a double-edged sword. Money was made available to compensate the owners of such property but not necessarily out of public funds to build replacement housing stock. All too often the displaced tenants, virtually powerless, were simply left to fend for themselves. In practice this meant moving into already overcrowded and substandard housing, often close by.

An improvement in the public sector came with the formation of the London County Council applying the terms of the 1890 Housing of the Working Classes Act. By 1914 the LCC had built accommodation for about 25,000 people. As so often in Victorian Britain charity and philanthropy played a role in improving the lot of the poor. Mention has already been made of various bodies which provided tenement-style accommodation for the 'Industrious Classes'. A problem that could be ascribed to charity is that it tackles the symptoms of inequality without addressing the causes and thereby actually perpetuates the issues involved. Between them statutory and voluntary sectors made some progress in improving the housing of London's poor during these years but even in the twenty-first century there is still a housing crisis of major proportions and plenty of London still has homelessness and substandard housing on a scale which is an affront to a supposedly civilized society.

Despite quantitative data identifying improvements in public health and general welfare, a sense remained that there were still districts in London populated by a threatening criminal underworld. These rookeries, which 'respectable' people entered at their peril, were characterized by squalor, immorality, despair and desperation. These perceptions were stoked by investigative journalists such as Andrew Mearns in his *Bitter Cry of Outcast London* (1883) and W. T. Stead in the *Pall Mall Gazette*. Of course, as journalists they wanted to dig the dirt. Readers generally wanted what was sensational and preferably gory, not what was for the best in the best of all possible worlds. Mearns tugged at the emotional heartstrings as this example shows:

> you have to penetrate courts reeking with poisonous and malodorous gases ... courts, many of them which the sun never penetrates, which are never visited by a breath of fresh air ... You have to ascend rotten staircases, which threaten to give way beneath each step ... You have to grope your way along dark and filthy passages swarming with vermin.

Stead was scarcely more measured in describing 'pestilential rookeries where it is a physical impossibility to live a human life' and rookeries which contained 'the stunted squalid savages of civilisation'.

Transport in Victorian and Edwardian London

At the beginning of the nineteenth century, London was a place in which most people walked. This was not necessarily a healthy activity because the streets were filthy. It was a moot point whether it was worse in wet or dry weather. There was always a liberal presence of human and other forms of ordure and filth of every description. When it was wet, this formed a loathsome adhesive quagmire which pedestrians could do little to avoid. When dry, it became a noisome dust which covered streets and buildings and swirled around in eddies entering clothing and bodily orifices.

Those who could afford to do so rode on horseback or travelled in their own horse-drawn conveyances, short-distance stagecoaches or hackney cabs. Often the best and quickest means was by boat on the Thames although this, of course, was not appropriate for all journeys. The river was favoured for trips between the City and Westminster and vice versa. None of these modes of transport was cheap. Nor was the horse-drawn omnibus introduced by George Shillibeer in 1829 cheap enough to cater for those of all incomes. This was an enterprising venture that ran from Paddington to the fringe of the City at Farringdon. By 1850 there were about 1,300 horse buses plying London's streets. Many owners of these buses gave then names as was the practice with stagecoaches. One rejoiced in the seemingly inappropriate name 'Autopsy'. There was cutthroat competition between operators. Many went to the wall. Eventually the French-backed London General Omnibus Company, commencing operations in 1856, emerged as the main operator of London's horse buses and a major component of what became London Transport in the 1930s.

Horse buses were succeeded by horse trams. Regular services dated from the 1870s. They carried more passengers, charged cheaper fares and operated for longer hours than horse buses. Their relative cheapness encouraged commuting into central London and their availability encouraged the growth of inner suburbs for those with regular work such as white-collar clerks and shop assistants. Many of them were avid to be seen as 'respectable' and they favoured districts like Holloway and Camberwell where new housing development was aimed at this clientele. In due course horse-drawn trams gave way to electric trams. These could carry considerably more passengers with very low fares and were used particularly by working-class Londoners not only to travel to and from work but also for pleasure and recreation. So popular did electric trams become that they were once mellifluously described as 'the gondola of the people'. A comprehensive tram system developed but with one seemingly insoluble drawback – the authorities would not allow

117

trams into the City or the West End. Many densely populated working-class suburbs benefitted from intensive electric tram services but the value of this very cheap form of transport was limited because it was unable to penetrate much of central London. The London County Council became the major operator of electric trams. Its first route opened on 15 May 1903 from Westminster Bridge to Tooting.

The introduction of the B-type motor bus in 1910 was the death knell of the horse bus. A variety of horse-drawn conveyances for hire had long been available in London. Although motor taxis appeared in the 1890s, it took many years before the last horse-drawn cabs disappeared from London's streets. Although railways and London seem inseparable it is easy to forget that in the nineteenth century, most goods and merchandise was hauled around London's streets by horses. Until the internal combustion engine became a practicality, the number of horses and people engaged in various ways with working with horses, increased steadily. The sound, the smell, the droppings of horses were everywhere. In the 1870s Gustav Dore produced an impression of traffic congestion in a view looking along Ludgate Hill towards St Paul's. He portrays a nightmarish gridlock of horse-drawn conveyances far worse than anything the M25 was later able to offer. The total chaos and confusion are not helped by the fact that someone is trying to drive a herd of sheep through the streets.

The Impact of Railways on London

London's first passenger railway was the London & Greenwich Railway (L&GR) opened in 1836 and London Bridge was its western terminus and therefore central London's first railway station. Its promoters wanted it to compete with steamboats on the Thames and with stagecoaches both of which carried significant amounts of what we would now call commuter traffic between the two places. In this function, the line was not a great success but the directors found to their surprise that they could tap into the leisure business. Many Londoners found it cheaper to take a steamboat one way and the train the other for an afternoon or evening out at Greenwich which was a very popular destination for pleasure seekers. The L&GR established a practice widely associated with many of London's subsequent railways. Public railways were incorporated by law. This gave them powers of compulsory purchase which enabled them to buy up and demolish properties that stood on the projected route. The L&GR made extensive use of such powers. Although many later railways used viaducts in their approaches to London, the L&GR was unique in that the entire line was built on viaducts. Viaducts were a feature particularly of lines approaching London on the flat terrain south of the Thames. Cuttings and tunnels were characteristic of the lines threading the Northern Heights on their way into King's Cross, Marylebone, Euston and St Pancras while Liverpool Street was approached with a combination of tunnels and viaducts.

With the London & Greenwich, railways started making their mark on London. Much more was to follow. As the *Building News* was to say in 1862:

> The invasion of the Metropolis by the 'Steam Horse' has, during the last quarter of a century, produced changes, not only in the physical features of the Metropolis, but also in the manners, customs, mode of living, and even in the thoughts of its inhabitants, which are almost incredible. For a century previous to the year 1834, stagnation was the order of the day; but then came the locomotive to London, and all was changed.

The *Building News* in 1870 was even more fulsome:

> What would London do now without a railway? What would become of the immense holiday crowds who are regularly whirled over the country, fifty miles and back, in a single day with eight hours at the seaside, if the railways were suddenly to shut up shop? Brighton and Southend became seaside extensions of the Metropolis, while Birmingham and Bradford could appropriately be described as outposts of the City ... It could be said that all England was a suburb of London, and each part of that real Greater London proceeded to specialize not only in its material but its aesthetic, intellectual, and emotional production; knowing that whatever it did not provide could be had a short railway away.

The construction of London's railways was hugely disruptive where they penetrated those parts of the metropolis which were already built up. Bodies, public or private, that supplied utilities objected to projected railways that would disturb the increasingly complex systems of subterranean pipes, sewers and gas mains, for example. The legal profession enjoyed a bonanza in the disputes surrounding compulsory purchase. A particularly emotive issue occurred when human remains in churchyards and other burial places had to be moved to make way for railways.

Whenever possible, the railways bought the cheapest possible land for their proposed routes, their stations, goods depots and other installations. Cheap land was often occupied by substandard housing, usually rented by poor people with no influence. Much of this property consisted of slums and, in buying it up, the railways fortuitously contributed to the process of slum clearance. Until the late Victorian period there was not usually any legal requirement for railway companies to rehouse those displaced. They were simply decanted into neighbouring districts where the housing was little, if any better, and which then became more overcrowded and pestilential. As *The Times* stated: 'The poor are displaced but they are not removed. They are shovelled out of one side of the parish, only to render more overcrowded the stifling apartments in another part.' Overall, the railways probably caused more harm than good for the dwellings of the poor. The impact was a major one because an estimate put the number of people displaced by railway construction at a minimum of 120,000.

Railway viaducts were visually intrusive but they also provided travellers with a grandstand view of the lives of the London poor. Charles Dickens provided a vivid description of the approach to London over one such viaduct in *Dombey and Sons* (1869):

> Everything around is blackened. There are dark pools of water, muddy lanes, and miserable habitations far below. There are jagged walls and filthy houses close at hand, and through the battered roofs and broken windows, wretched rooms are seen, where want and fever hide themselves in many wretched shapes, while smoke and crowded gables, and distorted chimneys, and deformity of mind and body, choke the murky distance … it was so ruinous and dreary.

He continued:

> Every garden has its nuisance but every nuisance was of a distinct and peculiar character. In one a dung-heap, in the next a cinder heap, in the third was a pile of whelk and periwinkle shells, some rotten cabbages and a donkey: and the garden of another had a pond of thick green water.

The railways proved critical in bringing to London the vast quantities of coal needed by industrial and domestic consumers. They broke the earlier monopoly enjoyed by coastal shipping and railway companies, especially the Great Northern, the Midland, and the Great Eastern developed intensive traffic flows bringing coal mostly from South Yorkshire and the East Midlands to marshalling yards where trains were broken down and wagons were then tripped around London to industrial users and to small coal depots whence coal was delivered by horse to domestic consumers. London only grew in the way it did because the railways were able to satisfy its almost insatiable demand for this fuel.

Likewise, the railways made a major contribution to supplying London with the huge quantities of meat its citizens demanded. The London & North Western and Great Western Railways in particular developed a sophisticated business importing cattle from Ireland, either as dead meat slaughtered at places like Birkenhead or brought live to London to be slaughtered there. The railways also brought huge quantities of fish to London. This was a highly perishable commodity and the railways were able to use their speed to get it to the massive London market in reasonable condition. There is debate as to the where in Britain fish was first fried with chipped potatoes. London is one contender for this honour. Whatever the truth, fish and chips became a staple item in the diet of working-class Londoners. It was cheap, sustaining and made a major contribution to improving the diet and health of ordinary Londoners.

Another highly perishable foodstuff was milk. As late as the 1860s vendors led cows through London's streets and milk could be had, fresh from the udder. These cows were grazed on any open land close to the metropolis or, if they were unlucky, in dismal, overcrowded byres in the slum areas, adding their own unique contribution to the heavy mix of odours emanating from such places. In 1890 over 80 per cent of London's milk arrived by rail. The transport of milk provided lucrative business for several railway companies, particularly those serving the wetter west of England and Wales. The London & South Western Railway and the Great Western Railway were the major players in this enterprise. In January 1884 alone the Great Western handled 52,293 gallons of milk in London. The availability of cheap supplies of fresh milk had a greatly beneficial effect on the diet and health of Londoners. Whereas in 1850 it is estimated that Londoners each drank about six gallons of milk a year, just before 1914 the figure had risen to about twenty-one gallons. Railways should be given full credit for their contribution to the welfare of London's populace.

The presence of railways encouraged the development of intensive market gardening in parts of London's hinterland. For example, carrots were grown in profusion around Biggleswade in Bedfordshire and arrived in London by the wagonload, courtesy of the Great Northern Railway. The railways did good business with another product created by Londoners: this was the euphemistically named 'nightsoil' which was the content of privvies. Added to this were massive quantities of horse droppings. Both human and equine waste made excellent fertilizer and went by rail to places such as Biggleswade where it was reprocessed and eventually returned from there to London as carrots. Similar recycling took place elsewhere. Some railway companies diversified their operations to include running fruit and vegetable markets. The Great Eastern Railway, for example, opened what became a thriving market at Stratford. In 1879, its first year, it handled 5,000 tons of railborne traffic. In 1887 this figure had increased to 33,000 tons.

Underground Trains Come to London

The Metropolitan Railway running from Bishops Road at Paddington to Farringdon Street on the edge of the City was the world's first underground railway. It opened amidst great celebration on 10 January 1863 and before long was carrying 25,000 passengers daily. It proved that underground trains could be a viable venture in London, it eased traffic congestion in central London and it generated a new phenomenon. This was the travel habit. People now made journeys for pleasure because an easy mode of transport was available when previously they might have stayed at home.

Critical factors in the choice of the route of the Metropolitan was the need for a quick transport link between the developing suburbs along the New Road (now the Marylebone and Euston Roads) and the City and the establishment from the late 1830s of important railway termini at Paddingon, Euston and King's Cross. These were to be joined by St Pancras and, much later, Marylebone. The other factor was chronic road congestion resulting from London's growth. Any railway serving inner London had to be built below ground, the cost of buying already built-up land being prohibitive.

The line was built on the then novel 'cut-and-cover' principle whereby a deep trench was excavated along which the tracks were laid, the trench then being partially roofed over. Roads or buildings could then be laid down along the route. To minimize the cost of compulsory purchase and compensation for damage, where possible the lines were built along and below the alignment of existing roads. Considering the scale of the engineering works involved, the building of the line was carried out remarkably easily. The only major incident occurred in June 1862 when the Fleet River burst into the workings.

From the start there was concern about the smuts and the smoke produced by the steam locomotives that hauled the trains in the early years. Certainly, stations like Baker Street which was entirely subterranean contained a poisonous and often almost impenetrable fug which caused travellers to cough, splutter and expectorate uncontrollably. The sulphurous miasma provided a happy hunting ground for pickpockets. Carriages were lit by oil lamps whose contents emitted a foul smell and dripped on passengers. Early underground travel was not for the faint-hearted. *The Times* added its weight to the doubters with sinister allusions to 'passages inhabited by rats, soaked with sewer drippings and the possibility that passengers would be poisoned by gases given off by ruptured mains'. However, despite apocalyptic predictions that building railways underground would disturb the Devil and incur his wrath and that the tunnels and cuttings would collapse, none of these things happened and the early Metropolitan was an almost complete success. It was so successful that the Hammersmith & City, much of which ran on viaducts and was in effect an extension, was opened in June 1864. The Metropolitan District and Circle Lines followed.

Also underground with a rather different concept was the first of London's tube railways. This was the City & South London Railway which was the first electric underground railway in the world to operate in deep-level tunnels. Initially the line was to run from King William Street near the Monument under the Thames and below Borough High Street to Elephant & Castle. It was soon extended to Stockwell. Public services started on 18 November 1890. Initially, small electric locomotives hauled carriages housing up to thirty-two passengers. They were not provided with windows on the basis that there was nothing to see; the carriages were also noisy and claustrophobic and soon became known as 'padded cells'. This short line was the predecessor of London's extensive tube railway system which became so vital to life in the metropolis.

The idea of tube trains caught on and all sorts of schemes were put forward for lines serving central London. Many never came to fruition. What developed was a series of uncoordinated lines which needed to be consolidated into an effective system of underground lines. The man who did this was Charles Dyson Yerkes (1837–1901), a thrusting American entrepreneur. He wanted an image of unity for the Underground and, inspirationally, he took on a young architect, Leslie Green (1875–1908), who put his stylish imprimatur on many of the stations on the system. The exteriors of these stations were highly distinctive, employing terracotta finishes the colour of oxblood and various architectural motifs. The interiors of his stations had concrete floors of crusted granite and walls decorated to shoulder height with bottle-green tiling, all with Art Nouveau influence. Although some of these buildings have been replaced, often tastelessly, there is still much of Green's work to be seen and it is usually now treated with the respect it deserves. It is interesting to note in view of the UK's uneasy relationship with countries in Europe that Yerkes, an American, ordered rolling stock for his lines from France and Hungary.

Even a casual look at a map of London may raise the question of why none of its major main line termini are conveniently located in its central core. A possible exception might be made for Charing Cross and, perhaps stretching a point, Victoria. The other stations are certainly peripheral. Their respective locations have been and, to some extent, are still inconvenient for travellers arriving at one station and wishing to travel from another.

Railway companies were profit-seeking businesses that needed space for their stations but were severely constrained by the cost of land in central London. There were also influential landowners who did not want railways with their noise, dirt and crowds bringing down the value of the exclusive fashionable residential areas that several of them had developed and which brought in handsome rents.

The idea of one or two large centrally located stations acting both as termini, departure and exchange points for the various existing and projected main line railways, was mooted early on. Discussions rumbled on through to the 1880s as congestion in London's streets became worse and worse. The advocates of a 'Grand Central' were to remain frustrated. This was because back in1846 the Royal Commission on Metropolitan Termini recommended that big main line stations be kept out of central London, particularly because of the road traffic they would have generated and the disruption and destruction of property that would have been needed for their approaches. The Commissioners designated an area they referred to as 'The Quadrilateral' as a 'no-go' area for major main line surface railways and their stations and other installations.

The idea did not entirely go away because in 1863 the London & North Western Railway proposed a terminus at Leicester Square as a central facility to replace Euston and in the 1870s the South Eastern Railway advocated a station of its own nearby. The partial solution to the difficulties of inter-station travel was the building of the sub-surface and later the tube lines. Perhaps London should be grateful that it was at least spared the even more appalling road congestion that would have been caused had there been one or two grand central termini.

London's Industries and Commerce

Manufacturing played a major part in London's economy in the nineteenth century but mostly in small industrial premises employing ten or fewer workers. In 1851 only seventeen establishments had more than 250 employees. Many of the small-scale industries had been inherited from the previous century or earlier. Shoe-making and clothing, for example, were traditionally located in the West End close to where the well-to-do customers tended to live. The nineteenth century saw the majority of these small businesses close down as consumers as a whole tended to switch to cheaper, lower-quality 'off the peg' products that were mass-produced elsewhere. However, many small businesses opened in the East End in what became known as the 'rag trade', selling clothes that were cheap because they depended on low-paid sweated female labour. Manufacturing industry tended to leave central London during this period. That which remained was still small scale but reflected the presence in London of very affluent consumers. North of Oxford Street and east of Great Portland Street were many small premises engaged in making items of high-quality furniture.

It should be mentioned that many new industries moved to London in this period but largely outside the central area. Sometimes located in substantial premises, they included electrical, locomotive and vehicle manufacture and the myriad of other industries attracted to London because of the sheer size of the market provided by its growing population. Shipbuilding, however, was an industry that had largely vacated London by 1914 with the decline of wooden vessels.

London's position as the world's largest and busiest seaport with all its associated activities and industries created huge numbers of jobs. Wharves and warehouses lined the Thames where it passed through central London although the new enclosed docks on sides of the river were downstream and again outside the central area. These docks tended to specialize in particular commodities. West India Docks, for example, handled rum, tea, hardwood, sugar, fruit and coffee. East India Docks concentrated on tea, silks, spices and porcelain. Downstream from the neighbourhood of the Tower were numerous riverside businesses such as flour-milling and sugar-refining, the raw materials arriving by water. Their products were often re-exported, obviously by using the Thames as their starting point.

London's retail operations underwent considerable change in the period under review. As early as the 1830s there was a very marked movement westwards of retail premises from the City along Holborn, Oxford Street, Fleet Street and the Strand into the area recognized as the West End. A new

'West End' further west in Kensington, Knightsbridge and Bayswater opened later. Oxford Street became a particular hub of retail and towards its western end saw the opening of London's grandest purpose-built department store in 1909, This, of course, was Selfridge's and it is no coincidence that it was built adjacent to stations on what became known as the Central Line, known in its early years as the 'Twopenny Tube'. By 1914 Selfridge's had 160 departments and employed 950 men and 2,550 women. The big stores used cutting-edge technology with glittering electric lighting, lifts, escalators and plate glass.

A retailer with smaller premises but which made a major impact, especially at London's railway and underground stations, was W. H. Smith with its bookstalls. Middle-class Londoners thought these stalls were highly disreputable because they sold cheap 'French' novels. No more need be said! Another newcomer was Sainsbury's. Its stores were then, of course, small but they used improved transport networks to bring a range of standardized food products to consumers.

The wholesale markets also experienced change. In 1855 the live cattle market at Smithfield was moved to Copenhagen just north of King's Cross, partly to reduce the nuisance of livestock being driven through the streets of central London. A replacement meat market opened at Smithfield in 1866. Some of the markets in central London were displaced when new streets and railways were built and others, such as Billingsgate, Covent Garden, Spitalfields and Leadenhall, were rebuilt. A few markets were opened on the initiative of rich individuals. Perhaps the best known of these was Columbia Market promoted by Angela Burnett-Coutts. This was housed in a grandiose building but proved to be a spectacular failure.

London was already famous for its street markets and most did a roaring trade in working-class areas although they found themselves being subjected to increasing regulation under public health and nuisance laws. There were, of course, rogue traders and the fact that they did much of their trade late on Friday and Saturday when workers had been paid their wages meant that they became associated with drunken disorder. Some of the street markets were huge. One in Tottenham Court Road had 333 regular stalls. Itinerant hucksters and hawkers of varying levels of probity and selling an extraordinary range of commodities walked the streets of central London.

Public Buildings

By the nineteenth century London had become the commercial heart of not only of the world's largest and wealthiest city but the financial centre of a worldwide empire the like of which had never before been seen. London not only served the financial needs of the empire but was also seen for much of the century as a secure and safe place for handling all manner of financial business on behalf of much of the then developed world. Merchant bankers in London became major world financiers and investors and the proceeds brought vast riches and prestige to the City.

At the same time the administration of Britain's vast empire and the growing functions of her own domestic government required a major expansion of official buildings in which these functions could be performed. Most were located in the Whitehall area. It was felt that that the size and appearance of such buildings should be commensurate with the importance of the functions with which they dealt so not only were they built on a grand scale but the most eminent architects of the time were employed to give them the required dignity. These included men of the calibre of Sir Charles Barry and Sir George Gilbert Scott.

At the eastern end of Whitehall was Trafalgar Square, the centrepiece of which was Nelson's Column, completed in 1843 – the lions were added later. The Square came to be regarded as the 'heart of the Empire' and from its earliest days was the location of political demonstrations, of celebrations of military and naval successes and of various public frolics and revels such as those of New Year's Eve.

In harmony with the concept of Empire and of London being its capital, its buildings grew larger and larger although perhaps in a ponderous and brash rather than an aesthetically pleasing way. The big hotel was a product of the Victorian era. The Langham, opened in 1865, was one of the first but was soon overtaken by behemoths like the Grand, the Victoria and the Metropole in Northumberland Avenue. It was also the age of giant emporia and shops in Regent Street such as Jay's, Peter Robinson's and Dickins & Jones astounded visitors from the provinces and abroad.

The urge to impress was replicated in the commercial world of the City. Many joint-stock banks and insurance companies had premises in the City or close by and were designed to give a sense of permanence and prestige. They drew on the fashionable if rather eclectic architectural styles then in vogue. When a replacement Royal Exchange was built and opened in 1844, it was in a Classical style while the headquarters of the Prudential Assurance Company in Holborn was a somewhat brash essay in the Gothic Revival Style.

The valley of the River Fleet had long been an impediment to traffic of all sorts between the City and Westminster and the West End. Holborn Viaduct was opened in 1869 and greatly improved communications across central London. Temple Bar was another obstacle to traffic and was removed in 1879. The new Houses of Parliament, replacing the burnt-out Palace of Westminster, were completed in the 1850s. Designed by Charles Barry, they were in a Gothic retro style which emphasized the supposedly ancient and hallowed nature of British political practices.

Perhaps the most spectacular public building of the era was that which housed the Great Exhibition of 1851. The Exhibition was basically a trade fair intended to showcase Britain's indisputable world lead in inventions, manufacturing and industry and to sell British goods particularly to the host of overseas visitors it was hoped to attract. Foreign goods were also on show but British ones dominated. A ground-breaking building containing 4,000 tons of iron and 400 tons of glass was constructed in Hyde Park and quickly dubbed the 'Crystal Palace' particularly because of the sparkling effect of the sun after rain had fallen. Not everyone was enamoured of the building, however, with one irascible critic describing it as 'neither crystal nor a palace'. The Exhibition was hugely successful and the railways contributed greatly by putting on cheap excursions which brought vast numbers from across the British Isles to London, many of them for the first time. After the Exhibition the building was eventually dismantled and re-erected on Sydenham Hill. Part of the profits went to the creation of a museum quarter in Kensington with such splendid institutions as the Science and Natural History Museums around the aptly named 'Exhibition Road'.

Victorian and Edwardian England society and public life appeared to be suffused with Christian ideology and influence. At the same time most of the Christian denominations were deeply concerned about what they saw as the widespread lack of religious belief and practice and they deplored the empty pews which were a feature of so many places of public worship. In order, as they hoped, to take the Christian message to the people, they engaged in an orgy of church and chapel building. Their efforts were frequently unrewarded. In 1851 it was recorded that less than 25 per cent of Londoners went to worship publicly on Sundays. This figure fell somewhat over the next sixty years. Church attendance was as high as 40 per cent in affluent areas and as low as 10 per cent or less in deprived districts like the East End. The pews remained stubbornly ill-frequented for many reasons, not least that the Church of England was perceived by many to be the bastion and justifier of a grossly inequitable society. In well-to-do areas a significant part of the congregation was likely to be composed of servants who were required to attend worship. Non-conformist churches and chapels were to be found in sizeable numbers in upper working-class and lower middle-class districts especially in east and north-east London. Many local residents had migrated from East Anglia where nonconformity had a strong hold. Worship at Catholic establishments ran at high levels in those areas such as Kilburn where there were large Irish populations. The building of Westminster Cathedral in central London in 1903 was an assertion of the continuing significant presence of Catholicism in the life of the capital and, indeed, the nation.

Establishing Social Control

When the nineteenth century began, London was an extremely violent and unsafe place in which to live and move about. It was notorious by continental standards. The resources for law enforcement were feeble and wholly inadequate. Parish constables and the 'Charlies' or night watchmen were no match for individual or organized criminals always prepared to use violence. How then was it that by the end of the nineteenth century the people of London had a reputation for being law-abiding and the metropolis as being relatively safe and secure for residents and visitors alike?

At the beginning of this period, the Victorian middle and upper classes felt insecure, scared by what they saw as the apparently infinite teeming hordes of lawless, anarchic and naturally vicious slum-dwelling poor. They remembered how a similar 'swinish multitude' had overthrown the French monarchy and aristocracy in the revolution of 1789 in a terrifying inversion of the natural social order. With political radicals in London forever attempting to stir up discontent and the presence of untold masses of the criminally inclined poor in London's population, methods had to be found of reducing the perceived threat to the lives and property of the rich and powerful. Few attempts were made to probe into links between poverty and crime. Measures were needed which established and asserted the rule of law and made them feel safe and they were part of the process of social control.

Poverty has never been an exalted state. Very much the opposite. The poor have always been punished for being poor. London's well-to-do were offended by indigents of all sorts. They were convinced that considerable numbers of people had no intention of earning an honest living for themselves and thought they had the right to be maintained by those industrious and respectable individuals of sufficient financial substance to pay rates. To cow the poor and needy of London and elsewhere, the Poor Law Amendment Act of 1834 was implemented. This decreed that 'assistance' would only be given to those who entered and resided in the forbidding new workhouses stipulated under the Act. Conditions were made so uncongenial in the workhouses to deter all but the most desperate from seeking entry. 'Outside' relief was not to be provided and it was hoped that the Act would force the lazy and feckless to support themselves through legitimate employment. Although outdoor relief was never eliminated, the Poor Law Unions always looked to minimize their expenditure and to stigmatize paupers and pauperism. The indigent lived in constant fear that they would be forced to throw themselves on the tender mercies of the Poor Law authorities. Poverty and its causes were not addressed and enormous human suffering resulted. The Poor Law was one of the means by which affluent London exercised some degree of control over a substantial element of its poorer citizenry.

The poor were perceived as a potentially criminalized mass. Another means of controlling them was to develop effective methods of policing. A start was made with the Bow Street Runners in 1750. Public policing was controversial because many influential people thought that a police force would act in a spying capacity on behalf of the government and undermine the supposed liberties of freeborn Englishmen. Crime was a boom industry in London in the eighteenth and early nineteenth century, the response of the authorities largely being to increase the savagery of the penal code. This did little to deter criminal activity.

The first regular police force was the Metropolitan Police established in 1829. This owed much to the doggedly persistent campaigning of the Home Secretary, Sir Robert Peel. Although uniformed, great efforts were made to ensure that they had a non-militaristic appearance: they were provided with truncheons rather than swords or firearms. It says much for the continuing power of the continuing power of the City that it gained a similar force but under its exclusive jurisdiction.

The initial response to the 'Peelers' as they were known was mixed. Many early recruits were semi-criminalized bullies. The poor saw them as stooges of the propertied classes – 'escapees' from their own ranks who then victimized the very people with whom they had been brought up. It is certainly true that much of the Peelers' early activity was in London's poorer districts but that was usually where life on the streets was at its most intensive. Over time, the 'Met' became a perhaps grudgingly accepted part of London life although there were occasions when they were on the receiving end of severe criticism, not least over their failure to solve the notorious 'Jack the Ripper' murders in 1888.

The establishment of the Metropolitan Police was followed by a decline in reported crime and increase in detection and prosecution rates so that by 1900 the streets of London were considered among the safest of the big cities across the globe. This process, however, was not a simple one.

There were periods when criminal activity surged upwards and middle-class Londoners in panic mode declared that the criminals were taking over. These occasions seem to have occurred most frequently when wages were falling and prices rising. Overall, London was a boom city which, while it attracted a large inward migration with consequent social volatility, meant that there was a growing job market and rising overall prosperity, admittedly not equally shared.

Town planning was used as a form of social engineering in the belief that if criminal rookeries like Old Nichol, Saffron Hill and Seven Dials were demolished or 'opened up' by having roads driven through them, their inhabitants, their antisocial behaviour and criminal culture would somehow disappear. The authorities have never been keen to make an objective analysis of the causes of crime and to set about tackling those causes. Clearing slums did not eliminate criminal activity but simply decanted their inhabitants into neighbouring districts where they continued to practise their wicked ways.

The end of transportation to the colonies, often for what today seem to us as trivial offences, meant that many new prisons had to be built. These were penitentiaries where prisoners had to undertake physically hard and often futile tasks, the intention to break their spirit rather than attempt to reform and rehabilitate them. New prisons included Millbank, Brixton and Pentonville. As late as the 1850s two semi-derelict and superannuated ex-men-of-war known as 'hulks' were still moored in the Thames housing convicts.

The introduction of compulsory elementary education helped to inculcate desirable attitudes and behaviour in young people and was another form of social control.

Public Disorder

London in this period may have gone some way towards becoming a safer place but it was by no means necessarily a settled and serene one. It maintained its long-standing reputation for public disorder which, on several occasions, provided a serious challenge to the relevant authorities. There were many political issues during the century which generated sufficient emotion to cause Londoners to take to the streets in sizeable numbers. There were also political activists, sometimes in penny numbers, who engaged in activities intended to subvert the political and social order, if necessary, by using terrorist tactics.

In the first half of the century the issue of political reform was high on the public agenda. With most of the population denied any effective political power a major flashpoint was inevitable. It was easy to portray those who advocated political reform as being sympathetic with what were seen as the worst excesses of the French revolutionaries. This indeed was the thrust of the repressive and reactionary governments in the years following the end of the French wars in 1815. However, most radicals emphasized peaceful political education and agitation for reform of the franchise, for freedom of the press and for the legalization of trade union activity. Groups like the Cato Street Conspirators around Arthur Thistlewood who in 1820 planned to assassinate the Cabinet in the belief that cutting the head off the body politic would spark revolution, were well outside the radical mainstream.

The more far-sighted members of the political elite were coming to realize in the 1820s that unless concessions were made on many issues, political radicals might decide that piecemeal reforms were not enough and that revolutionary measures were needed. The Reform Act of 1832 was preceded by enormous rallies in London whose organizers and speakers were mostly middle class but with crowds largely composed of working people. All wanted the right to vote. These meetings largely went off peacefully although London's well-to-do were always scared that mass gatherings of the lower orders were a prelude to possible insurrection. In the event, the Act conceded the franchise to relatively small numbers of mostly middle-class men and was greeted with anger by huge numbers who felt let down and frustrated because the right to vote had not been extended to them.

It was out of this disappointment that the Chartist movement emerged and developed in the 1830s and 1840s. This was a mass movement for radical change which, had it been implemented, would have created a system of universal male suffrage and a parliament more able to act on behalf of ordinary people than any such institution before or since. The implications of Chartism were revolutionary although most of its supporters eschewed violence and believed in 'moral force': persuasion based on reason. It was a genuinely national movement with London being only one of its centres of support. One tactic of Chartism was the drawing up of a petition or charter embracing six proposals for political change. This charter, hopefully with millions of signatures appended, would be presented to Parliament who would then enact the proposals in the form of legislation. This was naïve because Parliament was composed of men who were not going to legislate away their own domination of the political system and all the power that went with it.

Frustrated by the way in which Parliament had contemptuously rejected earlier petitions, the Chartists decided in April 1848 to hold a peaceful monster meeting of supporters from across Britain, on Kennington Common. Fortified by speeches from the leading lights there would then be a march to Westminster carrying the monster petition bearing at least five million signatures. This was history repeating itself as farce. Had there been ten million or more signatures, Parliament would have remained impervious to this demonstration of popular feeling. A photograph of the mass meeting on Kennington Common is believed to be one the earliest known of a large crowd.

Despite most Chartists rejecting the use of physical force, 1848 was a particularly sensitive time given the wave of revolutions across Europe. The political establishment was taking no chances and it over-reacted to the demonstration scheduled for 10 April. Almost the whole Metropolitan Police Force was on the streets along with about 85,000 volunteer special constables armed with anything from ancient fowling pieces to truncheons. Troops were on hand, mostly kept out of sight, guarding notable public buildings such as the Bank of England. They were equipped with cannon. In the event, heavy rain somewhat dampened the ardour of the huge crowds who turned up at Kennington. When the bedraggled demonstrators got close to Parliament the police persuaded them to disperse in exchange for which the petition would then be presented to Parliament. When it was clear that many of the signatures were simple forgeries, the petition was once again summarily rejected. It was the ignominious end of Chartism as a mass movement.

The events of 10 April were a fiasco and perhaps an indication that despite the inequalities and injustices of mid-Victorian Britain there was no general taste for political revolution. From this time large-scale political meetings and demonstrations became less common in London partly because Parliament, wisely if not very willingly, conceded a wide range of social and other reforms over the next decades. Economic growth and a general increase in prosperity particularly from the mid-1840s to around 1880 contributed to reduced levels of political discontent and unrest and a period of relative stability. The very diversity of London's industries and the 'melting pot' nature of its burgeoning population meant that it lacked the sense of community and class consciousness which was a feature of many provincial mining and industrial communities. The multicultural nature of London's population and its dispersal over an increasingly wide geographical area meant that its working class did not identify themselves as Londoners nor as members of a class with shared interests.

133

Outdoors and on the Streets

Away from the fashionable streets and squares particularly of the West End, the streets were a seething melting pot, a kaleidoscope of London life, much of it seedy, often threatening, but full of vitality, always fascinating and in various degrees active throughout the twenty-four hours. It never really went to sleep.

A street sight peculiar to the first quarter of the twentieth century was the saloop stall. These were to be found in odd corners across London's historic core. It was a small kitchen table on wheels, with cupboards and fitted with an urn for the making of the saloop which was an infusion of sassafras, sugar and milk, sold at three halfpence a bowl. This was cheap and made it popular with many workers and passersby. Apparently, saloop was a favourite of boy chimney sweeps who would hover around the stalls and if they could not buy it, would have to be satisfied by sniffing its tantalizing aromas.

Walking the streets and bawling out their wares were all manner of itinerant vendors. There was a sizeable demand for those selling broadsheets containing 'Last Dying Speeches and Confessions'. Those purported to be the best sellers were ballads that reported murders in the goriest detail, real or massively enhanced and accompanied by images intended to grab the imagination.

Vying for attention and spare coppers were those playing the hurdy-gurdy, the pan pipes or scraping away on a fiddle. There were even genuine musicians and singers of real talent but somehow down on their luck who gave snatches from Italian opera while singing for their supper. Singers of sentimental ballads could usually gain an audience. Other street entertainers included those with performing animals: Frenchmen with hares who could play musical instruments such as kettle drums and Germans with canaries which gave displays of military exercises. A notable character in the 1820s was the 'Flying Pieman'. He sold puddings, not pies; he had gained his name from the speed with which he ran round the streets, only slowing down slightly when making a sale. Bawling 'Hot, hot, hot – pudding hot' he ran like a lamplighter. His wares sold so well that his tray was emptied several times a day. Although he had a shop in Smithfield, he preferred to go out to his customers rather than wait for them to come to him. He was an early form of 'Stop Me and Buy One'.

One of the sights of London that always drew a crowd of spectators in the early part of the nineteenth century was the departure every evening of the mail coaches from the inns that acted as their base. Thomas De Quincey (1785–1859), the critic and essayist, described the sight in fulsome terms:

The absolute perfection of all the appointments about the carriages and the harness, their strength, their brilliant cleanliness, their beautiful simplicity and the royal magnificence of the horses ... Every part of every carriage had been cleaned, every horse had been groomed ... Can there be horses that bound off with the action and gestures of leopards? ... What stir – what sea-like ferment! – what a thundering of wheels! – what a trampling of hoofs! – what a sounding of trumpets!

There were many 'road hogs' on London's crowded Victorian streets. Hansom cabs and pirate horse-drawn buses were notorious for the reckless way in which they were driven and speeds exceeding ten miles per hour were common and accidents many. Runaway horses were another hazard, being entirely unpredictable. Penny-farthings could move very fast given the chance and many pedestrians were mown down by these contraptions. The more modern type of safety bicycle appeared in the 1880s. While not so fast, it also took its toll of pedestrians, mainly because it was small, inconspicuous and much quieter, inattentive walkers simply not seeing them quickly enough.

In the early decades of the nineteenth century the streets were made somewhat brighter by use of new-fangled gas lighting. The first gas-lit streets may have been Pall Mall and Whitecross Street and soon the use of gas spread to the main streets. This benefitted the public who were less likely to have accidents or be the victims of crime. As a correspondent to *The Times* wrote:

notwithstanding the wetness of the evening, and other unfavourable circumstances, we were both pleased and surprised to see that part of the street illuminated with at least twice the quantity of light usually seen, and that light uniformly spread, not merely on the footways, but even to the middle of the street, so that the faces of persons walking, the carriages passing, etc., could be distinctly seen.

Many writers were impressed by the street markets, especially in winter when the days were short. De Quincey again:

There are hundreds of stalls and every stall is illuminated by the intense white light of the new self-generating gas lamp, or else it is brightened up by the red smoky flame of the old-fashioned grease lamps. One man shows of his yellow haddock with a candle stuck in a bundle of wood. Some stalls are crimson with a fire shining through the holes beneath the baked chestnut stoves ... while a few have a candle shining through a sieve. These, with the sparkling ground-glass globes of the tea-dealers' shops, and the butchers' gas-lights streaming and fluttering in the wind like flags of flame, pour forth such a flood of light that, at a distance, the atmosphere immediately above the spot is as lurid as if the street was on fire.

Among the creatures of the night who inhabited the streets were the Bucks, successors to the previous century's Mohocks. They were louts and bullies, mostly members of the aristocracy, who enjoyed overturning saloop stalls and other items used by street vendors. They also enjoyed plaguing the lives of the night watchmen or 'Charlies' who patrolled the streets and basically represented the thin line of law and order before the introduction of the Metropolitan Police. Having the sense of entitlement that went with their affluent upbringing, they nevertheless modelled their activities on those of the least respectable of the lower orders. The Bucks swaggered along the street, trying to catch people's eyes and then inviting them to a fight or to indulge in a robust exchange of views. In Tudor times an invitation to fisticuffs was given by biting the thumb, in the eighteenth century by cocking the hat or jerking the thumb over the shoulder, implying birth out of wedlock. Early in the nineteenth century the challenge was signalled by putting a thumb to the nose and later by jerking two fingers upwards. It is interesting to note how often sanctimonious middle-class moralists spoke disparagingly about the behaviour of the 'lower orders' but excused that of upper-class louts as little more than high spirits.

The rookeries such as St Giles (near the present-day Centrepoint) and the Holy Land of Seven Dials continued to send forth their hordes of beggars importuning alms. They came in many and frequently ingenious forms. They included the genuine maimed and blind and others operating under false colours. There were ragged women with barefoot, piteous-looking children who were frequently hired for the day. Any number of old soldiers and sailors displayed grievous bogus or even genuine wounds and amputated limbs. Some accompanied their begging by a little nifty pickpocketing if the mark came too close. The rookeries contained academies where boys and girls were trained to learn the skills necessary for a lifetime of low-level street crime. There they would learn the 'kinchin-lay', 'cly-faking' and 'wipesnitching' and how to 'nim a ticker'. Every racket had its own description: the housebreaker was a 'Cracksman', the footpad a 'Rampsman', the street thug a 'Bludger', 'Bug Hunters' waylaid and robbed drunks, a pickpocket was a 'Buzzer', women who enticed children into their houses to strip them of their clothes were 'Skinners', counterfeit coiners were 'Shofulmen' and gamblers with cogged dice were 'Charley-Pitchers'.

Artists flocked to London, many eager to capture and record the complexity and diversity of the world's premier city. London was always a place of moods, but few captured the seamy side of London life with such virtuosity as the Frenchman Gustav Dore (1832–83). He had a dark, almost nightmarish style admirably suited to the portrayal of the dark streets, the low life and the menacing atmosphere of the rookeries and notorious districts like the Ratcliffe Highway, just east of the Tower. Dore made skilful use of fog and murk in leaving us a record of London's underbelly.

Charles Dickens recorded London's fogs for posterity: *Bleak House* contains a classic evocation of what Londoners would later call 'The Smoke'.

> Implacable November weather ... smoke lowering down from chimney pots, making a soft black drizzle, with flakes of soot in it as big as full-grown snowflakes ... dogs, undistinguishable in mire. Horses, scarcely better, splashed to their very blinkers. Foot passengers, jostling one another's umbrellas, in a general infection of ill-temper, and losing their footholds at street-corners, where tens of thousands of other foot passengers have been slipping and sliding since the day broke adding new deposits to the crust upon crust of mud, sticking at those points tenaciously to the pavement, and accumulating at compound interest. Fog everywhere. Fog up the river ... fog down the river, where it rolls defiled among the tiers of shipping. Fog creeping into the cabooses of collier-brigs; fog lying out on the yards and hovering in the rigging of great ships; fog drooping on the gunwales of barges and small boats ... Chance people on the bridges peeping over the parapets into a nether sky of fog, with fog all round them, as if they were up in a balloon, and hanging in the misty clouds.

The Thames could be described as one of London's streets because so many people used it for the purpose of getting around the metropolis. Every year many drowned in it, by sheer accident or sometimes by sheer stupidity. It was less common for people to drown in London's streets. One afternoon, around 1820, a giant vat of beer at Meux's brewery in Tottenham Court Road exploded without warning and the force burst other vats nearby open. A tsunami of over 10,000 gallons of beer coursed down the street towards the rookery of St Giles. It washed away carts and their horses and demolished several houses and flooded others. At least eight people perished.

Deeply regretted by most London inhabitants, at least in London's less fashionable quarters, was the abolition of the pillory soon after Victoria came to the throne. It was not long before public hangings at places like Tyburn and occasional public floggings and the ducking of convicted pickpockets also ended, much to the chagrin of the crowds who were robbed of popular entertainment and an excuse for a jamboree. Public executions and the use of the pillory had clearly become no kind of deterrent to criminal activity. Indeed, when popular miscreants stood in the pillory or were hanged, huge crowds turned out to wish them well while enjoying the sight of their suffering. Miscreants who, for whatever reason, were popular with the crowd were cheered and the hangman jeered. The opposite happened if the victim was unpopular. It was common for pickpockets to harvest rich rewards in the packed crowds. Ravening masses were no longer treated to the sight of convicts undergoing humiliating, agonizing punishment and sometimes terminal punishment, this being part of the civilizing process but widely resented on London's streets.

The Pubs of Victorian London

London's pubs as most people probably perceive them are Victorian and Edwardian. Many of them are thought of as 'gin palaces'. In considering such establishments, it should be remembered that eighteenth-century London had been blighted by the myriad of problems associated with the distilling and consumption of cheap gin, much of it adulterated and frequently poisonous. The habit had been so prevalent that at its peak it was undermining the ability of tens of thousands of Londoners to do anything useful with their lives. Hogarth's famous illustrations *Gin Lane* and *Beer Street* expressed the views of the legislators that gin was evil and beer somehow virtuous, if only by comparison.

To tackle the gin-drinking craze head on, the Beer Act was passed in 1830. This allowed anyone to set up a beerhouse after paying a token fee. The intention of the Act was achieved. It was to undercut the sellers of gin by opening thousands of additional drinking places in which very cheap beer was available. While this could be seen as encouraging, in the consumption of alcoholic drinks, beer was of nowhere near the strength of the gin it was intended largely to replace. The Act was not fully thought through. While it certainly saw off binge gin-drinking, the poor, in seeking temporary oblivion from their squalid lives, packed out the beerhouses instead. Thousands of these cheap drinking places were set up in the poorer working-class districts and were almost as squalid as the dens of desperation they replaced.

In 1869 the Act was repealed and vast numbers of these debauched establishments closed down. The brewers decided to clean up the image and reality of drinking establishments and the phrase 'public house' was coined for establishments which allowed the consumption of alcohol but in a controlled way and in more salubrious surroundings. Many kinds of drinking establishments were set up offering a wide variety of facilities and among these were the so-called 'gin palaces' of which examples may still be seen in London today. These were frequently grandiose in scale and opulent in their furnishings and fittings. The brewers were offering a sprat to catch a mackerel. Most of their clientele lived in miserable, poorly lit and frequently insanitary conditions and the gin palace was designed to lure them out into well-heated, bright surroundings where they could enjoy a drink in convivial company.

Historians generally consider that the first gin palace was Thompson & Fearon's, opened in 1831 in Holborn. The latest technology was employed in these establishments using a combination of gaslight and plate glass often with etched decorative motifs and mirrors to give an illusion of greater space. Superbly crafted mahogany partitions and bar fittings, stained-glass windows, roof mouldings of Lyncrusta and Anaglypta cleverly imitating plasterwork, came together to flatter the drinker and make him (it was mostly him) feel he was indeed in palatial surroundings. Over the period to the 1900s these gin palaces tended to become increasingly fancy and impressive, huge eye-catching buildings dominating their neighbourhood and often with enormous lamps above the entrances from the street.

They provided a carefully controlled drinking environment and contributed to a new sense that drinking in a public space was no longer disreputable.

Immigrants in London

Britain was a pioneer in the process of large-scale modern industrial development. Based on this early start, she became the world's dominant economic power for a period of decades in the middle of the nineteenth century.

The resulting growth meant that some immigration was to be encouraged to meet likely rising requirements for labour and at other times to create a surplus which could have the effect of moderating wage demands among the indigenous workforce.

The emergence of highly repressive regimes on the Continent led to political refugees of a liberal or socialist political persuasion coming to Britain during the century. Inevitably, many of them took up residence in London. Mid-nineteenth century Britain had a not wholly justified reputation for political tolerance. She was at the height of her general confidence and was prepared to provide a home for small numbers of revolutionaries and others whose views were not seen as a threat but were unlikely to have been acceptable had they been voiced by the native population. Among these exiles, some of whom lived in London for many years, were the Italians Garibaldi and Mazzini, the Hungarian Kossuth, the Russian anarchist Kropotkin and the revolutionary socialists Marx and later Lenin. All were escaping potential persecution in their own countries and, if not necessarily accepted with open arms by the political and social establishment, were tolerated because they were believed to be generally harmless.

The tolerance extended to this motley crew was in marked contrast to the various waves of poor immigrants whose numbers and poverty made them seem a real threat to the living standards of working-class Londoners. The first to arrive, from a trickle in the 1830s to an absolute flood in the 1840s, were the Irish. The irony was that their desperate plight, when the potato crop on which they were so dependent failed, was primarily the fault of absentee English landlords who insisted that they continued to pay their rent despite having little or no income with which to do so. Most were evicted if they did not pay up. Many of the landlords resided in London, enjoying opulent lifestyles.

Between 1790 and 1890 the population of Ireland was nearly halved. Some managed to get to the United States but others made the shorter journey to mainland towns and cities, especially Glasgow, Liverpool and London. Being penniless and at the bottom of the social ladder, they had little option but to find living accommodation in the very worst slum districts. In London the Irish were concentrated in several areas, the largest perhaps being around Tottenham Court Road and Charlotte Street. Their dire poverty meant that when a death occurred, the cadaver often had to be kept in the house until enough money had been found for a funeral. A doctor called out to treat a patient in an Irish house wrote: 'a horrible stench arose from a corpse which had died of phthisis twelve days before, and the coffin stood across the end of the bed ... This was a small room not above ten feet by twelve feet, and a fire always in it … being the only one for sleeping, living and eating in.'

Despite the searing poverty in which they lived, Irish men were capable of extraordinary physical effort and there was much navvying work available for them as London expanded so rapidly in the Victorian period. They were also employed in all manner of unskilled and semi-skilled work. They met with much resentment from indigenous workers because their presence as cheap labour pushed down wages and they were also used as strike breakers. Resented, the Irish certainly were but such was the expansion of the British economy that there was an almost continuous demand for their labour. Indeed, it could be argued that the country's economic growth partly depended on the cheap labour the Irish provided.

If the Irish people living in London did not stand out in appearance from the rest of the poor, the same could not be said of the large numbers of Jews who arrived in London. They elicited the full force of native xenophobia. There had long been a significant Jewish presence in London and many of them had made a success in fields like business and the arts. Middle-class Jews had become an accepted if not wholly welcome element in London's multicultural society.

From the middle of the nineteenth into the early years of the twentieth century, Jewish populations in Russia and Eastern Europe were subjected to savage persecution and pogroms. Many Jewish people had little option but to flee. Although the objective was often to reach the United States, many arrived and stayed in London. Unlike the Irish, the Jewish arrivals brought with them a consciousness of having been persecuted throughout history. This engendered a defensive state of mind, a kind of siege mentality in which, more than other groups of immigrants, they felt the need to settle in close-knit communities. Many arrived with just the clothes they stood up in. They had little option but to move into districts already containing some of London's worst housing. Two of these were St George's, south of the Thames, and Whitechapel.

Whole streets were taken over by the newcomers and they took on a very distinctive character. Jewish districts had their own synagogues, shops selling their specific requirements, close-knit social networks and even their own newspapers. They spoke their own languages and most made little attempt to learn English. Native Londoners resented the beards and seemingly strange apparel of Jewish immigrants, their air of self-containment and exclusiveness and the way in which they put their stamp on their surroundings. They also resented their determined efforts to better themselves through their own efforts. Since most Jewish arrivals were unskilled and jobs of that sort were declining in late Victorian and Edwardian London, they were forced to find their own means of putting bread on the table. Many became itinerant street peddlers but the employment with which they became most associated was in the sweated trades, particularly the making of readymade clothes – the 'rag trade'. This kind of work was characterized by long hours, appalling working conditions and very low pay. The employers in these trades were usually Jews themselves.

Aversion to the Jewish presence built up from the 1870s in the more uncertain economic conditions that followed the boom of the mid-century. It was all too easy to blame an easily identifiable minority of people of foreign extraction for the problems of society such as crime, unemployment, bad housing and disease. Jews were made into scapegoats for the ills of society. Some Conservative MPs formed the British Brothers League to demand immigration controls and were part of a vicious and hysterical anti-Semitic campaign in speeches and printed media. One writer described Jews as: 'the scum washed to our shores in the dirty water flowing from foreign drainpipes'. He went on to extol 'racial purity' and hold forth about the unique and elevated qualities of the 'English race'.

In 1905 the Conservative government succeeded in getting an Aliens Act onto the statute book with the intention of controlling the influx of destitute immigrants. By 1910 immigration was in decline and a host of other issues facing Britain and her standing in the world edged immigration towards the bottom of the political agenda.

Chapter 8

London 1914–2000

A Tumultuous Century

The start of the twentieth century saw London at the height of its influence as the largest city in the world and capital of the largest empire in history. Between 1914 and 1918 London experienced the first aerial bombing which would be a precursor to more extensive and devastating bombing some twenty years later which left thousands dead and many homeless. In the interwar years London expanded in area and population as a suburban boom stretched into neighbouring counties. High-rise housing became a contentious issue and the skyline of central London was shaped by an increasing number of tall buildings in the latter part of the century. Protests and demonstrations, over both domestic and global issues, continued a long tradition. By the 1960s 'Swinging London' became the capital of fashion but this was followed by de-industrialization, which hit many industries, especially the docks. The old problem of congestion continued to worsen while a number of projects transformed London's transport networks: the M25, Channel Tunnel, Gatwick and Heathrow airports. Cultural life boomed, as did the diverse range of leisure activities. In typical and traditional style, the capital came through the upheavals, adapting and reinventing itself, as the world's greatest city.

London and the First Blitz

In 1914 London continued to be the most populous city in Europe with over seven million people, as well as the financial centre of the world. Unlike some cites in Europe that experienced social or political upheaval during the First World War such as Berlin (starvation), St Petersburg (revolution) or Paris, which was close to the conflict, the disruption to London was not on the scale of the Second World War. However, Jerry White claims (*Zeppelin Nights: London in the First World War*, 2015) that the First World War left a deep and lasting imprint on the city, and 'continued to have consequences down to the twenty-first century'.

When war was declared on 4 August 1914, London became the hub of total war. Enthusiastic volunteers queued in large numbers at the central Recruiting Office at Scotland Yard. The capital produced a large part of the nation's munitions where many women left domestic service to work in the armaments factories. Soldiers on their way to the front passed through London and many of the wounded were treated there. War created full employment as well as food shortages and it gave licence to the self-appointed moral guardians who were quick to clamp down on entertainments, drink and any other type of behaviour of which they disapproved.

Everyone was expected to do their patriotic duty in whatever measure possible. Even the popular 'must-have Christmas gift', the toy soldier, was accompanied by the boast that they were 'British-made'. In 1914 Gamages department store in Holborn advertised their 'Great Christmas Fair and War Tableaux' encouraging people not to 'forget the British Patriot's Wartime Motto, Buy as Usual', also adding, 'Bring the Children to see the Great Miniature Battle … English and Allies versus the German Army in our large toy hall', complete with 'field guns and Howitzers fired by real gunpowder, [with] trenches and barbed wire'.

Within weeks of the outbreak of war the government requisitioned over 300 buses and their crews for use in France and Belgium. In addition, some 1,300 London General Omnibus Company (LGOC) vehicles were sent abroad and around 2,500 LGOC drivers and conductors volunteered for the war effort, many having been in the 'special transport reserve'. The drain on transport meant there was a shortage of buses and drivers especially from 1916 when men were conscripted. There was also a return to horse-drawn buses in London, which had ceased in 1914.

In 1914 the Defence of the Realm Act (DORA) was introduced. This gave the government unprecedented powers to intervene in people's lives. Curfews, censorship and restrictions on movement were imposed whilst whistling for a London taxi was banned for fear it may be mistaken for an air-raid warning. DORA, along with the Aliens Restriction Act, limited the civil liberties of non-British-born subjects who had to obtain permits if they intended to travel more than five miles. Germans became enemy aliens at the outbreak of war and many feared internment, whilst those owning shops and businesses suffered sporadic looting and violent attacks on their shops. Over half the German population of England and Wales from the late nineteenth century lived in London with many of them well established in parts of the East and West End. Charlotte Street, north of Oxford Street, was the main West End thoroughfare of the German community and was referred to as 'Charlottenstrasse'.

Germanophobia went beyond persecuting people. There was a rooting out of all associations with Germany from surnames to sausages (Sainsbury's 'German Sausage' became the 'Luncheon Sausage'). Such hysteria persuaded King George V to change his name from Saxe-Coburg-Gotha to Windsor in 1917 and Prince Louis of Battenberg changed his name to Mountbatten. Pub signs were switched. The King of Prussia in Tooley Street became the King of Belgium, which proved quite apt as some 250,000 Belgian refugees came to Britain (90 per cent returned after the war) with about one-third settling in London. Newspapers poured out stories about German spies and demanded an intensification of internment. When a German torpedo sank the UK-registered ocean liner, the *Lusitania*, about eleven miles off Ireland, riots intensified. In London some 2,000 shops and properties were attacked. *The Manchester Guardian* of May 1915 reported that 'damage was especially extensive in the area near the East India Dock, where over sixty German shops have been attacked. Terrified Germans who were found hiding under beds, were thrown out into the street, beds and all'.

By 1917 London was under martial law, nightlights were darkened and, in a foreshadowing of the Second World War, anti-aircraft guns boomed out into the air. Britain was attacked from the sky for the first time, early in 1915.

Zeppelin aircarft bombed London between 1915 and 1918, killing 668 people. In September 1915 a single airship inflicted serious damage around Lincoln's Inn and in June 1917 Gotha bomber aircraft killed 162 people, including 18 children in Poplar.

A fervent recruiter for the war effort was Arthur Winnington-Ingram, Bishop of London from 1901 to 1939. He called on men 'to band in a great crusade ... to kill Germans. To kill them, not for the sake of killing, but to save the world; to kill the good as well as the bad; to kill the young men as well as the old'. His fervour did not please everyone including Prime Minister Herbert Asquith who described the bishop's comments as 'jingoism of the shallowest kind'. Winnington-Ingram was not alone among senior Anglican clergy in his bellicose rhetoric from the pulpit. There were others who saw the conflict as a holy war including the Archdeacon of Westminster and Chaplain to the House of Commons, Basil Wilberforce, who was possibly even more belligerent than Winnington-Ingram.

On 11 November 1918 an armistice was signed and hostilities on the Western Front ceased. The Cabinet Room at 10 Downing Street had been the nerve centre of Britain's war effort and it was here shortly before

11 o'clock that the Prime Minister, Lloyd George, made an appearance at one of the first-floor windows to tell an excited crowd: 'It is over! The war is won!' Celebrations took place throughout Britain and many parts of the world with huge crowds gathered in Trafalgar Square. The following year a temporary Cenotaph in Whitehall was erected for a peace parade and in 1920 it was replaced by a permanent structure, designed by Sir Edward Lutyens, as the United Kingdom's official national war memorial.

Between the Wars

The interwar years saw London grow in population and area. A suburban expansion extending beyond the boundaries of the old London County Council into surrounding Middlesex, Surrey, Kent, Essex and Hertfordshire, effectively became Greater London by 1939. (Greater London was officially created in 1965 when the traditional LCC definition of London was any area within fifteen miles of Charing Cross). London's population grew by three million reaching 8.7 million by the late 1930s but it was no longer unique. Other world cities were growing faster with New York reaching 11.6 million.

Suburban growth was a distinctive feature and far ahead of other capital cities. In 1915 the term 'Metroland' was coined by the Metropolitan Railway to describe a stretch of countryside north-west of London, marketed as a land of idyllic cottages. From the late nineteenth century to 1939 the population of the outer ring of London grew from just under one million to over four and a half million. This expansion brought with it the development of new houses, roads, tramways, rail links for commuters, and industries whose boundaries now stretched west from Hayes to Dagenham in the east, and south from Croydon to Enfield in the north. In addition, many important venues were located on the outskirts including the Empire Stadium in Wembley, opened in 1923 to hold the British Empire Exhibition in 1924.

As the capital's population grew, inner London experienced a net loss from its peak in 1901 of four and a half million to around half of that figure over the next eighty years, clearly reflecting a migration to the suburbs. Despite this shift central London saw many attractive developments including entertainment, shopping and building. Regent Street, which was rebuilt in the 1920s, was owned by the Crown Estate who stipulated that the buildings were to be dignified in scale and had to have stone-built facades. In keeping with its high-class requirements, the new Regent Street included department stores with plate-glass window displays, and a 1,400-seat cinema.

The West End saw an increasing American influence typified by shops (Selfridges 1909, Woolworth 1910), hotels, apartments and cinemas, which showed mainly Hollywood films. American influence had certainly had a huge impact on some of the grand hotels. William Waldorf Astor, 1st Viscount Astor, was inspired by the American tradition of offering not just rooms but a place for passers-by to stop for dinner, afternoon tea or a drink, when he established the Waldorf (1908) in Aldwych. Likewise, the impresario, Richard D'Oyly Carte, having seen the opulence of American hotels during his visits, was motivated to build the luxury hotel, the Savoy, on the Strand.

One of the most significant cultural developments of the twentieth century was film and the West End provided a natural home. Two of the earliest West End cinemas were in Soho, the Electric Cinema Theatre (named in 1909 by the Metropolitan Police as the 'worst' cinema in their district) and the National Bioscope. Not surprisingly Soho became associated with the film industry very early on with more than twenty film companies established on Wardour Street by the First World War. Production and distribution companies had offices there including Pathé News, Warner Brothers, Rank Organisation and Hammer Films – later Hammer House (named after William Hinds – stage name Will Hammer – after his home, Hammersmith), whilst nearby, Soho Square became the headquarters of the British Board of Film Classification (BBFC). By the late 1940s there were around 100 film companies on Wardour Street.

After the war bigger cinemas opened in the West End with decorative architecture, cafés, orchestra and the latest films. The Tivoli on the Strand took over from an old music hall, a practice that was occurring with many cinemas. The Odeon, which was part of the Oscar Deutsch empire (his publicity team claimed Odeon stood for 'Oscar Deutsch Entertains Our Nation') opened in Leicester Square in 1937. Also in Leicester Square, the old Empire Music Hall was rebuilt as the Empire in 1928 and had a capacity of around 3,300 seats, a Wurlitzer organ and was the first cinema in the UK to be fully air conditioned.

Wartime restrictions were lifted in 1921 when the Licensing Act replaced DORA and the new licensing laws established set times and restricted hours for opening compared to those before 1914. Drink was allowed until after midnight as long as it was accompanied by food. This led to many new luxury nightclubs with their glitzy, and often extravagant, décor opening in the West End. The Kit-Cat Club (1925) in Haymarket claimed to be the 'most luxurious Luncheon, Dinner and Dance Club in the World'. It became one of the most famous late-night haunts in London with a membership that included princes, cabinet ministers, dukes and peers. For its grand opening it featured the famous Dolly Sisters who had been appearing at the Moulin Rouge in Paris. Other clubs included the Cave of Harmony on Gower Street and the London Club, near Baker Street, which offered billiards (forty tables), cabaret, dining and dancing. Between 1920 and 1924 The Criterion in Piccadilly Circus with its Italian roof garden, became a favourite haunt of high society. The Trocadero, which opened in 1896 on the corner of Shaftesbury Avenue and Windmill Street, introduced cabaret in the mid-1920s and continued every night until the Second World War. Live music flourished and musicians from all over the world played in many of the London clubs.

In post-war London the Jazz Age blossomed. Associated with this was a set of young socialites, aristocrats and middle-class bohemians known as the 'Bright Young Things' who partied in many of the fashionable places in the West End. They were defined either by their irresponsibility or free-loving pleasure-seeking. At a time of economic recession with hardship looming, the idea of privileged young people living it up didn't impress everyone.

For those who could not afford the high-end nightclubs or parties there were many drinking clubs particularly around Soho and also the café culture which had grown out of the coffee houses from around 1900. The café provided a precursor to the milk bar, which first opened in Fleet Street in 1935 selling exotic milk 'cocktails' such as 'Bootleggers'. It was Hugh McIntosh, an Australian and ex-miner, who came up with the unlikely idea of having a milk bar in London. Whilst many thought the idea ridiculous, he soon opened a further eleven bars in the capital.

From the 1920s to the 1960s the dance hall was only second to the cinema in popularity for working-class people. The 'palais de dance' became the adopted name for modern dance halls with the Hammersmith Palais in 1919 marking the beginning of the boom. Working-class people could, for an affordable price, enjoy the luxury as well as the escapism. In 1919 it was reported that 'dancing establishments in London are crowded morning, noon, and night ... whilst dancing halls are booked up for months ahead' (*Dundee Evening Telegraph*). In 1928 the *New Survey of London Life and Labour* reported that 'dancing as an active recreation appeals to many people of all classes ... the dance-halls are within the range of nearly everybody's purse, and typists, shop assistants and factory girls rub shoulders in them'. The more expensive venues featured leading dance bands such as Ambrose and his Orchestra at the Mayfair Hotel and Jack Hylton at the Savoy Hotel.

Dance bands found a forum at the newly constructed Broadcasting House in Portland Place, north of Oxford Street. Opened in March 1932, the 1930s style building, redolent of a cruise ship, was described by the *Architectural Review* of 1932 as the 'new Tower of London'. Its first musical programme featured bandleader Henry Hall and the BBC Dance Orchestra. Others followed: Billy Cotton, Geraldo, Joe Loss and Jack Hylton became celebrities as the new medium of radio reached five million licences by the 1930s. The BBC was formed in 1922 by a group of leading wireless manufacturers including Marconi whose studio in the Strand was where daily broadcasting began. Two years later people heard for the first time a familiar sound that endures to the present day, the six electronically generated 'pips' to mark the start of every hour on BBC radio. By 1929 John Logie Baird was broadcasting some of his first experimental television broadcasts from studios near Covent Garden.

In 1926 the General Strike, which lasted nine days, took place. The Trades Union Council (TUC) was outraged by the government's intention of reducing miners' wages. Many industries came out in sympathy but there were also clashes between strikers and strikebreakers. Many of the latter included upper-class volunteers who treated the occasion as a lark. Reactions to the strike in London varied. Among those places most supportive were industrial areas, particularly the docks in east and south London, and inner boroughs. Public transport was disrupted with the tube closing and trams and buses hardly running apart from those operated by strikebreakers, as in the case of the London Omnibus Company, which had eighty-six buses driven by middle-class volunteers. A key industry was the docks and the government moved quickly to break the strike there. Troops, armoured cars and volunteers assembled in Hyde Park in order to escort lorries to the docks. Such a show of strength meant there was little the strikers could do as fighting broke out in Camden between pickets and police. Support for the strike was strong at King's Cross and Euston stations where everyone including women cleaners joined the strike. An attempt to drive the trains by incompetent strikebreakers backfired when the cylinder head blew off an engine. Violent fights took place in Southwark throughout the strike and in Tooley Street thirty-two people were arrested after a police baton charge.

Adding to the volatile atmosphere were right-wing mobs including the fascist group National Fascisti who supported the strikebreakers whilst a significant number of British Fascists joined the Organization for Maintenance of Supplies. The intervention by these embryonic groups was a foretaste to bigger showdowns to come. Ten years later, in 1936, a larger violent clash between the British Union of Fascists (BUF), led by Oswald Mosley, and anti-fascist groups erupted in what became known as the 'Battle of Cable Street' in the East End.

London Underground

In between these political events, Harry Beck, a technical draughtsman (1902–74), created the most recognizable diagrammatic transit map in the world (or schematic): what we now call the London Underground map. Born in Leyton, Beck drew the diagram in his spare time while working at the London Underground Signals Office. He based his idea on the circuit diagrams he drew in his job and showed the Tube network as a neat diagram of coloured, criss-crossing lines instead of emphasizing distance and geographical accuracy.

When Beck submitted his idea in 1931 the publicity department rejected it as it was thought to be too radical compared with previous designs. Harry persisted and resubmitted it the following year. This time his design was given a trial run of 500 copies and distributed to selected stations. In 1933 his design received full publication and proved to be enormously popular and did what it set out to do – convey information easily and effectively to commuters.

Unfortunately, Beck did not receive full recognition in his lifetime for his contribution. His name appeared in the bottom left-hand corner of the publication but London Transport claimed the copyright. Beck received a small bonus (believed to be just over £5) for his design. Recognition came after his death and his iconic 'map' has become a worldwide inspiration for designers.

Over the years London's Underground network has grown with the Jubilee line (opened 1979 and extended in 1999) thus bringing the number of underground stations to 270 (and counting). Further developments have included the Docklands Light Railway (DLR), the Elizabeth Line and the Northern Line extension to Battersea. Ninety years on Harry Beck's design remains the standard by which other metro maps are judged. The seventeenth-century illustrator Wenceslaus Hollar, best known for his topographical works, has been described as the man who drew London. There are many artists who could stake a claim to that accolade but at least Harry Beck can be credited as the man who drew London in the context of modern twentieth-century designs.

London could boast the world's first underground railway, opened in1863, with much of the central London network completed in the first fifty years through private initiatives. However, it was greatly expanded during the first half of the twentieth century, particularly with the changeover to electric trains. The Underground acted to 'pull together' the remarkably disparate collection of 'villages', which constitutes London. It stimulated and sometimes directly caused the growth of vast tracts of London's inner and more distant suburbia including, of course, Metroland so affectionately mocked by Sir John Betjeman (1906–84).

In 1933 the Underground as well as all of London's public transport, buses, trams and trolleybuses, came under public ownership, where decisions regarding services could be fully coordinated. The London Passenger Transport Board took control of sixty-one bus companies, seventeen tramways and five railway companies. It set about a programme of extensions to the tube system and modernization of rolling stock, stations and other facilities. In addition, it also created an immediately recognizable house style for the system, with close detail being paid to design issues as disparate as station architecture and the moquette used for seating.

Since the Second World War, new lines have been few and slow in coming. The Victoria Line (opened in 1968) and the Jubilee Line were both extended and have set new standards for automation. In 1999 the Jubilee Line was extended to London's Docklands, facilitating regeneration and the growth of the Canary Wharf business district. Controversially, maintenance of the infrastructure and rolling stock passed into private hands.

Without question the London Underground has had an enormous social, economic and cultural impact on the metropolis and has provided a ready means for people to get around quickly and easily, particularly in the central parts of London. It assisted the regeneration of areas of inner-city decay, for example, in the Bermondsey district of south-east London with the building of the Jubilee Line. It has given the world the immortal Beck's diagrammatic map of the system, a concept copied globally. It has expressed itself in stations of the highest architectural merit such as Park Royal and East Finchley and the monumental headquarters block of 55, Broadway with its sculptures by Henry Moore and Jacob Epstein. More modestly it has given us the distinctive glazed terracotta station fronts, the colour of oxblood, and the Art and Crafts faience work of the architect Leslie W. Green. These date from the 1900s and many of them can still be seen on the Bakerloo and Piccadilly lines. London Transport and particularly the Underground have created a constant demand for advertising and poster art of the very highest quality.

There are also a number of disused, or 'ghost' stations on the Underground. Aldwych (opened as the Strand Station in 1907) was formerly on the

Piccadilly Line as well as the terminus of a short branch from Holborn until it was closed in September 1994. It is well preserved and has been used as the location for TV and film productions. British Museum Station was located at Bury Place near the Museum and opened in 1900. With the opening of Holborn Station in 1906 less than a hundred yards away it was decided to combine the stations in 1933. During the Second World War platforms were bricked up to protect those sheltering from passing trains. Among former stations with substantial remaining evidence at street level are Aldwych, York Road, South Kentish Town and Brompton Road. Just visible from passing trains are parts of such stations as St Mary's (Whitechapel Road), York Road, British Museum and City Road.

On a more tragic note, the Underground has experienced a number of accidents, derailments, fires and terrorist attacks during its history. Two accidents in particular were responsible for a high number of fatalities. On 28 February 1975 the Northern City Line section of Moorgate Station was the scene of the worst ever accident involving a train on London's Underground. The reason why the disaster occurred has never been satisfactorily established. In the early morning a southbound train entered the terminal platform without showing signs of decelerating and crashed at about 40 mph into a thick concrete wall marking, literally, the end of the line. A massive rescue and recovery operation was launched, working in appallingly hot and confined conditions. It took over four days to bring all the bodies out. Forty-three people died and seventy-four were seriously injured. In November 1987 a large fire broke out in King's Cross St Pancras station killing thirty-one people from the toxic fumes and extreme heat of the blaze. The fire had been caused as a result of a discarded match or cigarette igniting debris and grease beneath the wooden escalators. This led to a more rigorous enforcement of the smoking ban on the Underground as well as the replacement of all wooden escalators.

The Approach of the Second World War

The First World War was to be the war that ended all wars. However, ominous signs of political instability lingered after 1918 in Europe. In the aftermath of the war over nine million people were made refugees with a diaspora of people finding new homes in other countries. In Britain the Aliens Act was passed in 1919, which obliged foreign nationals to register with the police and restricted where they could live as well as their employment rights. By the late 1920s, with rising unemployment, foreigners were banned from certain jobs including working for London County Council. German communities, persecuted during the Great War, left their locations, notably Fitzrovia. Many foreign communities existed across parts of London; for example, Jewish and Irish settlements could be found in the East End, Chinese in Limehouse, Italians in Clerkenwell, Holborn and later Soho. In fact, Soho provided homes for many groups including Greeks, Belgians, Russians, Africans and Indians.

The shadow of fascism that took hold in Germany, Italy and Spain found fragments of support elsewhere. It became a real and dangerous threat to foreign communities, especially Jewish, who were vulnerable to racist attacks. By the late 1930s more Jews sought refuge in Britain as persecution worsened in Germany.

On the eve of the Second World War London was the capital of the British Empire. It was remarkable that such a small area consisting of the West End as the seat of government and the City with its financial institutions accounted for so much of the world's wealth. In addition, there was the tonnage and trade that passed through its docks. However, the Blitz was to change not only Britain's global prestige but also so much of London's landscape. Thousands of tons of bombs rained down on the capital accounting for around 30,000 lives lost – nearly half of Britain's total civilian deaths for the whole war. Well-known landmarks were hit including Buckingham Palace and the Houses of Parliament. Some areas were so badly damaged they had to be rebuilt after the war.

War was declared on Germany on 3 September 1939 although preparations had been going on for some months. Most British adults had been issued with gas masks, families were encouraged to build air-raid shelters, blackouts were enforced, some 600,000 children were evacuated, there was a large-scale culling of cats and dogs, and sirens helped people to take to shelters. Resources for the war effort were vital, especially the need for iron and steel and most of the London squares did their duty by contributing their iron railings. Belgrave Square became a tank park, St James's Square was dug up and given over to vegetable growing, and air-raid shelters were built in Soho and Manchester squares. George Orwell, writing in 1944, felt strongly about the exclusive nature of the squares: 'When the railings round the parks and squares were removed, the object was partly to accumulate scrap-iron, but the removal was also felt to be a democratic gesture ... the public could stay in the parks till all hours instead of being hounded out at closing times by grim-faced keepers.'

Air raids were anticipated and so Air Raid Precautions (ARP) were put in place. Shelters varied from the Morrison, a cage-like construction erected in the house, and Anderson, a small and cheap shelter that could be erected in the garden. The latter was designed in 1938 and named after Sir John Anderson, Home Secretary, with the first Anderson shelter erected in a garden in Islington, in February 1939. Around Bermondsey and London Bridge the numerous railway arches acted as air raid shelters for thousands of residents. Londoners also flocked to the Underground stations in large numbers to escape the ferocity of the Blitz between 1940–1.

In the months that followed the declaration of war London remained relatively quiet. People started to drift back to the capital and many evacuated children were brought back home in this period known as the 'phoney war'. Within weeks of nothing happening cinemas, pubs, theatres and sporting events reopened. Dance bands played at West End clubs and hotels and New Year's Eve 1939 was celebrated at the Savoy. The Windmill Theatre in Soho, well known for its nude tableaux, carried on regardless through the war despite being bombed in 1940. Its famous motto, 'We never close', was humorously modified by others to 'We never clothed'.

However, this false dawn was about to change. From September 1940 until May 1941, Britain was subjected to a sustained enemy bombing campaign – the Blitz. In the late afternoon of 7 September 1940 ('Black Saturday' as it became known), over 300 German bombers advanced up the Thames estuary, targeting the docks in the first of fifty-seven consecutive nights of bombing. Although the raid initially came to a halt, it gave way to a heavy night attack lasting eight hours, which left the East End and parts of the City in flames as well as killing over 400 people. During September the Strand was bombed as were the shops on Oxford Street. On 13 September Whitehall and Buckingham Palace were hit (the latter on four separate occasions). Londoner Hilda Neal wrote in her diary, 'Bond Street and Park Lane bombed yesterday; much damage … but people are carrying on.' Conscious of the class disparities in the bombing the later Liberal Party Leader, Clement Davies, noted that 'Everybody is worried about the East End, where there is much bitterness … if only the Germans had had the common sense not to bomb west of London Bridge there might have been a revolution … As it is, they have smashed about Bond Street and Park Lane and readjusted the balance.'

In December Luftwaffe bombers dropped over 600 incendiaries over the City and the East End. The entire ward of Cripplegate was razed in firestorms, and destruction and damage were wreaked upon the Guildhall, fifteen Wren churches, Westminster Abbey, the Law Courts, the Tower of London, Southwark Cathedral, the General Post Office, BBC Broadcasting House, a number of railway stations, schools (which disrupted education) and St Paul's Cathedral. BBC's Broadcasting House suffered two direct hits, causing widespread damage, several deaths, and many injuries. On the night of 15 October 1940 millions of listeners heard live on air a bomb being dropped as the news was about to be read.

During the war the Tower of London continued its tradition of executions. Granted most of those executed there had been in earlier times and included notables such as Anne Boleyn, Thomas Cromwell, Thomas More and Archbishop of Canterbury William Laud. However, eleven people met their end at the Tower between 1914 and 1941. The last one was Josef Jacobs in August 1941. He was a German spy who was captured in a field at Ramsey in Huntingdonshire shortly after parachuting in. Wearing his flying suit, and carrying a radio transmitter, £500 in British currency and a German sausage, he was convicted of espionage, taken to the Tower where he was blindfolded, seated in a chair and shot by a firing squad.

The famous image of St Paul's Cathedral in flames came to symbolize the Blitz on London. Herbert Mason, chief photographer for the *Daily Mail*, took the photo on 29 December from the top of the *Mail*'s building whilst watching the fires across the City. He waited hours for the smoke to clear before getting his iconic photo. After some retouching and cropping out of surrounding buildings it was then published on the front page on 31 December. One of the German incendiary devices had lodged in the roof of the cathedral and when the lead of the dome began to melt, it dislodged the bomb, which fell to the floor of the Stone Gallery, allowing fire fighters to smother it with sandbags. Nearby in Fleet Street, St Bride's Church had a fire-bomb penetrate the roof and destroyed much of the interior of the church including the famous bells, which melted. It was by good fortune for Wren's spire, which reputedly inspired the modern wedding cake, that it survived.

Heavy bombing raids continued across London, with many incidents occurring in Southwark. On the night of 17 February some 300 people were taking shelter at an arch in Stainer Street near London Bridge Station, which had been converted into a shelter containing a medical aid post. At each end of the shelter was a pair of ten-ton steel doors. At 10.25 pm a high-explosive bomb exploded in the medical aid post, hurling the steel doors into the shelter. To add to the mayhem the water and hydraulic mains burst which contributed to 68 people being killed and 175 injured. Many had been crushed by the steel doors and were beyond recognition. A plaque on Stainer Street commemorates the bombing.

Southwark suffered heavily during the Second World War but attempts were made to keep businesses continuing as best as possible. This was the case around Borough Market and other makeshift spaces where growers from farms in Kent and Essex made their pitches and traded by the light of oil lamps in an area that backed onto Southwark Cathedral. Breakfasts could be had around Borough High Street, London Bridge Station and St Thomas Street at small cafés where a cup of tea and a sausage sandwich were a welcome relief. Nearby, Guy's Hospital suffered bomb damage, but still operated and remained open, treating over 3,000 air-raid casualties throughout the war.

An important part was played by the deep-level tubes during the Second World War, not only sheltering vast numbers of Londoners but also storing war supplies and valuable works of art. By October 1940 about seventy-nine tube stations were being used as shelters. Aldwych Station used the operational platform as a public air-raid shelter and the disused platform and tunnel to house some of the valuable artefacts from the British Museum including the Elgin Marbles.

The government was deeply reluctant about the use of underground stations, fearing the development of a 'deep shelter mentality'. Mass Observation (the social research organization founded in 1937) reported in April 1943 on a study of tube life that some families had 'established themselves permanently in the shelters, having abandoned their homes altogether. Children almost three years old had never spent a night at home'.

According to TfL (Transport for London) Corporate Archives Research Guides (World War II), the number of people sheltering by October 1940 was 124,000, with 2,750 at King's Cross alone. With numbers increasing as the months went on, the London Passenger Transport Board (LPTB) had to take control. Initially the priority was to make sure people left the stations before tube services resumed in the morning. By 30 November 1940, Westminster City Council became the first local authority to introduce the issuing of shelter reservation tickets which stipulated certain rules including: arrive after 1830, leave by 0700, don't stand in groups, keep away from the platform edge, control your children, take your rubbish home, cooperate with staff and when near a moving train stand still. In February 1941 sprays and compressors for aerial disinfection were provided with particular attention given to the elimination of mosquitoes. Hygiene was an issue and 'Elsan' chemical portable toilets were provided at shelters as well as buckets, although demand exceeded supply. For example, at Holborn there were just four Elsan toilets and four buckets for a station that could hold 4,600 people. Some 24,000 bunks were installed at various stations as well as cigarette machines and canteens, which provided a refreshments service, the first opening at Hyde Park station in October 1940.

Several stations were hit including Marble Arch (twenty killed), Trafalgar Square (seven killed), Bounds Green (nineteen killed) and Green Park Station and Sloane Square were damaged. Bank Station received a direct hit by a bomb in January 1941 which penetrated the road surface and exploded in an escalator machinery room killing fifty-six people and injuring sixty-nine. The huge crater left in the road had to be covered with a makeshift bridge to allow traffic to pass. At Balham Underground station a bomb fractured water and sewage pipes causing flooding, which led to the deaths of sixty-eight people.

The worst tragedy came in March 1943 when 173 people (twenty-seven men, eighty-four women and sixty-two children) were killed and ninety-two were injured in a crush whilst attempting to enter Bethnal Green Station in what is believed to be the largest loss of civilian life in the UK during the war. As the siren sounded at 8.17 that evening, hundreds of people ran to the Tube station where some 500 people were already sheltering. Ten minutes later loud noises outside panicked many who were entering the station; there was pushing, shoving and then a surge forward. A dimly lit staircase and wetness caused by rain during the day caused people to slip and within seconds over 300 men, women and children were crammed and crushed into the tiny stairwell. Rescuers found it almost impossible to help. In nearly all cases death was due to asphyxiation with virtually all dying within ten to fifteen seconds of being crushed. It was not until 1946 that a report was finally released. What caused the panic was the salvo of rockets fired from nearby Victoria Park by an experimental anti-aircraft weapon.

The Blitz lasted until May 1941 – 243 days of sustained air raids culminating in an all-out attack on 10/11 May. Over 500 bomber aircraft launched a devastating raid, killing over 1,400 people and seriously injuring 1,800. Severe damage was wreaked to railways, bridges and many famous landmarks. Ten thousand buildings were destroyed or badly damaged. In the Houses of Parliament, the Commons Chamber was hit, and the roof of Westminster Hall was set on fire. Thousands of tons of high explosives had been dropped on the capital. However, a brief respite from the bombing came as Germany turned its attention east to the Soviet Union. During the two-and-a-half-year period known as 'The Lull' there were sporadic raids on London but the intensity of the Blitz had ceased for the time being and daily life in London gradually started to improve.

During the Blitz, first-aid posts had been set up to deal with minor injuries, while overworked medical staff treated more serious injuries in bomb-damaged hospitals. Mortuaries were kept busy and children who had been orphaned had to be cared for. Damage to water pipes, cables and gas mains caused further disruption and danger with cases of people drowned whilst sheltering in cellars. As women were not allowed to join the Home Guard, the Labour MP, Dr Edith Summerskill, established an unofficial Women's Home Defence and by 1944 women were allowed to become Home Guard Auxiliaries.

Food rationing was introduced in January 1940 with the purpose of making sure there were fair shares for everyone during a time of national shortage. Items such as fruit and vegetables were not rationed and were often in short supply. Everyone was given a ration book with coupons; basic foods including meat, cheese and sugar were directly rationed whilst other items like tinned foods, dried fruit and biscuits were rationed according to a points system. There were priority allowances of milk and eggs, which were given to children and expectant mothers. Shortages increased and long queues formed, which led to a call for people to grow their own food, a scheme known as 'Dig for Victory'. Shortages also led to a black market, which gave rise to spivs as depicted in the *Dad's Army* character Private Walker, a romanticized cockney spiv. As raw materials were required for the war effort, it meant that other items were in short supply including clothing and furniture. Rationing continued after the war and eventually came to end in 1954.

The image created by the 'Blitz spirit' was one of endurance, getting through and all pulling together. There was no doubt that such a spirit genuinely brought many people together in a shared sense of struggle and hardship. However, the reality was more complex and varied over time and place. Home Secretary Herbert Morrison summed up the transition from fear to adjustment: 'After a few days the first horror of the raids wore off and people became adjusted to the new conditions of shelter life.'

There was also a darker side to the Blitz, as some saw opportunities to enrich themselves by taking advantage of the wartime restrictions. With the blackouts and people out finding shelter, criminals seized the opportunity to raid houses for valuables. A black market in many types of goods grew including the selling of coupons whilst some shopkeepers kept 'special' supplies under the counter. One particular scam during the Blitz was for thieves to dress up as an ARP warden and smash their way into shops. Some unscrupulous crooks used vehicles disguised as ambulances for their getaways. By the end of 1940 the number of cases for the despised activity of looting was over four thousand. Other contemptible crimes involved stealing jewellery and belongings from the victims of bombings. For example, in March 1941, the Café de Paris at Leicester Square was bombed, killing thirty-four people. Rescuers at the nightclub were shocked to find that looters were among them stealing brooches and rings from the bodies of those who had recently died. Other long-established practices continued. The 'Piccadilly Commandoes' could be mistaken for a volunteer force but it was a nickname given to prostitutes who plied their trade around Soho and catered for the needs of soldiers departing for the front.

One of the most sinister incidents came in the winter of 1942 when four women were murdered, three of them terribly mutilated, by a serial killer who came to be known as the 'Blackout Ripper'. The murders, along with two attempted attacks, were committed over six days in February by 27-year-old George Cummins, in the West End. His first victim, Evelyn Hamilton, was found dead in an air-raid shelter in Montague Place on 9 February. Over the next three days Cummins claimed three more victims: Evelyn Oatley in her flat in Wardour Street, Margaret Florence Lowe in Gosfield Street, Marylebone, and Doris Jouannet in her flat in Leicester Square. Cummins attacked two more women but they escaped and in so doing he left clues to his identity. He was arrested shortly after and his trial lasted just one day due to the overwhelming evidence against him, with the jury taking only thirty-five minutes to come to a decision. Cummins was hanged in Wandsworth Prison on 25 June 1942. Later it was shown that he had murdered two other women during air raids in London, in October 1941.

Air raids resumed between January and April 1944, in what became known as the 'Little Blitz' where London and south-east England came under attack in retaliation for the bombing of German cities. Targets included Westminster Hall, the Houses of Parliament, Embankment, Pimlico, Westminster Bridge and New Scotland Yard. Although victory beckoned with the D-Day landings in Normandy on 6 June 1944, London would have to suffer yet more deadly assaults. This time they came from over 3,000 highly destructive flying bombs, the V-Weapons or 'Doodlebugs' as they became known. The first one to hit London came on 13 June and struck Bow, East London, destroying nearby houses. These pilotless aircraft, which could travel up to 400 mph, made a buzzing noise, which stopped before they exploded. Long-suffering Londoners would have to put up with yet more danger and destruction.

During the V-1 campaign Croydon received many hits whilst the Guards' Chapel at Wellington Barracks, Westminster suffered one of the worst attacks when 119, mainly servicemen, were killed with more dying later. More Morrison shelters were issued and by July some 1,700 people had been killed and over a quarter of a million houses damaged or destroyed. Many places around Westminster were bombed between June and August with Pimlico receiving particular damage. A well-known photograph from the Imperial War Museum shows a police constable (PC Frederick Godwin) offering sympathy to an elderly man sitting on a pile of rubble. The man had just returned from taking his dog for a walk to find he had lost his wife and home to a V-1 flying bomb. More was to come.

Between September 1944 and March 1945 more than 1,000 V-2s (the world's first ballistic missile) were launched against London. Discharged from Europe, the V-2 could strike the capital without warning in five minutes. On 8 September the first V-2 struck Chiswick, killing three people. In London most landed in the East End but they also hit Westminster, Marylebone and Hyde Park. One eyewitness noted that 'with these things [V-2s] you get no notice. They come like bolts from the blue ... they travel faster than sound ... if you hear the bang, you are out of danger'. The attacks continued through the winter and in March 1945 129 died in a strike on Smithfield Market. However, the attacks were nearing the end; some 90 per cent of the casualties from V-2s had been in London. Despite the thousands of deaths, injuries, traumas, hardships, homelessness and destruction, London and its people had not been bombed into submission.

The war ended on 8 May 1945, designated Victory in Europe Day (VE Day). Although there was much rebuilding to be done that would wait a little longer. There was euphoria and rejoicing as spontaneous celebrations took place all over the country. Large gatherings attended services at St Paul's Cathedral, while thousands assembled in the West End. Prime Minister Winston Churchill met the King at Buckingham Palace and later broadcast a victory speech to the nation. There was a proliferation of Union Jacks as people waved and displayed them in the streets and outside their houses. The *Daily Mail* reported: 'London, dead from six until nine, suddenly broke into victory life last night. Suddenly, spontaneously, deliriously. The people of London, denied VE Day officially, held their own jubilation,' whilst *The Times* commented that after six years of blackouts, 'Large bonfires ringed London and most public buildings were floodlit'.

The following day was a public holiday and the celebrations continued. In the days and weeks that followed parades took place. On 10 June King George VI addressed former Civil Defence workers in Hyde Park. Londoners gradually adjusted to the realization that the disruption and suffering had come to an end although the war continued in the east. When that conflict ended in August 1945 there were more celebrations for the Victory over Japan (VJ Day). Now the serious issue of rebuilding and rehousing thousands of people had to take place.

Post-war Visions

The Second World War took a huge toll on London, accounting for almost 30,000 deaths and a further 50,000 seriously injured. More than 20,000 bombs had fallen on the capital, destroying or damaging beyond repair 116,000 buildings and an estimated one million houses as well as famous landmarks and irreplaceable historic buildings. We have a reliable record of where bombs were dropped as they were recorded and mapped for London County Council.

In the aftermath of war, London's landscape was peppered with bombsites, many of which were put to various uses. Several parks were developed from such bomb sites whilst others were used to bury the bombed debris. An unexploded bomb was found in Hyde Park as late as 2018. Carparks were created from some of the craters. The NCP, the UKs largest and longest-standing private carpark operator, saw the potential for developing such sites. In Red Lion Square, Holborn, they bought a bombsite for £200 and converted it into a carpark in 1948.

However, greater plans had to be drawn up for rebuilding London, as after the Great Fire of the seventeenth century. The Greater London Plan 1944, sometimes referred to as the Abercrombie Plan after Patrick Abercrombie (1879–1957), professor of town planning at the University of London, had been prepared as a blueprint for reconstruction after the war. Included in the plans was a more careful definition of the 'Green Belt'. In addition, there were plans to build inexpensive flats in the West End as well as the redevelopment of the South Bank as a cultural centre.

The General Election of 1945 saw the Labour Party win a landslide victory, taking forty-eight out of sixty-two seats in London. Labour were committed to making social and economic changes, including a comprehensive system of social welfare especially the creation of the National Health Service, and a National Insurance Act that provided sickness and unemployment benefits for adults. Retirement pensions and a large house-building project intended to provide millions of people with high-quality homes, were also part of their programme of reforms.

An area in the City of London faced with reconstruction was between Moorgate and Aldersgate, which had been flattened in just one night of bombing. Out of the ashes eventually came the Barbican, Europe's biggest reconstruction project. The Barbican, located on the north of what was once Roman Londinium, shows remains of the old London Wall. Another part of the wall can be seen in an underground car park (Bay 52) near the Museum of London.

Discussions about what sort of redevelopment should take place began in 1952 although work did not start for quite a few years. Built between 1971 and 1982, the Barbican Centre comprises two theatres, a concert hall, a library, an art gallery, three cinemas, a conservatory, offices, restaurant, shops and foyers. In 2001 the Barbican Centre became a Grade II-listed building. Adjacent to the Centre and part of the complex is the Barbican Estate, an upmarket residential complex of around 2,000 flats and houses.

Uniquely placed in the Barbican is the church of St Giles Cripplegate, which stands surrounded by parts of the London Wall, a bastion, a lake, the Museum of London and a residential housing complex. St Giles is one of the few remaining medieval churches in the City of London despite suffering a number of fires in 1545, 1897 and devastating bombing during the Blitz. A Norman church of 1090 stood on this site. The church has many famous associations including Oliver Cromwell, John Milton, John Foxe and Sir Martin Frobisher.

In 1948 London held the Olympic Games for the second time, which became known as the 'Austerity Games' owing to the difficult post-war economic climate. No new venues were built and the games took place mainly at Wembley Stadium. Three years later, in an attempt to lift the spirits of the nation the Festival of Britain was held in the summer of 1951, attracting more than eight million visitors. The idea for an exhibition of British products and design had been suggested during the Second World War. 1951 was an appropriate date to embrace the Festival as it coincided with the centenary of the Great Exhibition. A twenty-seven-acre site on the South Bank, which had fallen into dereliction, provided the location for the Festival. One of the most notable features on the site was the Royal Festival Hall, the first public building to be built in London after the war (it was also the first post-war building to be awarded a Grade I listing).

A series of pavilions displayed Britain's achievements as well as the largest dome in the world (at the time), standing 93 feet tall with a diameter of 365 feet, which held exhibitions on the theme of discovery. Further west Battersea Park became home to the fun-fair section of the Festival. Over 2000 events took place in many cities and towns across the country, which proved popular. The Festival ran from May to September, and although it had its detractors, few pretended that the Festival of Britain would have an enduring or international significance. For most it was seen as light-hearted, enjoyable and not too serious. Its intention was, as stated by the festival director, Gerald Barry, to be 'a tonic for the nation'.

Smog

The term 'pea-souper', a very thick, yellowish or black fog caused by air pollution, was particular to London for centuries. In 1871, *The New York Times* noted that 'the population [of London] are periodically submerged in a fog of the consistency of pea soup'. Fogs were not unique to Britain but they became much worse with the Industrial Revolution when factories and coal fires emitted large volumes of gases into the air. These emissions worsen when mixed with water and air causing polluted fog or smog, which in turn leads to breathing problems. November and December of 1952 had been very cold and by 5 December Londoners were huddled around their coal fires trying to keep warm. Smoke from the chimneys would normally disperse into the air but an anticyclone hovered over the capital, trapping the pollution close to the ground. This led to a toxic sulphurous blanket forming, which enveloped London for the next four days, causing chaos and thousands of deaths. In the absence of a wind to disperse the soot-laden smog, a noxious air mass reeked of rotten eggs.

Pedestrians could only see a few metres ahead and in many cases could barely see their feet. Many wheezed their way around covering their mouths and noses from the toxic air. People spoke of having to hold on to buildings in order to navigate their way. River traffic on the Thames came to a halt, as did flights and trains. Vehicles were abandoned as it became impossible to see and conductors had to walk ahead of the bus with a torch. Many services were cancelled, including ambulances, leaving people to walk to hospital. *The Manchester Guardian* of 9 December reported that lamp posts had 'become invisible ... The city police have put on their white coats again for the hazard of point duty ... The smash and grab men are harvesting fast ... motoring along Fleet Street and the Strand is a black nightmare at walking pace'.

Despite the disruption there was no sense of panic. London was used to fog. However, as the smog retreated some four thousand people had died according to official estimates while recent research suggests that it may have caused as many as 12,000 deaths. Public pressure was exerted on government to deal with any further problems, although the government's reaction was sluggish. They claimed the high death toll was a result of a flu outbreak and it took some months before an inquiry was ordered. A series of laws was introduced to avoid a repeat of the situation, including the Clean Air Acts of 1956 and 1968, which banned emissions of black smoke and decreed that there must be a conversion to smokeless fuels.

However, the transition away from coal took years; meanwhile deadly fogs periodically occurred.

In the months preceding and following the Great Smog was the accession (February 1952) and coronation of Queen Elizabeth II (June 1953). The coronation, held in Westminster Abbey, was the first to be televised, thus prompting millions of people to watch and listen to the event. People shared the occasion with those who had TVs while many others bought or rented TV sets (later surveys based on sales etc., suggest that for each TV showing the coronation, an average of seventeen people were watching). Street parties were held and the streets were packed with people waiting to see the processions, notably the Royal procession which wound its way round the West End from Buckingham Palace to Whitehall.

Swinging Sixties

Historian Roy Porter commented that the war had one beneficial effect: 'it dynamited some of the stuffiness of the capital's traditional cultural life.' He was referring to a largely male, loosely aristocratic and establishment world associated with the West End clubs, as well as Bloomsbury with its refined and raffish literary set and Soho with its bohemian culture of jazz and poetry. As the 1950s gave way to the 1960s, the post-war baby boomers were coming of age to benefit from the growth in the range of consumer goods. Coupled with more disposable income and the abolition of National Service in 1960, they could enjoy the music, fashions and culture that defined the decade. The editor of *Vogue* magazine wrote in 1966, 'London is the most swinging city in the world.' Similarly in the same year *Time* magazine ran a feature with the headline, 'London: The Swinging City' on its cover. *Time*'s feature was accompanied by images that were assumed to represent 'swinging London': a red Routemaster bus, a disco, Big Ben, a Mini (car), a female model with Union Jack sunglasses dressed in a miniskirt, and even Prime Minister Harold Wilson making an appearance. It was as though London had moved from its dark post-war days to become a place of colour and excitement with a changed identity. It was now home to some of the biggest style icons and models, notably Jean Shrimpton and Twiggy.

Paris had been the centre of the fashion industry with haute couture garments but that was about to change. A combination of youth and affluence created a demand and taste for fashions. Boutiques sprang up in Carnaby Street, Soho and King's Road in Chelsea. Thanks to shops like Lady Jane, Lord John, and The Mod Male, Carnaby Street was constantly packed with young people. Glaswegian, John Stephen (1934–2004) became known as the 'King of Carnaby Street'. In 1967 he and his partner Bill Franks, were responsible for a chain of fifteen shops in this fashionable street leading Stephen to boast, 'Carnaby is my creation.' Designer Mary Quant, whom the *Sunday Mirror* dubbed the 'most successful young fashion designer in the world,' opened her small shop, Bazaar, in 1955 in the bohemian King's Road, Chelsea. She was credited with popularizing the iconic miniskirt and hot pants. Quant said she named the skirt after her favourite car – the Mini.

The influence of London fashions during the 1960s was significant and proved to be an enduring legacy on later styles from mods to punk and beyond. Discos and nightclubs also flourished. Discothèques, a Parisian import from the early 1960s, proved popular. Jazz singer and writer George Melly described the Saddle Room in Mayfair as the 'most fashionable discotheque in London'. By the 1970s more live music venues sprang up in pubs, halls and clubs with places like Camden establishing a reputation for the diverse range of gigs on offer, from folk and rock to jazz.

Changes

In the sixties, big ships were still docking in the old Pool of London as far as London Bridge but the skyline was changing. The old towers and buildings would give way to even taller ones and glossy developments would appear along the riverside. Once there had been cranes, barges, timber yards, tanning yards, warehouses, a large vinegar manufacturer, at least two large breweries, hatters, hawkers, drapers, porters, labourers, a 'skin market', factories that made soap, lead and patent medicines and of course a whole variety of river occupations. Famous names with manufacturing premises at the riverside included Hartley's jams, Peek Freans, Oxo and Spillers. These were all major employers for much of the twentieth century. Raw materials for many of these industries were unloaded at the wharves just below London Bridge along Tooley Street.

It was during the 1960s that significant industrial changes started to take place. Docklands is an area along the River Thames covering around nine square miles of riverfront, centred on the boroughs of Tower Hamlets, Southwark, Lewisham and Greenwich. Much of Docklands had experienced heavy bombing during the war and hadn't fully recovered from that devastation. The capital's port facilities were superseded by operations at Tilbury, which became one of Europe's largest container ports. Large container ships and tankers were to dominate freight shipping and were also threatening to create redundancies. By 1967 the upper docks were declining and the Port of London Authority (PLA), whose operations cover ninety-five miles of the Thames, from Teddington to the North Sea, sold off stretches of the riverside including St Katherine Docks, where a hotel, yachting marina, restaurants and apartments were built. Shortly after, twelve miles of docks from Waterloo Bridge to Woolwich came up for grabs. By the 1970s changes in transportation brought redundancies and signalled the decline of the docks. Warehouses were left empty and places in East London became derelict.

From 1981 the London Docklands Development Corporation (LDDC, an urban development corporation that operated between July 1981 and March 1998 to secure the regeneration of the London Docklands) was invested with a large degree of planning. The LDDC had extensive powers to purchase and sell land compulsorily. Much of the land they gained, which had previously been public property, was sold to private developers at knockdown prices. Vast amounts of speculative capital and property developers with prestige constructions led to a transformation of the Docklands landscape around a huge expanse of mud and concrete that was turned into a high-rise skyline of glass and steel. Land prices soared from £70,000 per acre in 1981 when the LDDC was set up to around £4 million within six years. Little wonder that north Southwark became a dream for property developers.

An alternative spin on these changes was presented in 1987 when Nicholas Ridley, then Minister for Environment boasted: 'Take a trip around London Docklands and see what has happened. In five years, it has been transformed from a desert of dereliction to a showpiece of British building, design, architecture and business. It has created thousands of jobs by stimulating private enterprise. Homes have been built and refurbished [*Listener* 3 December 1987].'

On both sides of Docklands, the river witnessed the transition of wharves into apartment blocks, disused jam factories into converted chic, riverside loft-living accommodation along with restaurants and high-rise office complexes. These developments reflected a stark contrast between those who occupied these conversions and locals living in the social housing of the old London County Council flats that remained. Docklands were regenerated economically but not socially. A 1996 survey found at least half of the population did not reap any benefits from the millions of pounds poured in. Traditional working-class areas like the Borough saw the local community destroyed in a short period as local shops and homes along Borough High Street were turned into office developments. Throughout most of the 1990s no council housing was built in Southwark. Regeneration, it seems, often led to gentrification.

It wasn't just the docks that suffered from decline. De-industrialization saw London suffer more than any other UK city. The 1960s and 1970s witnessed an increase in factory closures and job losses as old established industries from soap making, electrical engineering and brewing to gasworks and vehicles shut down. Even the old glass company, Whitefriars, established in 1680 in the City before moving was closed down in 1980. Fleet Street, synonymous with newspapers, was still dominant in 1970 but over the next fifteen years it disappeared from the famous location. In the mid-1980s media magnate Rupert Murdoch moved the production of his papers, *The Times*, *Sunday Times*, *News of the World* and *The Sun*, to a non-union plant at Wapping. It was not long after Murdoch's exodus that other newspapers embraced the changes and vacated Fleet Street to locations in east London.

Another historic location that faced demolition was Covent Garden. It was becoming apparent as early as the 1920s that the famous piazza was becoming too congested for wholesale trading. By the late 1960s Covent Garden was suffering severe traffic congestion, which made distribution almost impossible. Hopes of redeveloping the area were restricted because the buildings surrounding Covent Garden were protected. In the 1970s, as the market moved to Nine Elms near Battersea, a public outcry and campaign mobilized to save the area. 'The Battle to Save Covent Garden' was a fine example of how people took on the powers-that-be against the odds and won. A plan drawn up by the then Greater London Council (GLC), under Conservative control (until 1973), intended to demolish much of Covent Garden and Seven Dials and with it some treasured cultural landmarks in order to make room for high-rise office blocks, conference centres and hotels. A group of campaigners, who later became the Covent Garden Community Association, began to organize against the GLC's plan. After languishing for some time, the central building re-opened as a shopping centre in 1980, establishing it as one of the busiest tourist attractions with cafés, pubs, craft market, restaurants and a variety of small shops.

Gentrification

Gentrification was a term that gained increasing use from the late twentieth century. The process of changing the character of a place via the influx of more affluent residents has a very long history. In 1964 sociologist and urban planner Ruth Glass coined the word gentrification (*London: Aspects of Change*), deliberately tongue-in-cheek, as a description for this process. She used the term to describe what she saw happening in certain areas of inner London, notably the borough of Islington, a predominantly working-class area, where young professionals were re-appraising the Georgian terraces and squares with a view to refurbishing them. She noted that stretches of the city, from Notting Hill to Islington, were losing their working-class character and becoming susceptible to only those who could afford to live there. Conversion of older houses into flats increased in the 1980s as property developers saw lucrative profits to be made and by the end of the decade such conversions were the single largest source of new dwellings in London. On the Monopoly board, first released in the 1930s, the Angel Islington square had a board price of £120 whilst in 2021 the average price of property was £784,836 according to SDL Property Auctions.

Inner city gentrification is not unique to London and is widely recognized as an international phenomenon. Gentrification has made victims of many working class, black and ethnic minority Londoners. Rather than benefit from artisanal bars and shops, they have found themselves displaced from their communities whilst those who reap the rewards are the very wealthiest of Londoners. Riverside developments in other cities have seen some of the highest levels of gentrification. In London developments in many former industrial zones have been redeveloped often as large-scale apartment blocks with notably high values in Woolwich and the Isle of Dogs. Further west, land in Fulham, Battersea and Brentford has been developed.

Central London has a population of mainly affluent people hence it is less vulnerable to wealthy incomers. However, some areas are ripe for gentrification including Southwark and Tower Hamlets. In May 2021 the *Evening Standard* reported that Tower Hamlets, Wandsworth and Newham had experienced the most gentrification of any of the London boroughs between 2010 and 2016.

A slice of London identity that sadly started to decline in numbers was the greasy spoon café. A number of newspaper articles appeared by the turn of the millennium lamenting how independent cafés were being pushed out and were slowly vanishing from the streets of London, subsumed as giants Starbucks, Costa and Café Nero spread, providing fierce competition and driving rents beyond the reach of smaller independent operators. Formica tables with edges worn away, fry-ups, mugs of tea, slices of toast, glass sugar dispensers, red and brown sauce bottles had a familiar appeal and were shared by so many from builders to bankers. Tastes and changes in food over recent years have also contributed to this decline and the greasy spoons have had to compete with the likes of smashed avocado on toast. Fortunately, some greasy spoons can be still sought out from Westminster to Borough High Street where a full value-for-money, all-day English breakfast can be enjoyed.

A defining landmark of the West End is Piccadilly Circus, one of the most famous road junctions in the world, as well as being synonymous with traffic and noise. For many visitors it is one of those memorable, welcome-to-London sights on ascending from the underground station in the evening and seeing the lights and bustle of traffic and people. It also featured in the introduction to the long-running radio series *In Town Tonight*. Beginning in 1933, this programme ran until 1960 and from 1955 was simultaneously broadcast on television to the accompaniment of the 'Knightsbridge March', composed by Eric Coates. Changes to the busy intersection of Piccadilly Circus had been mooted in the 1960s and 1970s with the aim of improving traffic flow. In the 1980s redevelopment work took place in order to increase pedestrianization hence the famous fountain was moved southward, which increased public access with the result of looking more like an urban square or piazza. In addition, the advertising screens are now more scaled down compared to the number that covered the surrounding buildings and bombarded vehicles and pedestrians with multiple messages.

Protest – Peaceful and Violent

London's long tradition of riots and protests continued in the 1960s and 1970s around issues such as apartheid and the Vietnam War. Resistance to the war in Vietnam had been gaining attention on American college campuses from 1965 and within two to three years many cities were supporting the movement. In March 1968, some 10,000 people protested in Trafalgar Square before marching to the United States Embassy in Grosvenor Square. Clashes ensued with more than 200 people arrested and fifty taken to hospital including twenty-five police officers. Also in the early 1970s, the first Gay Pride marches took place in London and at the same time the Women's Liberation Movement held a series of marches through central London demanding equal pay.

Other protests included the right to work and right to take industrial action, notably in support of the dockers who went on strike in 1972. The Civil Rights movement in the US inspired black Londoners who felt increasingly vulnerable from racist attacks and intimidation from the right-wing National Front. After the Second World War immigration reflected our imperial past when migrants from the West Indies, Africa, India and

Pakistan settled in particular areas including Brixton, Notting Hill, Southall and Camden. Racial tensions flared during the 1980s notably in Brixton and Broadwater Farm, North London.

Terrorist attacks on London by Irish republicans had occurred since the 1860s and intermittingly in the 1930s and 1940s. These attacks became more sustained throughout the last decades of the twentieth century. The Provisional IRA emerged in December 1969, as a result of a split within the IRA and the broader republican movement. In March 1973 the Provisional Irish Republican Army conducted its first operation in England, planting bombs in a number of places including the Old Bailey and Whitehall. Central London fell victim to further attacks, notably in July 1982, which saw four soldiers killed in Hyde Park, and seven bandsmen in Regent's Park. Further atrocities occurred in December 1993 when six people were killed whilst Christmas shopping at Harrod's. Financial institutions in the City were targeted in the 1990s with explosions at the Baltic Exchange, St Mary Axe (1992), killing three people, injuring ninety-one others and severely damaging the building and surrounding area. Following these attacks security systems were put in place, dubbed the 'ring of steel', consisting of checkpoints and CCTV cameras staffed by police. High levels of security became a familiar feature in parts of London vulnerable to acts of terrorism, particularly from Islamist groups in the following century.

The 1980s proved fertile ground for the coming together of protests and music as punk took off, and bands expressed anger at the government and the lack of economic opportunities. Large-scale fund-raising concerts were organized to raise money for poorer regions of Africa, notably Live Aid at Wembley, which featured many leading bands. With the election of Margaret Thatcher's Conservative government in 1979 came the privatization of a number of government-run industries. Protests continued throughout much of the decade culminating in the introduction of the Community Charge ('Poll Tax') in 1989. In addition, the GLC (the main local government administrative body for Greater London from 1965 to 1986) was dissolved, which led to the management of London's services falling to the local boroughs or Parliament. This situation remained until the creation of the Greater London Authority in 2000.

From Big Bang to Millennium Dome

The City of London was transformed during the 1980s in what became known as the 'Big Bang', a reference to the deregulation of the stock market designed to create new wealth for the capital. How London benefitted from these changes is debatable. It certainly increased jobs in the financial sector and the annual turnover of shares traded through London rocketed. On the other side, according to Martin Vander Weyer, business editor of *The Spectator* and former investment banker, the Big Bang 'destroyed job security and collegiate trust and made millionaires of some very undeserving people ... it encouraged ill-conceived takeover deals ... while doing nothing to protect or boost the savings and pensions of ordinary people'.

Whatever the opinions, the 'Big Bang' did have a visible impact on the City with the construction of new mega-offices. Lloyd's Building was opened in 1986 and Tower 42, more commonly known as the NatWest Tower, formally opened in 1981. Standing at 600 feet, the NatWest Tower was considered to be the first London skyscraper. Ten years later One Canada Square in Canary Wharf came along. It was clear that the new buildings were not easily accommodated within the confines of the old City hence a number of firms moved east to the Isle of Dogs. However, some traditional financial institutions remained, including the Bank of England and the Mansion House. The London Stock Exchange moved to new premises in Paternoster Square in 2004 as the old exchange became redundant mainly with the deregulation of the Big Bang. New computer systems and dealing rooms were needed but the Stock Exchange, which was established in 1571, continues its presence in the City.

If London had been the 'capital of swing' in the 1960s it became the capital of 'cool' in the 1990s. In 1996 *Newsweek* magazine described London as 'the coolest place on the planet'. What invited such attention? Changes had been taking place including a lessening of the IRA bombings as a result of the Good Friday Agreement and a new period of peace. A 'New Labour' Government was elected in 1997, ending thirteen years of Conservative rule, and were quick to embrace the idea of 'Cool Britannia'. Architectural and cultural developments were taking place, as was the growth of clubbing particularly around Smithfield and Southwark. The Eurotunnel, which opened in 1994, gave central London a faster connection to Europe as well as an increase in younger visitors. There was a large influx of international money coming to the capital and tourist locations now included Notting Hill and Camden.

Also in the 1990s, London's dining scene transformed with the opening of high-profile restaurants like Planet Hollywood where Londoners were prepared to spend on eating out, even if some of it was on overpriced burgers. Nonetheless, there had been a rediscovery of local produce and entrepreneurs who could make their names as celebrity chefs were opening restaurants on a regular basis. Long-established restaurants like the Ivy, which opened in 1917 on West Street in the West End, was transformed by two ambitious restaurateurs in the late 1980s to become one of London's most famous restaurants. According to Peter Harden (with his brother Richard founders of the restaurant guide, *Harden's*), the 'big restaurant groups came to dominate the top end of the London restaurant scene' in the 1990s. However, he adds, that trend began to change drastically and the independents fought back.

There is always a flip side with London. Expensive restaurants and lifestyles were beyond the reach of many. Unemployment was high in certain areas as was homelessness and crime. Soaring house prices made it difficult for the less well off. In 1990 the average price for a house in London was £84,000; by the end of the century it was £164,000 and rising. Put into context, average house prices in the UK increased in the twenty-year period since 1996 by 281 per cent whilst in London the figure was 501 per cent.

It's probably fitting that the chapter should almost end with a comment for bibliophiles. In 1998 the British Library was opened by the Queen at its new premises (listed a Grade I building in 2015) on the north side of Euston Road between Euston Station and St Pancras. Estimated to hold over 170 million items, including books, journals, manuscripts, maps, newspapers, magazines, prints and drawings, sound recordings and music scores, it is one of the largest libraries in the world.

The twentieth century ended with a huge fireworks display on the River Thames including what was called the 'River of Fire' and, more controversially, the opening of the Millennium Dome. Up to three million people gathered to see the River of Fire launch 200-feet-high flames above the water and shooting along the river from Tower Bridge to Vauxhall Bridge. Many were disappointed, stating that the flames went up maybe about fifty feet high but were then instantly overtaken by the fireworks display. The organizers insisted that the River of Fire was lit and it did travel down the Thames as planned. Despite this the criticism was not as strong or on the scale as it was for the Millennium Dome. The Dome was not helped from the start when thousands of VIPs who were invited to celebrate the New Year were made to queue for an hour in the cold as security checks took place at Stratford tube station. One of the many criticisms of the Dome was that no one could decide what it or the festival was about, or make sense of what was in it. Nonetheless, one favourable review came from the *Daily Telegraph* columnist Boris Johnson who said he would eat his hat if it wasn't a triumph (Rowan Moore, *The Guardian* 1/12/19).

Chapter 9

Twenty-first-century London

From Promises to Pandemic

At the beginning of the new millennium the London Plan of 2004 (a regional planning document first published in 2004) boasted that London was Europe's financial capital and the world's most culturally diverse city. There was a mood of optimism about economic growth and wealth-creating opportunities.

The first two decades of the twenty-first century saw London's population increase to 8.8 million people (officially surpassing its 1939 population peak), a multitude of building projects were undertaken, notably in the City, and property went up in both price and height. Property development made housing unaffordable for many as well as displacing people from their native city. There were huge developments in rail transport, as well as an attempt to reduce the volume of traffic and pollution by the introduction of a congestion charge in 2003. In 2012 London became the first city to host the Olympic Games three times with Stratford in East London the chosen site. In 2016 Sadiq Khan became London's first Muslim to be elected as Mayor of London (re-elected in 2021). The new century also brought tragedy with brutal terrorist attacks and a devastating pandemic.

Reshaping the Landscape

From its Roman foundations London's landscape went through many changes as well as a degree of continuity. A medieval street plan consisting of winding alleys, and marketplaces was one legacy and the rebuilding after the Great Fire was another. Georgian London witnessed the planning of elegant squares and the expansion of the suburbs, a process that continued into the twentieth century. So much of what we understand as London was a creation of the Victorian era and this was reflected especially in the huge public works and building schemes and railway developments. Wars devastated many parts of the capital in the twentieth century, which led to a large-scale rebuilding programme in the post-war period. A defining feature of the London skyline in the twenty-first century has been the proliferation of tall (perhaps super-tall) towers. The City, whilst the oldest part of London, looks the newest when viewed from Bankside.

In the late twentieth century architect Richard Rogers campaigned for the City to be 're-energized by enlightened architecture'. He proposed that the underused resource of the River Thames should be regenerated, an idea that appealed to London Mayor Ken Livingstone who made Rogers an advisor. A promise was made that a hundred public spaces would be formed as well as proposals for the construction of tall buildings. An important consideration in such projects was protecting the views of St Paul's Cathedral, the Tower of London and the Palace of Westminster. As the Tower and the Palace of Westminster are World Heritage Sites (not St Paul's Cathedral), the UK government has an international obligation to protect them although UNESCO has made complaints to the UK government for allowing the construction of tall buildings near these sites.

In 2000 Ken Livingstone became the first elected Mayor of London. He had shown a fondness for tall buildings but was criticized by Boris Johnson who said he would oppose the creation of a 'Dubai on Thames'. That was before Johnson was elected to the office of Mayor in 2008. He then became a convert, leaving a legacy for the record number of applications for tall buildings during his period in office (2008–16). On an international scale, London lags far behind many major cities in the number of tall buildings and is unlikely to turn into Shanghai or Dubai on Thames any time soon, although that may be little consolation to those that oppose such structures.

International cities began building skyscrapers in the 1880s but London did not follow as enthusiastically. In fact, Londoners referred to them as 'tall buildings,' meaning buildings of at least twenty storeys. The first decade of the twenty-first century saw London become, arguably, the pre-eminent international city for ambitious architecture. One of the early buildings was the 'Gherkin'. Located in the the City, 30 St Mary Axe, nicknamed the 'Gherkin' (much to the annoyance of its owners), was completed in 2003 and became a recognizable landmark as well as London's first ecological tall building. Its origins go back to 1992 when an IRA explosion damaged the Baltic Exchange, which had to be torn down. It was decided to build a larger tower in its place and construction began in 2001. Whilst tall buildings have not always been to the liking of many, the 'Gherkin' proved to be more acceptable and liked more than most. However, it soon became dwarfed by other projects. More tall buildings followed including the 'Cheesegrater' (122 Leadenhall Street), 70 St Mary Axe (the 'Can of Ham'), Heron

(Salesforce Tower, 110 Bishopsgate), 22 Bishopsgate (Twentytwo or the Pinnacle), Strata SE1 and 20 Fenchurch Street ('The Walkie-Talkie').

'The Walkie-Talkie' experienced some unfortunate teething problems when, in 2013, the light reflecting from the building was held responsible for melting parts of a parked Jaguar car. This was clearly an embarrassment to the developers who apologized and paid for the repairs. In 2012 the Shard, or Shard London Bridge, was completed. Designed by the Italian architect Renzo Piano it is the tallest building in the UK, standing at a height of 309.6 metres (1,016 feet). People either love or loathe it. I walked past London Bridge often as the structure gradually grew and wondered, given the surrounding area – a hospital, cathedral, railway station, the nearby Thames and a complex of small shops and businesses – how a structure that tall could find room to fit in. It did by using some innovative engineering methods, which included top-down construction, where foundations are dug while the core is built up (a first for the UK). Given its height, it has become something of a challenge for various individuals to climb or jump. In 2013 six women from Greenpeace climbed the building and unfurled a flag in protest over Arctic oil drilling. BASE jumpers (those jumping from objects using a parachute) have made a few descents including a man in 2016 that eluded security to glide down with relative ease.

As with many parts of London the deindustrialization of factories, warehouses, and offices saw the abandonment or 'regeneration' of many areas. On Bankside old warehouses were converted into flats, penthouses and shops. A middle-class shift to the area followed from the 1990s as *The Times* commented, not very tactfully, in 1998: 'five years ago, hardly anyone lived between Waterloo and Tower Bridge except council tenants.' As with much of the south bank of the Thames, the Borough has seen extensive regeneration. Declining light industry and factories have given way to residential development, shops, restaurants, galleries and bars.

Celebrations greeted the opening of the new century with a number of new projects along the Thames, notably the Millennium Dome, the Millennium Bridge, the Millennium Wheel/London Eye and Tate Modern Art Gallery on Bankside. Some of these were less successful, notably the much-derided Millennium Dome at Greenwich, although it evolved some years later into the more successful O2 Arena. Bankside, stretching more or less from Blackfriars Bridge to London Bridge, was transformed with a range of cultural and architectural changes.

The Millennium Bridge was the first pedestrian bridge built across the Thames as well as the first Thames crossing since the completion of Tower Bridge in 1894. Opened in June 2000, it connected St Paul's Cathedral with the Tate Modern but the opening of the bridge soon proved to be precarious due to its well-known wobble. Within forty-eight hours it had to close and it took two years of structural modifications until it was finally reopened in February 2002. Despite this it became one of the most successful millennium projects with an estimated 10,000 users a day. It also, along with the nearby Tate Modern, played an enormous role in the regeneration of Bankside. The Tate, with four million visitors a year, was helped in 2001 by the restoring of free entrance to galleries and museums.

Further west along the river, adjoining Jubilee Gardens, is the London Eye (formerly the Millennium Wheel), which opened in March 2000. The Eye, which occupies the same riverside site as the 1951 Festival of Britain, was intended as a temporary attraction, with a five-year lease, but it proved to be so popular it was kept in place. After some initial financial difficulties, it became the most popular paid tourist attraction in the UK with nearly four million visitors per year. Another boast for the Eye is that at a height of 135 metres, it is one of the tallest observation wheels in the world.

Tate Modern occupies what was once Bankside Power Station. The imposing power station had generated electricity from 1891 to 1981. Up to the Second World War there had been many complaints of smoke nuisance and, by the late 1930s, the station was considered inefficient, old and polluting. It was rebuilt in two phases between 1947 and 1963, and was originally designed by Sir Giles Gilbert Scott. In 1981 the station was closed down and lay derelict for fourteen years. In 1995 the Swiss architects Jacques Herzog and Pierre de Meuron won an international competition to convert the power station into an art gallery. The old turbine hall was turned into an impressive entrance and display area and the boiler house became the galleries. Tate Modern, which displays all the significant art movements from the twentieth century, was so successful that within four years of its opening it was struggling to contain the numbers of people that wanted to visit. A new extension was completed in 2016, increasing its size by 60 per cent and making it one the world's most visited modern art galleries.

One of the main arguments for tall buildings has been that with a growing urban population, a shortage of houses and a limited amount of land, there is nowhere to go but up. Nearly 90 per cent of completed towers in London in 2019 are residential. An alternative argument is that high-rise buildings use more energy per square metre than low-rise equivalents and emit twice as much carbon, according to research by University College London.

Criticism and controversy over tall buildings in London predates the present century. The Senate House in Bloomsbury was built in 1937 and the first wave of tall buildings in London emerged in the 1960s, notably the Post

Office Tower (177 metres) in 1964 and the controversial, thirty-four-storey Centre Point in central London, which remained vacant for many years. Much earlier, in 1888, Queen Anne's Mansions, a fourteen-storey block of flats, was built in Westminster and invited many complaints, including one from Queen Victoria who said it was blocking her view of the Palace of Westminster. Six years later the flats prompted the setting of a height limit of thirty metres, as it was felt dangerous to build above that level in the event of fire.

Tragically, in June 2017, the twenty-four-storey Grenfell Tower flats in North Kensington fell victim to such concerns. A fire, caused by a malfunctioning fridge freezer on the fourth floor quickly spread as a result of the cladding on the building. The fire burned for some sixty hours killing seventy-two people.

A criminal investigation was brought by residents who felt that both the Royal Borough of Kensington and Chelsea and the Kensington and Chelsea Tenant Management Organization were liable to corporate manslaughter. Grenfell also raised the issue of class disparities. Emma Dent, who was the MP, reported that there were huge differences in parts of the borough in terms of life expectancy, health, child poverty and income. In the poorer area of the borough average income was £15,000 per year compared to £100,000 in nearby wealthier parts. Whilst this gap may be more extreme than many other areas, it should be no surprise as London has the greatest wealth inequality in the UK.

The proliferation of tall buildings has had its critics and so has the issue of affordable housing in London. Since the Right to Buy policy of the 1980s and the practice of Buy to Let from the 1990s the number of homes available for social rent has reduced. London's population grew by 74,000 per year in the first fifteen years of the twenty-first century compared to a growth of 60,000 per year between the wars. However, this was not matched by a growth in housing with 43,000 new houses per year built in Greater London in the interwar period compared to 12,000 to 22,000 between 2000 and 2015 (figures quoted in R. Moore, *Slow Burn City*). There has also been the issue of the rich buying houses in Knightsbridge and Kensington to use as their 'London home' for a small part of the year, thus creating areas that become lifeless due to a lack of permanent residents. Affordable property continues to be a problem as many people increasingly find London too much of a luxury to live in, especially in times of austerity.

Between 2007 and 2009 the country was hit by a global financial crisis, which involved huge bailouts and subsidies and a political scandal involving many outrageous expenses claims by MPs at Westminster. London, as the financial and political centre of the UK became a target for criticism although neither of the events had much to do with Londoners themselves. London is responsible for almost a quarter of the nation's economic output but the capital's continuous growth and perceived political dominance have been a cause for some concern and criticism for centuries. William Cobbett described the capital in the 1820s as the 'Great Wen' (a cyst), Lord Rosebery (Prime Minister, 1894/5) called it a 'tumor, an elephantiasis', whilst writer, Thomas De Quincey was horrified by the 'labyrinth of London' with its vast populace, which he described as a 'pageant of phantoms'. Many of the criticisms persist and are as fashionable as ever. This is not to deny there are some elements of truth in such comments. Jack Brown, lecturer in London Studies at King's College, London University, has not only dispelled many of those myths but also argued passionately for how much the nation needs London (*The London Problem*, 2021).

And what of that most ancient part of the capital, the City of London? The landscape may have changed but the City continues to maintain its independence as it has done for centuries. It has survived waves of Victorian municipal reforms and twentieth-century local government changes. The Bank of England was given its independence by the New Labour government but the same government did not modernize the City of London. Even when a bank bailout to the tune of £1.6 trillion was made in 2008, the City was not held to account. Writing in the *Financial Times* (29 November 2014) Lord Glasman argued that the

> City of London needs to be held to account by the citizens of London and its inheritance made available for the good of the city. Maybe it is time, after 2,000 years, for all of London to become a city, for the Guildhall to be its parliament and for there to be one mayor of a united city who lives in Mansion House.

One doubts that the City of London Corporation, after centuries of self-government, will surrender its privileges anytime soon.

High-speed Disruption

In 2009 the UK government proposed a Y-shaped rail line named High Speed 2 or HS2 (HS1 being the Channel Tunnel Rail Link). Work on the controversial project, intended to link London, Birmingham, Leeds and

Manchester, was scheduled to begin in 2017, reaching Birmingham by 2026 and attaining full completion by 2033. These projections have proved to be overly ambitious and unachievable, as have the costs. The projected cost was initially £32.7 billion and then increased to over £120 billion and rising by 2021, making it, as the writer and journalist Simon Jenkins stated, the most extravagant infrastructure project in Britain's history. One bone of contention is the decision to use Euston instead of linking it with HS1 at King's Cross/St Pancras, which also has more underground connections.

Further disruption has been caused to flats, residents and businesses around the area of Euston. Complaints from locals were made about the levels of noise, destruction of ancient plane trees, loss of community and the need to be rehoused. Expanding Euston Station has also seen the loss of part of the old burial ground known as St James's Gardens (some 61,000 burials took place there between 1788 and 1853) where thousands of graves have been exhumed. Amongst the graves are those of Captain Matthew Flinders, who led the first circumnavigation of Australia and is credited with giving the country its name, and Lord George Gordon, who led the anti-Catholic Gordon Riots of 1780.

The Crossrail line has its origins, at least, in the 1940s and was first proposed to Parliament in 1991 but rejected. Construction started in 2009 on the central section and connections to existing lines that will become part of the route. In 2016 it was rebranded as the Elizabeth Line along with the line's purple colour theme. It is Europe's largest construction project with over 100 kilometres of rail line passing through forty stations, from Heathrow and Reading via forty-two of new tunnels under central London. Delays have beset the project; however, the Elizabeth Line officially opened on 24 May 2022. As with many large undertakings excavation gave archaeologists an opportunity to explore what lay beneath London's streets. Tens of thousands of items were found spanning back fifty-five million years. Among the findings were the graves of Great Plague skeletons at Liverpool Street station, Black Death skeletons in Charterhouse Square, Farringdon and also bison, reindeer and woolly mammoth bones, Roman coins and leather shoes from the Tudor period.

In 2000, an upgrade to St Pancras Station began as the new terminal for the Eurostar service to Europe. Both King's Cross and St Pancras (adjacent to each other) were subject to major developments in the twenty-first century. The area around King's Cross established a reputation for being seedy, rundown and frequented by prostitutes. In 1996 the decision to move the Channel Tunnel Rail Link from Waterloo to St Pancras became the catalyst for change. There was a major clean up with King's Cross Station which received a much-needed £500 million restoration, including a new semi-circular departure concourse, opened in 2012. Nearby, an underused industrial wasteland was transformed, utilizing the canal-side setting into an area with public squares and gardens, shops, bars, restaurants and a new campus for an art and design college. King's Cross Station became well known for its association with films and books, notably *Harry Potter* of which there is a merchandise shop and an ever-present queue at the fictional platform 9¾. Other films shot there include *Mission Impossible: Rogue Nation* (2015) and *Wonder Woman* (2017). For some earlier images of the area *The Ladykillers* (1955) includes views over the railway tracks and gasholders of the neighbouring Imperial Gas Works surrounded by worn-looking residential streets.

Terrorist Attacks

The title of the short British propaganda film directed by Humphrey Jennings made in 1940, *London Can Take It*, has become a defiant rallying cry during periods of adversity from the Blitz to terrorist attacks. On the 6 July 2005, London celebrated as it won the right to host the 2012 Olympic games, just beating the long-term favourite, Paris, to secure the world's biggest sporting event. Tragically, the celebrations were cut short the next day as London was hit by a number of terrorist attacks which saw fifty-two people murdered, and over 700 injured, whilst hundreds more suffered psychological trauma.

Four suicide bombers had set off by train for London from Leeds and Luton arriving at King's Cross by early morning peak time. Three of the four bombs went off just before 8.50 am on Tube trains that had departed King's Cross. The four terrorists, carrying backpacks, split up at King's Cross and boarded east- and westbound trains on the Circle Line and a southbound train on the Piccadilly Line. Twenty minutes later the bombs exploded within two minutes of each other. They occurred at Aldgate (killing seven people), Russell Square (killing twenty-six) and Edgware Road (killing six). The fourth explosion was set off on a crowded bus at Tavistock Square (killing thirteen).

In the minutes following the explosions on the underground trains, there was chaos and confusion as passengers were plunged into total darkness. The response from the emergency and transport services was fast and effective, especially for those seriously injured. One eyewitness who survived the King's Cross/Russell Square explosion shared her experience with the Report of the 7 July Review Committee:

Not long after the bomb went off, we all tried to stay quiet to hear for help, all we could hear were the screams from the other carriages, to our horror we then heard a train, thinking it was coming towards us people were screaming … no one knew we were down there. That was the scariest part of it (apart from thinking I was going to burn alive) – not knowing.

At Tavistock Square a survivor recalled:

The floor went completely up to my seat, and I'm in mid-air … I looked behind me and everybody and all the seats had vanished. I just went into flight mode … I hit the side of the bus on the way down … I was just screaming … All my clothes were hanging off me where they had all shredded.

London has suffered many terrorist attacks in the past but the 2005, or 7/7, bombings constituted the worst attack on London since the Second World War. A memorial to the victims, comprising fifty-two stainless steel pillars, is located in the south-eastern corner of Hyde Park.

Two further attacks occurred in 2017. The first was on 22 March when a terrorist, acting alone, drove a vehicle over Westminster Bridge near the Houses of Parliament. He mounted the pavement and began driving into pedestrians indiscriminately and then left the vehicle and stabbed an on-duty policeman to death before being shot dead by police. Four other people died as a result of the attack and fifty were injured. A second attack took place on 3 June at 10 pm when a van driven by three terrorists randomly ran into people on London Bridge. The terrorists then launched a knife attack, killing eight people and seriously injuring forty-eight others before the terrorists were shot dead.

Demonstrations/Protests

Demonstrations, protests and the occasional riot continued into the new century with a continuity of old concerns and some pertinent to the present, including the global problem of climate change. The conservative grouping, the Countryside Alliance, demonstrated in 2002 to preserve 'traditional rural lifestyles' including fox hunting. In 2011 students demonstrated against increases in fees and public sector cuts.

1968 had seen worldwide demonstrations against the war in Vietnam. In the twenty-first century the worldwide protests focused mainly on issues of environment and climate change. However, another war in 2003 became the focus of the largest political demonstration in UK history (estimates vary from 750,000 to two million). Demonstrators marched through central London to Hyde Park to protest about the looming war in Iraq.

The City of London's reputation for being one of the main centres of international finance made it a target for the G20 demonstrations on 1 April 2009, which gathered at the Bank of England to celebrate 'financial fools day'. Protesters took on a number of issues including the banking system (bonuses), the war on terror and climate change. Violence broke out which resulted in many arrests, windows smashed, and complaints were made against the practice of 'kettling' (where large cordons of police officers contain a crowd within a limited area). A bystander was killed, which led to a manslaughter charge against a police officer.

Smaller-scale protests took place in October 2011 when hundreds of people set up tents outside St Paul's Cathedral. Inspired by the Occupy Wall Street protests, they called for a change in the political system, opposed payments to large banks, and promoted democracy and global equality. Giles Fraser, then canon of St Paul's, welcomed the protesters but later resigned his post after they were evicted a few months later. Fraser said he could not sanction any policy that used force to remove the Occupy demonstrators.

Inspired by the Occupy movement and civil disobedience, the Extinction Rebellion (XR) was officially established in the UK in May 2018. The aim was to draw attention to the climate crisis and to use non-violent disobedience to influence government action in order to avoid an environmental disaster. A few months later they blocked the roads outside the Houses of Parliament, marking the beginning of a series of planned 'civil disobediences' In August 2021 Extinction Rebellion began their fifth mass protest over a number of days as they blocked busy junctions around Covent Garden and Leicester Square. Their protest coincided with a major review by the UN's Intergovernmental Panel on Climate Change (IPCC), which confirmed that the burning of fossil fuels was driving the climate crisis, causing heat waves, floods and storms. As part of the protest, they erected a giant pink table near Leicester Square.

Coinciding with the emergence of anti-global movements there has been a change from the usual historical routes of protests, which used to include Trafalgar Square and Hyde Park. More recently places that have financial organizations or large chain shops are targeted. The demonstrations organized by the Global Carnival Against Capital in 1999 included the novel idea of a mass bicycle ride through the City of London.

Diversity

As the 2004 London Plan reasserted, the capital was the 'world's most culturally diverse city', something it had been for many years. Diversity, it seemed, was replacing multiculturalism as a term but the ugly taint of racism continued. This was notable in the high-profile case of Stephen Lawrence, a black British teenager who was murdered in 1993 in south-east London. In the wake of the crime, the police were accused of corruption and being 'institutionally racist'.

London's multicultural communities have enhanced the city's restaurants with very diverse and distinctive flavours. Foods and restaurants vary from Chinese, Thai, Japanese, Indian, Bangladeshi, Korean, Vietnamese, Lebanese, Ethiopian, Egyptian, Nigerian and Moroccan to Italian, French, Argentinian and Mexican and, of course, British. Some are concentrated in certain areas such as Lebanese in Edgware Road, Chinese in Chinatown, Soho, and Afro-Caribbean in Brixton. Places like Soho, Camden and Borough Market offer a wide range of world foods.

In the last two decades of the twentieth century the process of gentrification gathered pace with less fashionable places experiencing something of a transformation. Shoreditch and nearby Hoxton began to see buildings and warehouses vacated by textile businesses and taken over by artists, notably those who became known as the Young British Artists, including Gillian Wearing, Gavin Turk and Tracey Emin. In 2010, Prime Minster David Cameron, announced plans to transform London's East End into a technology hub that would stretch 'from Shoreditch and Old Street to the Olympic Park'. Restaurant chains began to move in and by the 2012 Olympic Games Hoxton had the appearance of a startup technology community. Shoreditch went through a transformation as Westminster Council's decision to restrict bars in Soho and Covent Garden helped to create the need for a new social quarter. A bespoke bar culture and young tech-savvy millennials arrived, contributing to what we now know as 'the hipster'. Trends come and go as new businesses move, rents go up, places change and people move on and find new areas.

Pandemic

After the 2016 referendum people voted to leave the EU after forty-plus years. 'Brexit' raised many concerns about how the capital, the City and trade would adapt. We still don't know what the significance of this decision will mean. The COVID pandemic four years later added further uncertainty.

In 2020 the COVID-19 pandemic struck the UK. In February the first case in London was recorded in a woman who had recently arrived from China. By the following month there were nearly 500 cases and twenty-three deaths. The scale escalated with deaths rising to 4,000 a month. In the early stages London was one of the most affected regions in England with Southwark and Westminster initially the worst infected places.

Underground services closed in March and some hospitals were so stretched they had no critical care capacity. In April the temporary NHS Nightingale Hospital, which provided up to 4,000 beds, was opened in the ExCel Centre in East London. The first national lockdown was announced on 23 March and central London resembled something from a science fiction film, the streets eerily silent and almost deserted.

Shops, pubs and restaurants closed, and commuters stayed at home. As businesses struggled questions were raised about the future of the economy and working practices. Was all that empty office space needed if people could work from home? By May, after the initial first wave of COVID, London had a temporary recovery in relation to the rest of the country. It was not to last. By the end of the year a new strain of the virus sent infection rates up again.

As expected, some of the city's poorest boroughs suffered the most, notably Hackney, Newham and Brent. It was suggested at the outbreak that it would take time to develop a vaccine, perhaps eighteen months. However, by December, 81-year-old Lyn Wheeler became the first person to receive a COVID-19 vaccine at Guy's Hospital (90-year-old Margaret Keenan was the first person in the world to be given the Pfizer COVID-19 at Coventry). In January 2021, the mayor, Sadiq Kahn, declared London a 'major incident' as infection rates reached around one in thirty in the capital. As more people received vaccines, there were cautious signs of optimism although there was a realization that COVID was not going to go away. On 19 July COVID restrictions were lifted in England, social distancing rules were abolished and whilst the law no longer required the wearing of face coverings, masks remained mandatory on London Transport until it was lifted on 24 February 2022.

With the removal of restrictions, people up and down the country returned to their city centres to find familiar places had closed and many businesses had folded. By early 2022, despite the threat of a milder COVID variant, Omicron, there was caautious return to something resembling normality. The virus had raised important issues about how cities could survive such events. History has shown that 'London can take it'. The capital has come out of crises such as war, fire, plague, disease, smog, the Blitz and terrorist attacks, and reinvented itself.

Throughout this book there has been an emphasis not only on change and continuity but also on the ever-contrasting aspects of London. The artist, David Gentleman, who has painted countless scenes of the capital throughout his long and distinguished career, and whose mural can be seen on the wall at Charing Cross Underground Station, summed up this contrast so well:

> London … is an astonishing city … increasingly cosmopolitan [with] wonderful parks and public spaces, museums, galleries, theatres and places to eat … despite the city's familiar traffic, expensiveness, deprivation, unfairness, social decay and dwindling international significance is its continually breathtaking and surprising beauty. (*London You're Beautiful*, 2012).

Sources

Books

Ackroyd, P. *London: The Biography*, Vintage, London. 2001.

Brooke, A. *Fleet Street: The Story of a Street*, Amberley, Stroud. 2010.

Brown, J. *The London Problem*, Haus Curiosities, London. 2021.

Cockayne, E. *Hubbub: Filth, Noise, and Stench in England, 1600–1770*, Yale University Press, New Haven. 2007.

Gatrell. V. *City of Laughter: Sex and Satire in the Eighteenth Century*. Atlantic Books, London. 2006.

Halliday, S. *Making the Metropolis: The Creation of Victoria's London*, Derby, 2003.

Hibbert, C & Weinreb, B. *The London Encyclopaedia*, Macmillan, London. 2008.

Hingley, R. *Londinium: A Biography*, Bloomsbury, London. 2018.

Jefferys, A. *London at War*, Imperial War Museum, London. 2017.

Lincoln, M. *London in the 17th Century*, Yale University Press, New Haven. 2021.

Merrifield, R. *London City of the Romans*, Batsford, London. 1983.

Moore, R. *Slow Burn City: London in the Twenty-First Century*. Picador, London. 2017.

Naismith, R. *Citadel of the Saxons,* Bloomsbury, London. 2019.

Oldsen, D.J. *The Growth of Victorian London,* London, 1976.

Porter, R. *A Social History of London*, Hamish Hamilton, London 1994.

Ross, C, & Clark, J. *London: The Illustrated History*, Penguin, London, 2011.

Sheppard, F. *London 1808–1870: The Infernal Wen,* London, 1976.

Shoemaker, R. *The London Mob. Violence and Disorder in Eighteenth-Century England*, London, 2011.

Stow, J. *A Survey of London.* Sutton, 1999.

Weightman, G. & Humphries, S. *The Making of Modern London,* London, 2007.

White, J. *London in the Nineteenth Century*, Jonathan Cape, London. 2007.

White, J. *London in the Twentieth Century*, Vintage, London. 2008.
White, J. *London in the Eighteenth Century*, Vintage, London. 2013.
White, J. *The Battle of London 1939–45*. Bodley Head, London. 2021.

Maps

V. Harding & C. M. Barron (eds). *A Map of Tudor London: England's Capital City in 1520*. The Historic Towns Trust. 2018.
Londinium: A New Map and Guide to Roman London. MOLA (Museum of London Archaeology). 2011.

Websites

Diary of Samuel Pepys. www.pepysdiary.com
Map of Early Modern London https://mapoflondon.uvic.ca/index.htm
Roque's Map of London 1746. www.locatinglondon.org/
Strype, J. *A Survey of the Cities of London and Westminster*, London, 1720. www.dhi.ac.uk/strype/
Proceedings of the Old Bailey, 1674–1913. www.oldbaileyonline.org/

Acknowledgements

Thanks to all those who helped in various ways to the completion of this book, particularly Rod Corston for his photographic expertise and in creating the map of central London. Rita Gibbard for proof-reading large sections of the book. Thanks go to Claire Hopkins, Lucy May, Laura Hirst and Chris Cocks at Pen & Sword for their helpful suggestions and support and Alan Murphy who initiated the idea of a series on city histories. Thank you to those who gave permission for the use of images and who contributed their own photographs.

Index

Adam, Robert and James 71
Aethelred, King 7
air raids 1, 53, 157, 159
Aldersgate 4, 73, 86, 99, 161
Aldgate 4, 17, 21, 46, 48, 59, 66, 73, 180
Aldwych 6, 7, 147, 151, 152, 156
Aliens (Act) 142, 144, 152
Anglo-Saxon Chronicle 6, 7
Antwerp 2, 10, 50

Baker Street 44, 58, 123, 148
Bank of England 40, 66, 95, 96, 133, 171, 178, 182
Bankside 11, 20, 21, 23, 39, 48, 66, 67, 82, 174, 175, 176
Banqueting House 53, 55
Barbican 5, 161, 162
Bartholomew Fair 64, 76
Battersea 2, 66, 150, 162, 167, 168
Bazalgette, Joseph 112, 114
BBC 149, 154, 155
Beck, Harry 150
bears 15, 21, 23, 24, 34, 45, 67, 82
Belgravia 69, 72, 106
Bermondsey 2, 38, 46, 151, 154
Bethlam Hospital 46, 72
Bethnal Green 73, 99, 106, 157
'Big Bang' 170, 171
Billingsgate 14, 26, 38, 41, 48, 75, 126
Bishopsgate 4, 56, 73, 175

Black Death 17, 22, 179
Blackfriars 4, 42, 46, 71, 96, 175
Blitz 143, 153, 154, 155, 157, 158, 159, 162, 180, 184
Blake, William 73
Bloomsbury 37, 61, 64, 67, 85, 96, 110, 164, 176
Boleyn, Ann 46, 155
bombing 143, 154, 155, 157, 159, 161, 162, 165
Booth, Charles 109, 110
Borough 11, 32, 38, 66, 75, 123, 156, 166, 169, 175, 177, 183
Boswell, James 76, 88
Bow Street 92, 96, 130
Brewing 27, 39, 167
Bridewell 12, 47, 83
British Empire 107, 146, 153
British Museum 71, 152, 156
brothels 15, 20, 21, 35, 56, 67, 76, 85, 89, 93, 99, 100, 101, 104
Buckingham Palace 71, 153, 160, 164
buses 117, 135, 144, 149, 151

cafés 147, 156, 167, 168
Carnaby Street 164, 165
Catholics 25, 45, 46, 47, 53, 54, 57, 59, 65, 72, 74, 86, 87, 92, 93, 95, 96, 97, 129, 179
Chancery Lane 1, 79, 88, 98
Channel Tunnel 143, 178, 179

Charing Cross 57, 65, 79, 87, 101, 124, 146, 185

Charles I 53, 54, 57

Charles II 56, 60, 65,

Charlotte Street 140, 144

Charterhouse 46, 179

Charteris, Colonel Francis 101, 102

Chartists 133

Chaucer, Geoffrey 21

Cheapside 8, 15, 23, 38, 41, 42, 77, 78, 79, 92

Chelsea 30, 81, 164, 165, 177

cholera 16, 112, 113, 114

Churchill, Winston 61, 160

cinemas 147, 148, 154, 162

City of London xi, 4, 7, 11, 12, 51, 54, 55, 57, 66, 93, 111, 113, 161, 162, 170, 178, 182

Clerkenwell 38, 82, 83, 98, 109, 153

coaching inns 31, 32

coal 29, 30, 33, 34, 38, 57, 58, 120, 121, 163, 164

coffee houses 41, 52, 55, 64, 76, 78, 97, 148

Cornhill 2, 42, 52, 77

Covent Garden 6, 37, 38, 42, 48, 53, 64, 75, 76, 79, 82, 85, 87, 88, 101, 126, 149, 167, 182, 183

COVID-19 183, 184

Cripplegate 4, 12, 21, 46, 73, 154, 162

Cromwell, Oliver 56, 57, 80, 162

Crystal Palace 44, 128

Daily Mail 155, 160

dance halls/bands 148, 149, 154

Danes 1, 7, 9

Defence of the Realm Act (DORA) 144, 146

Defoe, Daniel 43, 59, 60, 69, 84

Dekker, Thomas 49, 60

Dickens, Charles 75, 95, 103, 120, 137

Docklands 150, 151, 165, 166

Dore, Gustave 118, 137

Downing Street 61, 145

Drury Lane 76, 80, 81

Dutch (War) 60, 65, 66

East End 29, 36, 39, 73, 92, 106-109, 111, 113, 125, 128, 150, 151, 154, 160, 183

East India Docks 35, 125

Edgware Road 2, 47, 180, 183

Elizabeth I 47, 50, 53, 73

Elizabeth Line 150, 179

Embankment 50, 115, 159

Essex xi, 6, 22, 25, 79, 146, 156

Euston 119, 122, 124, 149, 172, 179

Evelyn, John 57, 58, 59, 60, 87

Farringdon 75, 117, 179

Fascism 149, 150, 153

Fenchurch Street 7, 59, 175

Festival of Britain 162, 172, 176

Fielding, Henry 88, 92, 96

Figg, James 82

Finsbury Circus 5, 63

First World War 105, 143, 147, 152

FitzStephen, William 15

Fleet River 63, 10, 122

Fleet Street 3, 46, 47, 51, 59, 63, 77, 79, 80, 88, 89, 100, 125, 148, 155, 163, 167

General Strike 149

Gentleman, David 185

Gentrification 110, 167, 168, 183

Geoffrey of Monmouth 3
Georgian 68–71, 75, 77–80, 83, 87,
    88, 167, 173
German(s) 78, 144, 145, 153, 154,
    155, 159
Gin Craze 86, 98
'Glorious Revolution' 45, 56,
    66, 85
Gog and Magog 3
Gordon Riots 37, 72, 87, 94, 95, 179
Gordon, Lord George 95, 97, 179
Gracechurch Street 41, 59
Graunt, John 62
greasy spoon cafés 168, 169
Great Exhibition 44, 107, 128, 162
Great Fire 34, 40, 41, 42, 48, 59,
    60, 71, 110, 161, 173
Great Plague *see* Plague
Greater London xi, 84, 105, 110,
    119, 146, 161, 167, 170, 177
Green, Leslie 123
Greenwich 12, 47, 118, 119,
    165, 175
Grenfell Tower 177
Gresham, Sir Thomas 40, 50
Grosvenor Square 29, 61, 169
Manchester Guardian 145, 163, 172
Guildhall 3, 5, 48, 59, 154, 178
Guy's Hospital 72, 155, 184

Hamley, William 70
Hammersmith 30, 123, 147, 148
Hampstead 2, 37, 63, 64, 81
Hampton Court 47, 48
Hawksmoor, Nicholas 72
Haymarket 67, 80, 93, 147
Henry VIII 45, 47
Highgate 2, 37, 64
Hogarth, William 74, 78, 82, 85,
    87, 88, 98, 100, 101, 138

Holborn 42, 50, 51, 63, 70, 74, 84,
    85, 113, 125, 127, 139, 144,
    152, 153, 156, 161
Hollar, Wenceslaus 48, 150
Hoxton 109, 111, 183
Houses of Parliament 3, 66, 128,
    153, 157, 159, 181, 182
Huguenots 29, 66, 70
Hyde Park xi, 44, 54, 107, 128, 149,
    156, 160, 161, 170, 181, 182

immigrants 66, 74, 139, 140,
    141, 142
Irish 28, 66, 74, 87, 92, 93, 95, 129,
    140, 141, 153, 170
Irish Republican Army (IRA) 170,
    171, 174

Jack the Ripper 109, 130
Jews/Jewish 10, 17, 18, 28, 29, 55,
    59, 66, 92, 141, 142, 153
Johnson, Boris 172, 174
Johnson, Dr Samuel xii, 88
Jones, Inigo 53, 64
Jubilee Line 150, 151

Kennington 94, 99, 133
Kent xi, 4, 8, 22, 25, 31, 146, 156
Khan, Sadiq 173
King's Cross 119, 122, 126, 149,
    152, 156, 179, 180

Leicester Square 53, 61, 124, 147,
    1158, 159, 182
lamps 50, 78, 123, 134, 139, 156
Lincoln's Inn Fields 37, 53, 80
Liverpool Street 1, 119, 179
Livingstone, Ken 174
Lloyd's 41, 171
Lombard Street 7, 18, 40, 41, 59

Londinium 1–6, 161
London Bridge 4, 7, 13, 14, 24, 35, 42, 48, 50, 71, 73, 118, 154, 155, 156, 165, 175, 181
London County Council (LCC) 111, 113, 116, 118, 146, 153, 161, 166
London Eye 175, 176
London Wall 1, 4, 5, 6, 7, 8, 10, 15, 41, 45, 86, 161, 162
Lord Mayor 20, 22, 55, 112
Ludgate 2, 3, 4, 8, 21, 59, 73, 79, 83, 118
Lundenburg 6

Machyn, Henry 46, 47
Magdalen Hospital 85, 102
Marble Arch 47, 50, 157
markets 30, 38, 41, 42, 66, 75, 77, 122, 126, 135
Marylebone 30, 38, 69, 70, 78, 81, 82, 119, 122, 159, 160
Mayfair 38, 64, 69, 70, 77, 78, 101, 102, 107, 148, 165
Mayhew, Henry 101, 106
Mearns, Andrew 106, 116
Metroland 146, 151
Metropolitan Police 84, 130, 133, 136, 147
Millbank 72, 131
Millennium Bridge 175
Millennium Dome 170, 172, 175
Milton, John 56, 162
Monument 86, 123
Moorfields 23, 60, 85, 95
Moorgate 4, 73, 89, 152, 161
Museum of London 161, 162

Newgate 4, 21, 41, 47, 70, 72, 73, 84, 103
Navy 36, 60, 97

Newgate Prison 38, 72, 95, 96
Normans 1, 8, 9, 10, 11, 162

Old Bailey 72, 74, 91, 100, 102, 103, 170
Olympic Games 162, 173, 180, 183
Oxford Street 44, 69, 70, 77, 78, 82, 87, 125, 126, 144, 149, 154

Paddington 30, 64, 117, 122
Peasants' Revolt 21, 22
Pepys, Samuel 42, 49, 57-60, 61, 63, 64, 87, 88
Piccadilly 41, 43, 69, 77, 87, 148, 151, 152, 159, 169, 180
plague 15, 17, 18, 45, 49, 52, 53, 58, 59, 60, 62, 74, 79, 185
Pool of London 14, 35, 109, 165
Poor Law (1834) 30, 113, 129, 130
Port of London 30, 165
Porter, Roy xi, 37, 68, 79, 90, 164
poultry 15, 40
protests 54, 60, 143, 169, 170, 181, 182
prostitutes 56, 76, 81, 82, 84, 85, 102, 159, 179
Public Houses 50, 100, 101, 111, 138, 139, 145, 154, 165, 167, 184
Public Health Act (1848) 112, 114
Pudding Lane 59
Puritan 53–55, 64

Quant, Mary 165
Queenhithe 7, 41

railways 31, 32, 33, 108, 115, 118, 119–124, 126, 128, 157
rationing 158
Red Lion Square 61, 161
Regent Street 71, 77, 127, 146

riots 19, 20, 37, 72, 81, 87, 91–96, 99, 145, 169, 179
River Thames 1, 2, 4, 6, 7, 10, 12–16, 25, 30, 32–36, 38, 39, 48, 50, 54, 55, 58, 59, 63, 67, 69, 71, 81, 112, 114, 117, 125, 131, 137, 163, 165, 166, 172, 174, 175
Romans 1, 2, 3, 4, 5, 6, 31
Royal Exchange 40, 42, 48, 50, 59, 84, 127
Russell Square 180
Russell, Lord John 26, 102

satirists 68, 87
Savoy 147, 148, 154
Saxons 1, 5, 6, 7
Scotland Yard 144, 149
Second World War 143, 145, 148, 151, 152, 153, 155, 156, 161, 162, 169, 176, 181
Seven Dials 85, 131, 136, 167
Shaftesbury Avenue 101, 112, 148
Shard 175
Shelters 74, 75, 154, 155, 156, 158, 159
Sheppard, Jack 83
shipbuilding 36, 39, 55, 67, 125
smallpox 16, 18, 66, 113
smog 58, 163, 164, 184
Soho 44, 59, 66, 67, 70, 87, 101, 147, 148, 153, 154, 159, 164, 183
Southwark xi, 4, 11, 13, 20, 21, 23, 32, 39, 41, 48, 51, 52, 64, 66, 67, 73, 74, 75, 83, 94, 95, 97, 100, 109, 149, 154, 155, 156, 165-168, 171, 184
Spitalfields 38, 39, 66, 73, 75, 126
St Bride's Church 51, 155

St Dunstan 3, 73
St Giles 66, 67, 73, 74, 100, 101, 136, 138
St Giles Cripplegate 12, 162
St James's 37, 42, 47, 64, 65, 67, 69, 77, 78, 84, 85, 153, 179
St Mary Overy 13, 43
St Pancras 30, 119, 122, 152, 172, 179
St Paul's 2, 6, 7, 8, 11, 15, 34, 37, 48, 51, 59, 61, 91, 155, 160, 174, 175, 182
Stead, W. T. 116
Stock Exchange 171
Stow, John 48, 53
Strand, The 6, 42, 48, 53, 71, 72, 76, 77, 79, 84, 88, 89, 104, 125, 147, 149, 151, 154, 163,
Swinging London 143, 164

tall buildings 143, 174, 176, 177
Tate Modern 175, 176
Temple Bar 50, 79, 106, 128
terrorists 131, 152, 170, 173, 180, 181, 184
theatres 29, 48, 42, 45, 53, 55, 63, 65, 67, 80, 81, 88, 92, 93, 111, 147, 154, 162, 185
Threadneedle Street 40, 42
Times, The 120, 123, 135, 160, 167, 175
Tottenham Court Road 64, 126, 138, 140
Tower Hill 4, 5
Tower of London xi, 1, 8, 48, 149, 154, 155, 174
Trafalgar Square 6, 127, 146, 157, 169, 182
trams 108, 117, 118, 149

Tyburn 23, 46, 47, 57, 64, 70, 72,
    77, 83, 84, 102, 138
Tyler, Wat 22
typhus 16, 72

Underground 1, 2, 115, 122, 123,
    126, 150, 151, 154, 157, 169,
    179, 180, 184, 185

V-1 rocket 159, 160
V-2 rocket 160
Vauxhall Gardens 81, 82, 172
Victoria, Queen 80, 176
Vikings 5, 6, 7

Walbrook 2, 15
Walworth, William 20, 22
Ward, Ned 76, 85
Waterloo 166, 175, 179
watermen 12, 13, 34
Wedgwood, Josiah 29, 43, 70
Wembley 146, 162, 170
Wesley, John 85, 86
West End 38, 43, 52, 66, 68, 69, 70,
    76, 87, 92, 104, 106, 107, 113,
    118, 125, 126, 127, 134, 144,
    145, 147, 148, 153, 154, 159,
    160, 161, 164, 169, 172

West India Docks 35, 125
Westminster 3, 4, 8, 10, 12,
    16, 19, 30, 32, 42, 47, 48,
    54, 55, 57, 61, 66, 67, 71,
    72, 73, 82, 87, 88, 95, 96,
    98, 117, 118, 127, 128, 133,
    145, 154, 156, 157, 159, 160,
    169, 174, 177, 181,
    183, 184
Westminster Abbey 8, 51, 54, 67,
    69, 154, 164
White, Jerry xi, 74, 143
Whitechapel 29, 66, 73, 109, 115,
    141, 152
Whitefriars 46, 167
Whitehall 12, 38, 47, 48, 53,
    55, 56, 127, 146, 154,
    164, 170
Wild, Jonathan 83
William the Conqueror 8
Winchester 6, 8, 20
Worde, Wynken De 51
Wren, Sir Christopher 60, 61, 72,
    154, 155

Yerkes, C. D. 123, 124

Zeppelin 143, 144